Braking News

One bus, two girls, 15 thousand kilometres,
715 million votes...

Braking News

SUNETRA CHOUDHURY

First Published by Hachette India 2010

ISBN: 978-93-5009-052-7

SRD

Hachette Book Publishing India Pvt. Ltd
4th and 5th Floors, Corporate Centre,
Plot No. 94, Sector 44, Gurgaon - 122003, India

Typeset in Adobe Garamond Pro 11/14.3 by
Mindways Design, New Delhi

Printed and bound in India by
Manipal Technologies Limited, Manipal

MIX
Paper from
responsible sources
FSC™ C043100

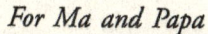

For Ma and Papa

1

In the Bylanes, for the Bylines

In the end, I suppose, it was probably just a blinding desire to be on air.

Nothing else can really explain why, that Friday evening towards the end of February, when I was called into the bosses' room, I instantly agreed to their suggestion that I hit the road for two months. In a split second, my fairly adequate ego had registered and processed an opportunity for potential airtime during Elections 2009 – at a time when newsroom budgets were facing a crunch and reporters like myself weren't even doing day trips.

My editors were surprised.

I mean, of course they knew I was a bit of what some people call an 'enthu cutlet' – one of those irritating workmates who despite having been in the business for ten years, still treats the office like an extension of the classroom; the sort who, when the teacher asks a question, almost falls off her chair as she eagerly thrusts up her hand. If there was an assignment going – whether in Jehangirpuri or Japan – I always wanted to go first. Or, at least, be *asked* first.

But then that's me – sort of over-competitive and maybe even eager-to-please.

Anyway, I was hanging around as usual that fateful Friday, looking, I imagined, gainfully occupied and absorbed in my work. I was sitting with my studio make-up on and staring at my computer screen, playing around with the articles for the set of headlines text:

'The Election Commission Now Plays Big Brother – Will Videotape All His Speeches.'

Will videotape. *Hmm.* Did that sound *urgent* enough?

How about: 'The Election Commission Comes Down Hard on Varun Gandhi; Orders Videotaping of His Every Move.'

Yes, much better.

Next story: 'Will Chiru Play a Spoiler in Andhra?'

Okay, so do we all know that Chiru is southern megastar Chiranjeevi? My south Indian colleagues would say yes but I wasn't too sure. And 'spoiler'? What other synonym could I use for that?

This was prep for the first prime-time show of the evening – the 8 o' clock show – and since I'd only been doing this slot for a few months I was very careful about every word that went in. I had less than five minutes per story. And even though an entire team worked on a prime-time bulletin, every presenter had to be very careful of what came out of their mouths. Sometimes, I'd seen desk hands laughing their heads off at what a presenter had written (and which they hadn't bothered to change). Often, this was due to a lack of time. But other times it was purely for their entertainment.

And even though it was obvious that I wasn't aiming to floor anyone with my creative intros, I didn't like the idea of walking towards the studio only to have the deskies cracking up behind my back.

'Sunetra, come in for a sec,' Sonia said just then, calling me to her room. Damn. Now what was wrong? I entered my boss's room nervously and found that Barkha was in there too. Neither looked at me; their eyes were fixed on the palm-sized TV screens in the room.

A few days ago, a journalism student had sent me a questionnaire for her thesis. The questions included:

Do you feel that there is a bias against women in media organizations? That women are associated with soft news and not crucial sectors like defence, diplomacy, finance? Have you noticed that women presenters are often pulled off air when there is breaking news?

I wanted to send the student a picture of Barkha and Sonia in office.

Barkha and Sonia are great looking presenters, true, but they are also totally and completely in charge of running the channel. They are both in their thirties, and they are so steely and tough that some male reporters refer to them as 'ball crushers'.

'Sunetra, Barkha and I have been talking about you,' Sonia said finally, without taking her eyes off the screen. I braced myself for a tongue-lashing. Just a couple of weeks ago, I'd had another meeting with Barkha and Sonia where they'd basically told me that I needed to pull up my socks. I'd been following the CBI for the last four years and according to them, I'd got caught in the minutiae of it all. 'The TV viewing nation doesn't *really* care about the number of times an official has been given an extension just because he's close to the minister,' Sonia had patiently explained to me. I hadn't disagreed and had promised to work on more saleable stories.

My channel was very clear. Our top stories *had* to be political. Many new-age editors in India had announced the death of the political reporter and the political beat, but at NDTV we still believed politics was our strength. Politics was always going to be the top headline of the day and so the political reporters' desk was paid maximum attention. I liked reporting on the psyche of politicians – and some of those minds are obviously fascinating! – but I was still struggling to find my special niche in the everyday routine of political reporting.

For instance, suppose you get to cover the big beat of politics – the Indian National Congress – well then, a Working Committee meeting of the party is considered a big deal. But for a TV reporter this basically means sitting like a watch-dog outside Sonia Gandhi's house and keeping careful track of which leader attends the meeting and which one chooses to give it a miss. My newspaper colleagues wouldn't even bother to turn up for things like that. They'd simply wait for the meeting to end and then work their phones. But us poor TV sods wait patiently around in the lawns – or on the street, or outside the gate – for the meeting to finish so we can file the spokesperson's uninspired briefing.

So, I really thought that Sonia and Barkha were going to do a bit of stock-taking as follow-up to our last chat. *How many political stories have you done, exactly, since our little chat last time, Sunetra?* Would the story about why Rahul Gandhi doesn't wear spectacles in election posters count, I wondered desperately, and then decided against mentioning that. There was no point in corroborating the other impression: that I only liked doing off-beat stories.

'Look, there's something we want you to do,' said Barkha finally. 'It is so exciting that I actually want to do it *myself*. But, of course, I *can't* – '

Uh-oh. I was immediately suspicious. This was classic sales sop to a gullible reporter.

' – We want you to take the NDTV studio bus across the country and do shows from various locations around the country.'

'It's an amazing opportunity, Sunetra. It's all on the road, and you get to decide where you want to go. Of course, it will have to be spots where the elections are due. At a rally, or the key constituencies...' Sonia listed the possibilities.

But I didn't need to hear any more, I was already nodding and beaming like crazy. The only thing I really registered were the words 'across the country' and that they wanted me to go. And I knew that this was about elections, I knew that this was about work, but all I could think about was Kerala, and how I would finally get to go there.

'Yes, yes, *yes*, yes, oh wow!'

Barkha thought I didn't understand the implications – 'It means that you don't get to come back home for the next two months.'

I beamed on, unfazed.

'You'll travel *only* in the bus, we'll make sure it is comfortable and you don't have to sleep in it. And there will be you and someone from Hindi as well,' said Sonia.

When I think about it now, I'm a little embarrassed by the superficial reasons for my instant compliance. I was just so happy that I was going to be gainfully employed in the elections. I would not be an MC-BC (that's 'mike carrier/bite collector' in TV parlance and not just the Hindi gaali you're thinking of!). I was free to gallivant about the country doing stories that I liked. If they gave me a show, it also meant that, among the barrage of political reportage coming in from across the country, my stories had less chances of getting lost.

My mind was racing. My visibility would be ensured, I thought, although I was hardly going to get top billing as far as prime-time slots were concerned. And yes, I had wanted to go to Kerala for the longest time. I remembered making a pitch to Barkha and Sonia during the Kerala assembly elections. 'Let me do the angle about whether having the highest literacy rates in the country changes the way that democracy works,' I had pleaded. They hadn't fallen for it then, but now I could go where I pleased and chase all the oblique stories I wanted.

'I didn't expect this reaction,' Sonia smiled as she took in how gleeful I was. 'We'll get the final clearance from Prannoy, and of course the bus still has to be modified and fitted, but you can start preparing for the trip right away.'

To be honest, on another level completely, I was wondering if I actually *had* the leeway to decline. I'd only tried to do that once at NDTV and I'm still smarting from the experience. It was in the summer of '07 when Sikh leaders started brandishing their swords because they were offended by the leader of a sect called Dera Sacha Sauda. Baba Gurmeet Ram Rahim had dressed up as Guru Gobind Singh and this was such a big sacrilege that Sikh leaders didn't just boycott the sect members, they wanted the leader arrested. Watching tensions rise on screen, my husband Sudeep called me and said that if I was asked to go, I should decline. 'It's not the time to act all emancipated, Sunetra, you will not be able to do it. It's going to be crazy and your channel should understand that.' His words, coupled with the images on screen, made me refuse the assignment when it was handed to me because I was genuinely spooked by the sword-wielding men and feared being caught in the middle of their battle with the security forces.

'*What* did you say?' Barkha had been vitriolic. 'Of *all* people, Sunetra, for *you* to bring up the gender factor in this coverage!' And I knew then that I shouldn't have listened to family on this. Because even though I ended up covering the Dera clash after that, I was mercilessly ribbed for the longest time for feeling scared for those few seconds.

Somewhere, that too was a factor in my emphatic agreement to the road trip.

I walked out of their room too stunned to focus on anything else. There was barely an hour left for me to hit the television studio. Usually, by this time, I'm at my stressful worst – a bit cranky, a bit touchy, and quite competitive. That day, however I completely let my co-anchor have his way with the show. He could have the glory of the starting headline, the clever line and all the so-called punch-lines involving Varun Gandhi, the Election Commission and Chiranjeevi. I looked at the screen as the words glazed and turned blurry.

'Are your headlines final?' the news-editor barked.

'Guess so,' I murmured distractedly, thinking only that I had to call Sudeep.

As soon as we had decided our lines with the editor I pulled out my mobile phone. 'They want me to travel the country in a bus for the next two months and I said yes,' I whispered to Sudeep.

'What? *When?*'

I felt a little guilty. Granted, I was no model wife, but maybe even I should have consulted him before gleefully accepting the assignment. 'In ten days' time. What do you think?'

What *would* he think? For as long as I've known Sudeep, there has only ever been one potential deal-breaker in our relationship. He wants us to drive to Leh from Delhi. He's been there before, lots of times, in fact. But he just wants to do the journey with me. Not by plane either, but a full-on road trip through the heart of Kashmir.

Sudeep has shown me innumerable photographs of the road we will take. The pictures look brilliant and I am charmed by his enthusiasm. But it is like looking at a beautiful, glossy brochure of a product I don't want to buy. There is this motorcycle ad which shows the very same road and every time it airs, he goes: 'Don't you see what you're missing? You are a reporter, you should always *want* to try out new experiences!'

I think the mistake people make is confusing a reporter with an intrepid traveller. The two don't necessarily go together. I've never been an adventurer, never been on a trek, and never climbed a mountain. In fact, I'm such a safety and comfort seeker that as a child I never learnt to ride a bicycle because I was too scared of falling off and looking silly. It's not something I declaim about in public but I honestly don't see this as a weakness. I believe a reporter's job is to observe what you see and tell it to the world and I do that just fine, thank you very much. So what if I tell my story standing at a safe remove, a short distance from the danger spot? I still tell the story.

As a professional journalist, I have carefully compart-mentalized my life. All the adventure that is necessary – be it rushing into a disaster zone or driving around it – is strictly on a *have*-to-do basis. I will only do it if my boss *asks* me to do it. When I'm on a holiday, I like beaches and hill resorts – predictable, dull and comforting. I don't care to waste time driving endlessly, preferring a quick flight or a train ride that will quickly get me to my destination; my holiday only beginning once I am there.

I blame my middle-class government family upbringing for my undeveloped travelling tastes. Unlike friends and colleagues who have been travelling since their early teens, I am one of those Indians whose school holidays were limited to being packed off to their grandmother's for the summer. My journeys, for most of my growing up years, were by the Tinsukia Mail (and later the North-Eastern Express) from Delhi to Guwahati, and from there a 3-hour road journey to Shillong. The train ride was a long one through the Hindi heartland and the Indian summer. Ma, Bhai and I would be seen off by Papa at the Delhi Railway Station and Ma wouldn't exhale till we arrived. Why was she anxious? Partly because she didn't like travelling without my father; and partly because Bhai and I were quite a pain.

Her travel anxiety has, unfortunately, been handed down to me.

Just as Ma marked each passing station: Aligarh, Allahabad, Kishanganj to Katihar and then Bongaigaon before reaching Guwahati, with progressively easier breathing, I punctuate every one of our journeys with the plaintive refrain – Are we there yet?

So naturally when I broke the news of my two-months-on-the-road trip to Sudeep he was a bit freaked. 'Are you kidding me?' he asked.

I wasn't.

'I cannot believe it. What did you tell them?'

Yes! Yes! Yes! 'I said fine, I'll go.'

'That's amazing, I can't believe it. You are damn lucky, damn lucky!'

After talking to Sudeep I went down to the green room on the first floor. It's always buzzing at this time of the evening – hair dryers blazing at burning heat trying to straighten rebel strands of hair, thick coats of pancake being slathered on faces, and, in every mirror, male and female faces preening intently. Anchors of the English, Hindi and Business channels are all packed in, vying with each other to get the attention of one of the make-up persons. (Many of them were also vying for the top spot on the prime-time shows that election.)

In our small green room – before we put on our nice faces – it's always difficult to hide any undercurrents of tension, not just among small-fries like myself but also among the big stars, those looking for their next big story. The make-up artists always know what is going on, and they love to gossip. I strained to listen in to the conversation in the next chair:

'Did you hear about that new slot?'

'Yeah, apparently, her show wasn't working but they couldn't piss her off so...'

'Really?'

'Yeah, I saw her closeted with...'

I wondered if they knew about my new show. I wondered what they would say. Would they think of it as an enviable assignment, or would they feel sorry for me, lurching about in a bus, up and down the country in the midst of a cruel summer?

I figured I wouldn't have to wait too long to find out.

Even if I was scared about leaving home for such a long time, scared about the sheer physical exhaustion that I was sure to feel in just a week's time, I couldn't afford to admit it. For now, I thought, I would just focus on Kerala and the other beautiful sights I was bound to see. I would focus on the fact that at the end of it all, I could claim: 'I have covered the entire country and I have seen how it works on the ground.' I was going to focus on the fact that I would be the journalist (vanity has everything to do with it!) who'd notched up the maximum number of kilometres on the campaign trail.

Yeah, baby, me and Rahul Gandhi! We would discover India together!

2

Two for the Road

The insomnia started that night.

As soon as I lay down, sinking back gratefully against the pillows and shutting my eyes, the thrill of an assured byline began to fade. The scale of the task I had taken on slowly grew larger, becoming this ominous dark thing. My mind went back to some of the other 'experiences' I'd had with longish assignments.

In 2004, for instance, I was still new to NDTV when three Indians truckers were kidnapped in Iraq by an unknown group of terrorists called 'Holders of the Black Banner'. It was a really big and really long-drawn-out story and involved a virtual stake-out at the homes of the three men. Basically, the Indian government was in diplomatic talks to negotiate the release of three men, Antaryami, Sukhdev Singh and Tilak Raj, but the captors drove a hard bargain. Sometimes, they would ask for the drivers' employer, a transport company called KGL, to pull out of Iraq. Sometimes, they would haggle over the ransom money. Every time the Indian mediators seemed close to a breakthrough in the negotiations, the kidnappers changed the terms of release. It was crucial to get the reaction of the victims' families on the course the negotiations were taking, so TV channels parked their reporters in these godforsaken towns.

When the story first broke, my part in it involved handling the copy and doing voice-overs for the morning bulletins, a few hours before they were telecast, in the night shift. I would come into work at midnight and sleepily track the story through my colleague's despatches from Una – the Himachal Pradesh town that bordered Punjab, which was home to two of the hostages, Antaryami and Tilak Raj.

The day my week-long night shift finished, I set off for home relishing the thought of the three days off I had earned. But as soon as I reached home my then editor (now the boss man of a rival channel) called.

'Sunetra, will you go to Una? The reporter there has some work in Delhi and needs to come back for the weekend. It's just for two days; you can come back after that.'

It wasn't the best of assignments but – I had learnt the hard way – saying no was not really an option.

Una is one of those dirty, characterless Indian towns that is not really known for anything other than acute unemployment. But the worst part of my visit wasn't the uninspiring town, or the really disgusting hotel I had to put up in, it was the mind-numbing lack of work. On the first day I did a story about the terrible unemployment in Una that was forcing local inhabitants to still look for work in Iraq, despite the kidnappings. Then, I did a mushy story about the hostages' families (not wholly original either; it had already been done by my colleague). But, after that, as the two days extended to six and we awaited news from Iraq, there was nothing to do. I realized that the colleague I had replaced had probably cited personal reasons just to escape. Nor did I blame her – it was hell sitting there in my hotel room and watching TV while my editor said, 'Wait till Sunday, wait for at least a week.'

When I'd finally languished through that long week and was starting to feel happy about my imminent return home, I received a call from the Delhi office. One of those daft minions on the assignment desk said: 'Sunetra, listen, there's a warning that the Parechu Lake in Tibet is about to burst and flood Himachal Pradesh.'

My whole attitude, frankly, was, 'So what's it gotta do with me?'

'You are the closest to Rampur, which is in the danger of being wiped out, so we want you to rush there.'

I think I cursed her and started to cry, saying that I couldn't go because I had no clean clothes. I had packed only for two days, remember?

In ten minutes, the editor called: 'What is it, Sunetra? What is it? Are you homesick?'

I must have been crazy because I actually thought that he felt sorry for me and sympathetic towards my condition. I sniffed a teary, 'Yes.'

'Then you *fucking* come back to Delhi and *fucking* stay in the air-conditioned office! Homesick, homesick!' he thundered, going ballistic, shouting me out of my self-pity.

I'd ended up staying for a fortnight longer and no, the floods never came, and no, I never cried again.

But that night, as I lay in bed thinking of a trip that would be at least four times longer, I remembered how pathetic I'd felt in Una – tears streaming down my face as I'd washed my clothes in that disgusting loo. What if I felt homesick again? I'd signed myself up for two months but I had never been away from home that long. The longest I'd been away from family was just 21 days.

And I also have an embarrassing history of having passed up an opportunity to stay back in England and going to university there after doing my A-levels during my father's stint in the High Commission. I chose to return to India with them because I didn't want to stay without my Mommy and Daddy, even at the age of eighteen. So, what if I turned all girly again and cried and wanted to come home? My reputation would be in shreds and I would never – *never, never* – be considered for anything remotely challenging again.

I knew that the loos on my Bharat Darshan trip would be much more squalid than any I'd had the misfortune of finding myself in before. Even, I shuddered to myself, dirtier than the loo in Darbhanga, Bihar. I had the pleasure of staying in that part of the world during the floods in 2000. The potty was a western one, which is totally disgusting because it involves more physical contact. Forget the stains and the state of the toilet seat – I can handle that; I just bandage it with reams of toilet paper – what I couldn't handle was the water that came out of the tap. It stank. For the week that I stayed there, bathing made me feel fresh as a drain.

'Good news for you, Sunetra. We have a tie-up with this five-star hotel chain. You can stay with them in whichever city they have a hotel.'

Okay, so that's not *really* how Dr Prannoy Roy, the Boss Man at NDTV, began his briefing with me the next morning but I'd be lying if I said that it was not a seductive factor for me. A factor I accept and am totally at peace with. As a newspaper reporter with *The Indian Express*, I clearly recall an incident where my colleague covering environment and rural affairs, went to cover a story in rural India. A senior editor would not stop admonishing her when he got the bills from a resort she had stayed at. She tried to explain to him that there had not been any other decent place to stay nearby but he kept saying, 'How can you go and cover a story about poor village people and stay in a five-star resort?'

I didn't have an answer then but now I would seriously disagree.

I mean, how does demanding a clean bed and toilet take away from the integrity of a reporter? I agree that empathy goes a long way but does it have to come from staying amidst the dirt and grime? I just think that I can do my work a lot better when I know that at the end of the day I will be guaranteed a place to wash and a bed unsoiled by some stranger's bodily fluids to sleep in. And although it's changing every day – especially in south India – budget hotels just don't give that kind of guarantee yet.

Of course Dr Roy's briefing was much more than just about the pleasures of a five-star stay. (And anyway I didn't get too happy because I knew how few small towns actually have a five-star chain!)

While international broadcasters had used concepts like a moving bus studio for elections before, it had never been tried in India. Also, a mobile studio travelling across India is an entirely different ballgame from driving across the United States.

They would never have to worry about basic things like roads, toilets, technical support in rural areas, and general safety.

Dr Roy was very clear: 'First of all, no Kashmir, no Naxal territory. It's just too dangerous and not worth it.' We were to travel in a hard-to-miss red bus with very, very expensive equipment aboard so it was no surprise that NDTV didn't want to risk taking the bus into hostile territory. 'Forget the bus, we want you guys to be safe,' Dr Roy said.

The plan according to NDTV was this: The election bus would travel roughly 50 kilometres every day for sixty days covering a distance of 3,000 kilometres, zigzagging through India. Two teams, consisting of an anchor-reporter and cameraperson, would produce a half-hour show every weekday from the bus, which was to be beamed live from a suitable location, i.e. a village charpoy or a chai shop.

The bus was to be fitted with comfortable seating for the entire crew and would be accompanied by another smaller vehicle – for narrow lanes that the bus would not be able to go through. We would stay the nights in hotels and not inside the bus. A lot of emphasis was to be paid to the exterior of the bus. It would have 'NDTV Election Bus' painted in huge letters on the side and would have flags on top apart from, of course, the satellite dish: our lifeline. I didn't fully appreciate at the time the role that the bus would play in our journey. The flags, the sheer size, and the impressive nature of the bus really drew the crowds in, at all the places that we visited.

To a lot of people, the fact that we had come out to see them was an assertion that their opinion mattered to the country; that NDTV cared enough to send their most show-offy thing to their town, sometimes to places where even local politicians hadn't bothered to visit.

'You will have full editorial control of this half-hour show,' said Dr Roy. 'You will decide what kind of segments you want. We don't want politicians to figure that much, unless they are really big. The programme should focus on the young people of that town; perhaps you could meet a local family and understand what they need from the elections. You could even add fun stuff that you see along your journey.'

I just sat nodding to everything Dr Roy said, absolutely thrilled, but also *very* scared. A whole-half-hour every day, produced entirely by me!

Up until then, I had thought that I would do a story a day and then present the other election stories from across the country. Basically, I'd envisaged lots and lots of travelling with just a few hours of work at every destination when we looked for a story.

Now, it seemed I would have to bust my butt working and never be sure whether I had produced quality work, worthy of a 30-minute show. I knew it was near impossible because I did half-hour stories maybe once a year. They all took me not less than a week, and a week where I worked day and night and wished I had more time. I know that in the BBC, and in other networks abroad, reporters sometimes took months, even a year to do half-hour shows.

And I, god help me, had nonchalantly agreed to produce one every day for two months.

🚌

I needed help from a professional – from someone who would tell me what to do. I couldn't keep hassling Dr Roy with my thousand queries, nor Sonia and Barkha, and I didn't really know anyone who had travelled the country on a bus. So I did the next best thing. I emailed someone who used to manage one of the biggest networks in the UK and also in Australia, and who had always been kind to me. In journalism, I'd been taught never to be ashamed to ask for help. So I did.

This is what he wrote back:

> You won't be able to roll into some far-flung place, find somewhere to set up, and then look for half an hour of content.
>
> Agree you'll need to plan the route according to the election phases.
>
> But also look for the issues which will be likely to determine the outcome of that phase, and pre-select the locations which could best bring out those issues.
>
> Certainly you'll need panel discussions with the local movers and shakers, and people in the street, so English language will also be something to think about.
>
> But you'll need to identify and line up the people you want to talk to, long before you get there, and also have a crew and a producer move at least one day ahead to pre-shoot material for the day you are live from there.
>
> So you'd need a package to open, on what the areas about, why you are there, and what they are concerned about, and how that area could affect the election outcome. How it voted last time. Why it may change. Why it won't. Democracy in action.
>
> You'll need some good maps (on air) and plenty of pre-planning and shooting before you fire up the satellite truck each day.
>
> And don't forget to organize security and audience control.

The first sentence made me baulk. Rolling into some far-flung place and then looking for content was *exactly* what I was going to do. Then the part about having a producer go ahead, a day in advance, to shoot material for me, made me want to laugh hysterically. And of course, no reporter in India had ever heard about using security for audience control so I wasn't even going to go there.

I was going to have to do all the dirty work myself. Not only was I going to have to lug a 10 kg tripod into the fields to shoot, I'd also have to look pretty and fresh for the camera in the evening.

I was nearly hysterical by the time I got home. The entire bus trip began to feel like a grand conspiracy to prove that I was a failure. Why had I been selected from among so many reporters in my organization? Was I the only fool who would agree to this? After all, one of my colleagues did say, 'You should tell them you'll only do this thrice a week. It's too much to do everyday. You are very brave to say yes.'

Brave, I thought, or foolhardy?

I think I would have driven myself to a nervous breakdown even before I left if Sudeep hadn't put it into perspective for me that night.

'First of all, it will be a good show. Not every day, perhaps, because every place will not give you great material But that doesn't matter. It's the opportunity of a lifetime. Do you know that people like me would just kill to do this? So stop cribbing and consider yourself very lucky.'

So I took his advice and got busy over the next two weeks.

First, I tried to do the easy thing by finding a route across the country on Google. (The search engine is so integral to a journalist's life and is the source of so many stories that I have friends who refer to it as 'Google Mata', a deity to which they submit themselves wholly.) I was looking for the equivalent of Route 66 in India; to follow a path that, maybe, some backpacker had taken. All I found was the route taken by some firang kids (trust them to have so much time on their hands!) who had clambered into an auto-rickshaw to drive from Nepal to south India.

The toughest part of this trip was that I had to select places that were (a) interesting as news stories, (b) not overexposed and, most importantly, (c) towns that we could reach *before* the people voted. My dilemma was the places that were going to vote in the first phase of elections on April 16th couldn't have been further apart. They were Chhattisgarh, Kerala, half the seats of Andhra Pradesh and Orissa and the entire north-east of the country. Now, I could choose the north-east as it was largely neglected and there would be so many stories to tell, but that would mean that I would have to completely ignore states like Kerala and maybe even Andhra Pradesh as there was no way I could go through expansive states like Uttar Pradesh, Bihar and Bengal to reach the north-east and then make my way back to the eastern coast of India. I had to quickly prioritize the states and decide which ones we had, for logistical reasons, to leave out. I mean, I could have flown into some places in order to cut time but that wasn't even discussed because we were bussing everywhere, remember?

So, despite my best intentions we had to kiss the north-east and Chhattisgarh goodbye, while Kashmir had already been ruled out by the Boss. It's something we received a lot of complaints about and yes, we are guilty of giving more importance to the Hindi heartland. But, surely, not being on the agenda is a compliment in a way. We cover Bihar and UP so much *because* they are so warped.

I also had to quickly abandon the original plan of 50 kilometres a day. I wasn't going to get anywhere if I just did such small distances. For instance, if I was in Madhya Pradesh, it would take me a week to cross the state even if I covered 200 kilometres a day. And it was the same for other large states like Andhra Pradesh. Not only would it be time-consuming, chances were the issues too would not be very different over such short distances.

So I resigned myself to the idea that sometimes we would just have to be a little sleep deprived and travel around six to eight hours after our show in the evening, to get to our next destination. I knew that it would be hard on the crew, especially on our drivers, but we hadn't much choice if we wanted to cover the country. Fortunately, there was only me in the team at that time, so there was not much dissent within the ranks!

Then there was the other area of concern.

I desperately needed to know who the Hindi anchor travelling with me was going to be.

I'd heard this story recently about two best friends who took a month off to journey through the remote forests of South America. They'd been friends all their lives but after travelling together for a few weeks they'd hated each other and finally went their separate ways citing irreconcilable differences over an iPod.

I was dreading the list of stars that our sister network would pull out to accompany me on this amazing journey. What if it was the male anchor who thought he was a Bollywood hottie? He didn't look anything special, Lord knows, but his self-important stories in the make-up room always began with, 'My friend Aamir said' and 'My friend Shah Rukh said' and 'Hrithik called me and wanted to know what he should do, so *I* told him...' etc. I mean, is it just me who is sceptical of the special relationship that some TV anchors claim to share with glamorous film stars? How is it possible for a TV anchor to believe that one lousy interview with a film star – who is nice because he wants good press – makes them chuddy-buddies for life?

Then there was the morose female anchor who was cynical about everything. If you got an exclusive story, she'd say: 'It's a plant; your source is only giving it to you because he's going to benefit from it.'

Or: 'I'm sure that has been done before.'

Or, when you were pissing in your pants with excitement because you'd landed what you thought was an *amazing* story she'd diss it immediately, or worse, play on your TV insecurities: 'Sunetra, how come so and so was given that slot and not you?' So you'd tell her exactly what your boss told you, which in your apparent naiveté, you actually believed. And she'd go: 'Really, do you *actually* believe that?'

I did, you vixen, till you went and totally messed my peace of mind.

Okay, so I'm exaggerating.

I just knew that I was going to have to spend weeks in the same room, in the same vehicle, 24x7, with one person. Actually the team comprised others, but the Hindi presenter would also be sharing my room (TV budgets weren't that big). And if the Hindi presenter decided that she was going to compete with me, then not only was it going to be hell but it would also bring out the beast in me. After all, competition makes people do stupid things.

There was this one time in 2004, when we were covering the 400th anniversary of the Guru Granth Sahib. It was a pretty big story and I was assigned to go to Amritsar, to the Golden Temple. Over the ten days of celebration, thousands of people from across the world converged at the temple – the prime minister and the president of India among them. We were broadcasting live from there from morning till prime-time in the evening and I was slotted to do a live despatch for Dr Roy's show at 9 pm.

It was a pretty big deal for a junior reporter like me, so I had many calls from the Delhi office confirming my location, checking my background, etc. My colleague from the sister network had to do his live report for the 8.30 show. I just remember coming to stand in front of the camera at 9 (15 minutes before I was slotted to go on air) and discovering that the talkback was missing. The talkback's basically an earpiece that allows the Delhi office to talk to you, to give you directions and, most importantly, lets the studio anchor ask you questions. It had just vanished! The cameraperson said that my colleague had used it last but he was nowhere to be seen. I was already hyperventilating when I called him, and he casually told me that he had put it in his pocket by mistake.

'Okay, I need it *now* because I go on air in five minutes!' I said trying to keep the hysteria out of my voice.

Guess what he told me? 'I'm sorry, security is not allowing me through.'

It's been five years but I am yet to get over that incident and the madness that ensued with me begging other networks stationed there to lend me their earpieces. Finally, I went on air with a mobile earpiece, but the incident scarred me for life.

Here I was going crazy mapping out a route for the *Election Express*. But what if, after all those hours, my co-anchor came on board to announce she wasn't happy with the places I had chosen? I had bought a map of India taller than myself and I would sit with it and my computer, switching from the National Highway map, to the Yahoo India map, to Google news, studying them every minute I had free. For the first week I'd mapped out Delhi to Bharatpur, which was the centre of the biggest agitation in Rajasthan. Then Agra which was about 50 kilometres away, followed by Gwalior, Shivpuri and Jhansi. It was a really cool route, I thought, because we were covering three states in just a week, and covering diverse issues like Gwalior being a VIP constituency, Shivpuri being one too but not as developed, and Jhansi showing the worst of Uttar Pradesh and also having other issues like drought, and the development of the Bundelkhand issue. If the co-anchor found fault with it, I would tear my hair out.

She had a say of course, it was her show too. 'But why should we go to Kerala and not Chhattisgarh?' she might demur. 'No one speaks Hindi in Kerala, and we hardly have a presence there so I don't want to go. Please change the route. We will now go to Raipur.'

Aaarghhh.

So, I decided to put my superpowers to play. I like to believe (because I have watched way too much Oprah and because I believe she is my spiritual Momma) that if I really want something, I can *will* it to happen. I kept praying for the one anchor with whom I had had no problems at all the

last time we had been on an assignment together to Haridwar
– Naghma Sahar.

🚌

Everyone had kind of warned me off before that trip. 'She's
such a diva'; 'She's a star who has been brought in at a really
huge salary from the other channel'; 'Do you know that the
Hyundai Accent she drives was given to her by office? It's
because she is their *biggest* star.'

Because no one bothers to talk about insignificant people
like me, I was curious about people like her; people who got
talked about all the time. I knew she was hugely popular
because there were massive street hoardings with her picture
plastered on them all over the city, and ads featuring her in
newspapers. For me, she was the original TV star. I thought
having a few tantrums went with the turf. But like many other
things about Naghma, this was a fabrication.

Naghma was aware of her star status – she could hardly
ignore it when she was being mobbed in the gallis of Haridwar!
– but she didn't let it interfere with her interactions with me
on that trip. We had agreed broadly on how to do things and
had got along just fine, and although the Haridwar Ardhkumbh
had been a long time ago, I remember feeling pretty peaceful
about that assignment.

'Oh Lord,' I telepathically beamed to the Superpower
Headquarters: 'Let it be Naghma this time around as well.'
But when I bumped into her in the make-up room, a few days
later, I wasn't sure my message had got across to the gods.

'Going anywhere for the elections, Naghma?' I'd asked
nonchalantly. We shared a joke now and then, but I wasn't
close enough to her to ask her about the big assignment. What

I wanted to say to her was: 'Please get them to send you on the *Election Express*. Please, please!'

'I don't know, yaar, you know how it is. I'm just going to Agra for a few days' leave and then, let's see,' Naghma replied.

That's what's so cool about her. While everyone else, including myself, was going blue in the face trying to get themselves a starring role in the elections, she was taking it easy. She would play it as it came and it didn't look like she was angling for anything, either.

Luckily, a week before we were scheduled to leave, while she was still on vacation, she got the call I was praying for so ardently. She called me instantly. 'Listen, I've just been told about this trip. I asked them what it is about and they said, ask Sunetra.'

Yes, there is a god!

I told her not to worry, that I had things under control and to enjoy the rest of her days off. I would fill her in when she came back.

Why tell her now that she would not enjoy another day off for a long, long time?

🚌

'It's going to be really, really tough.'

I was having lunch with a colleague from our rival channel TV Today, Ravinder Bawa. During the 2004 elections, Ravinder had travelled across the country by road, like we were planning to do, but had basically gone from the extreme north of the country to the extreme south. 'We were also staying in hotels but sometimes we couldn't make it to one and had to spend the night in the car,' she said. 'By the end of it, I was dead.'

Bawa is the coolest, motorcycle-riding female journalist that I know. If she was calling something tough, I knew it was tough.

I was really scared now because I knew that not only was my journey longer, I was also going to have a live show to handle at the end of it, every day, while Bawa had just filed a story. But then she said something that was really encouraging: 'That trip has been the highest point in my career.'

It was time to stop worrying and to just take control of the situation. I was about to complete ten years as a professional journalist. I needed something big to celebrate. I was ready for the highest point of my career and I was determined to make this road trip work.

3

The Show Gets on the Road

When you're a newspaper reporter you pretty much fly solo – you meet your contacts, you get a story, you decide its worth, you sell it to your editor and once it makes it to the page, the glory is pretty much all yours.

In TV, it's not quite the same. Yes, the glory – or infamy as the case might be – might still be yours but it's definitely not in your hands. You are dependent on every single person in your team to deliver, to make sure that you don't end up looking like a performing monkey on camera. Monkey or daft cow – I've looked like both on several occasions, so I know how important this is, and naturally I was anxious about the team that would be assigned to me.

The biggest god for any reporter is the cameraman. If you want your story to be seen by people other than your cameraman and your editor, in other words, by the TV-watching public, then it has to have not just good pictures, but great ones. Pictures – we've been told by numerous TV professionals – are the most essential element in a story and if you don't have those you can pretty much pack your bags and go home. There are many colleagues I've worked with who think that cameramen are essentially people who weren't good enough to be reporters. They make their disdain known by not helping them carry their stuff, by talking down to them, by basically just treating them like coolies.

Some cameramen resign themselves to this treatment and work on, not complaining, but not producing brilliant work either. Others, insidiously, get their own back.

For instance, they might choose to overlook telling the reporter when she's having a really bad hair day, and casually refrain from suggesting that she tie up her hair to avoid looking like a helmet-headed horror. Or they might choose to shoot her at an angle suggestive of a triple chin and an urgent need for corrective liposuction. Or they'll make the reporter stand facing the sun in 45 degrees Celsius while they take their own sweet time pretending to configure the most appropriate piece-to-camera frame.

Oh, they know where it hurts and they hit hard.

Because I was not a diva and not high enough in the scheme of things, I couldn't demand the best or the most-sought-after cameraperson, or anything superlative in that department.

'Please assign someone who is excited at the prospect of travelling all over the country,' I had pleaded with the Camera Boss Man. 'Someone *so* enthu, he wouldn't mind giving up sleep for the next couple of months.'

Either I was one of those reporters who was branded non-cameraman-friendly or, to sustain enthusiasm over sixty days was just not possible, because the withering look the Camera Boss Man gave me, made me realize this was a tall order.

There was just about a week to go, and the Camera Boss Man was still shrugging his shoulders, with a shifty expression in his eyes and a hollowly unconvincing reply every time I confronted him in office: 'We are still looking.'

Hell, maybe it *was* me. While being supremely demanding of others, I am quite aware that I am not much of a joy to work with. My first and biggest problem is that I always think that the story I am working on is *the* biggest story in the world. I like to think that this is illustrative of my dedication to my job but some think otherwise. My friend Nirmala Ganapathy loves to tell a particular story of the time when we were both working on the city desk of *The Indian Express*.

It was the evening of September 11, 2001 and we were both in the newsroom where people had just witnessed two planes crashing into the Twin Towers in New York. Everyone was screaming, glued to the TV, calling their friends and relatives in America. Some reporters were being despatched to get reactions from communities in Delhi. But I was sitting at my terminal, trying desperately to zone out the din and file my story.

'Sunetra, why aren't you watching all this?' Nirmala kept asking me. 'Your story is probably not going to make it.'

Understatement of the year.

But there I sat, resolutely keying in a story about how the Ministry of Health was about to make Ayurveda part of the MBBS syllabus, quite convinced of its earth-shattering implications!

The story did make it, by the way.

Just two months later.

The other team member whose importance cannot be denied is the engineer. His role is a bit tricky because he *really* is an unsung hero and he knows it. TV cameramen may not be seen on air but their role is so obvious that the good ones know they are stars. Like reporters, they have skills that are quite tangible. When a team comes back from a conflict zone, the cameraperson becomes as celebrated as the reporter and while the public may not see them, the industry certainly acknowledges their worth.

But despite the engineer's work being crucial – what would you do if the engineer doesn't line up your satellite, for heaven's sake? – he is largely missing from the limelight.

I learnt the value of a good engineer the first time I had a broadcast van at my disposal. To explain, I'll again have to go back to the story of the Parechu Lake in Tibet and the floods that never came to Himachal Pradesh in 2004.

Usually, when you see TV people covering an event, you see them rooted to the same location all day. This is because it is a heck of a job finding a location, setting up the van, tracking the dish, pulling out the heavy cables and getting ready to go on air. It takes a lot of energy and enthusiasm to do this repeatedly, as part of the demands of ever-rolling TV bulletins. The engineer on that trip was a man who didn't speak much – I still don't know much about him – but he smiled easily, was mild-tempered and equable, and shared my concern for clean clothing.

But the reason I will never forget him is because the man would never say that something could not be done. Every couple of hours, we would quickly pack up and move to another location that told a different aspect of the story. When I'd ask him if it was possible for us to move again, would he have enough time to set it up, etc., he would always give me a definitive – 'I need ten minutes'. Not the classic cover-your-arse response – 'I'll try,' which makes me want to tear my hair out and hyperventilate at the same time; if it works, then hell, everyone should be grateful; if it doesn't, hey, I never made any promises.

'Sunetra, we found you someone, and he says he's pretty excited about going on the trip,' Camera Boss Man told me in the newsroom three days later.

I think he was more relieved than I was.

I called Mohammed Mursalin immediately.

'Hi Mohammed, have you heard of the wonderful adventure that we are about to go on?'

Mohammed, at twenty-eight, was about three years younger than me. He was married and had a baby girl who was just about a year old, and he was still willing to go on such a long and tiring journey; certainly that proved his enthusiasm. He'd joined NDTV much after me and, clearly, appeared to speak much less than me as well:

'Uh-huh,' was all he managed.

'You do know that they expect us to do a half-hour show every day, right?' It was almost as if I was trying to scare him off. 'They expect us to get to a place, to find enough stories, to line them up and then shoot them in a way that they can be edited really quickly?'

'I know,' he sounded calm. 'Don't worry, we'll do it.'

I spoke to other colleagues and they all told me that Mohammed was a good cameraman. That was all I needed to know – I had a co-anchor I liked and a solid cameraman.

I was feeling pretty chuffed about the assignment now. A few days ago I'd met someone who knew the business inside out, and he'd advised me that if I couldn't sleep at night then I would do well to spend those hours planning ahead. Planning for everything – finding out how much time it would take to get from the last destination to the next (don't forget, in some parts of India you can do 100 kms in an hour, and in others the same distance takes five hours), calling up local contacts, quizzing them about stories and issues, making a list of possible stories and personalities from those areas, and possibly fixing appointments with politicians when we visited their area.

So while I had already pinpointed some interesting stories that I wanted to do in all my first-week locations, I didn't necessarily want to spurn the sympathy that some of my co-workers were laying on me:

'We all heard about your big journey,' they'd say sympathetically and I'd immediately launch into this plaintive number about how I was going crazy and how I would have a breakdown with the amount of work and how I was only going because there was a chance that I was going to become Kate-Moss-skinny.

Actually, this last part was kind of true. I thought that since I was going into villages, I wouldn't get proper nutrition; that we'd probably have to live on bananas and carry crates of mineral water on the bus for the interiors. I pictured myself 10 kilos lighter, with well defined cheekbones, my jeans hanging from my hips, looking like one of Rachel Zoe's pack.

My weight-loss dreams were actually based on the first election story that I had covered in 2000. The Samajwadi Party leader Mulayam Singh Yadav's son Akhilesh Yadav had just returned from Australia (where they speak English, a language his father wanted to do away with in his 2009 manifesto) and wanted to try his hand at a by-poll election.

My paper thought it was just the right kind of off-beat political story for them, but they decided to send along their most politically naive reporter. I was summarily packed off to Uttar Pradesh's Kannauj with the paper's most politically astute photo-journalist, Praveen Jain. (After all, they couldn't risk a complete flop show.) If I started to fall apart under pressure of a political story, Praveen, they reasoned, would pull it together and avert a total disaster.

So, Praveen actually was my first teacher in the Art of Survival outside the Delhi office or the Art of Surviving the Jungle of Indian Politics.

We were on the Shatabdi Express, headed towards Lucknow, and I was watching, a little embarrassed by my colleague's behaviour, as he stuffed his bag with all the crap they give on the food tray, stuff that no one bothers with – four Marie biscuits, powder milk sachets, and tea bags. After staring for a little bit, I came out and asked Praveen why he was doing this.

'We're going into the interiors, darling, don't know when we will get food again.'

I wanted to tell him that even if I was dying of hunger, *I* wasn't going to be caught eating milk powder, but wisely didn't. Praveen Jain is from Rohtak in Haryana and he's worked his way up the hard way. If anyone knew about roughing it out, it was probably him.

Besides, it sounded pretty glamorous: *Oooh! I'm going to go to a place where we will not get any food! Oooh! I'm a tough reporter now!*

But, believe me, when we sat in the car eating hard-boiled eggs all through that assignment, weight loss or not, it certainly didn't feel half as cool.

I met Naghma five days before we were scheduled to leave.

'So tell me, how are we going to do this?' she said.

I gave her the lowdown.

'Are they going to send replacements in two or three weeks?'

'I don't know about you, but they have made it very clear to me and my cameraman that there will be no replacements at all.'

'Two months? But that's too much! I'll just ask them for a replacement in some time,' Naghma said, horrified.

I felt sorry for her; she'd had much less time to prepare for the journey ahead than I did. But in keeping with her trademark calm, Naghma looked completely unfazed.

We went over the itinerary for the first six weeks. I was a little anxious because it was so close to the departure date and I didn't want her to totally disagree on some of the destinations I had chosen. I carefully explained the rationale behind each place and some of the stories we could do there and the appointments that I had already fixed.

I think she sensed how anal I was about the route and agreed with me on most places. 'But shouldn't we spend more time in Uttar Pradesh, isn't that where most of the election colour is?'

We were touching Agra and Jhansi in the first week, I told her, and then perhaps on the way back to Delhi from

Bihar, we could visit more places like Rae Bareli and Aligarh, whatever she wanted, really.

'I've never been to Varanasi, I really want to go there.'

I knew how she felt. If we were going to be going on this back-breaking trip, we may as well visit some of the places that we had always wanted to visit, do some fun stories, take a boat-ride on the Ganga, perhaps. 'I don't think we can go there, Naghma. If we do then we'll miss the Andhra Pradesh elections, Kerala, a lot of other things. You tell me, how do we do it?'

Naghma just sighed loudly.

My editors were a bit more upbeat when I showed them the plan the day before we left. 'It sounds great,' beamed Sonia. I think that was the first time that she had no suggestions for me nor did she make any changes in our itinerary or any of the stories. 'Enjoy your last night of city life and have fun,' is all she said.

Enjoy your last night of city life?

Memories of a certain night out in 2002, before an impending Aligarh visit, had permanently marred that. It was summertime. I was single but, sadly, living with my parents. I was seeing Sudeep at the time and we'd decided to meet two other friends for dinner because I was leaving on an assignment the next day.

I have never been known to handle my drink but as friends are forever optimistic about one's skills, and because they do not understand the meaning of the word 'no', and also because journalistic assignments are *meant* to be tided over with lots of alcohol, glasses of daiquiri were followed with wine and tequila. Before I knew it, I was throwing up in the foyer of the Ambassador Hotel in Delhi. My friends got me home by 2am and I lay in bed with a head that was on a roller-coaster ride. Barely two hours later, the photographer accompanying me came to pick me up. My friends had promised me that I would sleep off my hangover on the way but the heat coupled with the UP road ensured that it was the worst ride of my life. Thank god for the healing powers of bananas in a reporter's life.

No, I didn't want to risk another bout of banana medication.

So I stayed in on the night of 20th March and moped about. I finished my packing in half an hour, having shopped earlier for a stack of kurtas. My friend from work, Neeta Sharma, had got her tailor to make me a few Patiala salwars to go with them – 'Please do not wear those short kurtas and pajamas like you do,' she had warned, shuddering at the thought of the sartorial blunders I might commit, thereby inadvertently attracting the attention of village rowdies.

Once the packing was done I looked mournful again.

'There's no point looking like you are sad about leaving me for so long,' said Sudeep, finally. 'You are dying to go.'

He was probably right.

There were some assignments before which I'd literally shed tears – all part of my coping mechanism! – but I couldn't wait to get started on this one. The adrenaline build-up had started three weeks ago and I was raring to channel it right.

🚌

Unfortunately, when we gathered early on Saturday morning at our designated departure spot, outside office, things were far from perfect. For one, our beautiful, shiny red, state-of-the-art bus was not ready. It could only notch up a top speed of 60 kilometres an hour so it was supposed to have left for Bharatpur early in the morning to wait for us there. But now there was no telling when we would arrive at our first destination. Typical. We were also supposed to have had an all-important dry run on Friday itself, which of course had not materialized. The plan had been to take the bus to Haryana, to shoot some stuff and uplink it back to Delhi to just familiarize ourselves with the bus. In the event that something was not working, it could be fixed well before our first show on Monday.

'Don't worry, it'll leave tomorrow morning. You guys carry on,' the engineering department told us cavalierly.

Theoretically, we didn't need the bus immediately but it's like when one aspect of your plan doesn't work, it usually means that other problems will soon follow.

And they did.

We were supposed to leave by 8am and my bags and Naghma's bags were loaded into the SUV but there was no sign of the cameramen.

'Where *are* you guys?' I was already exasperated when I called them.

'Umm, we are just getting our equipment together,' said Naghma's cameraperson, Nishant. He and Mohammed were to travel with us in the car. Why couldn't they have done that before? It was so unprofessional to make us wait like this.

After four hours and considerable heart-burn, we were finally ready to go. The back of the car was stuffed with equipment and I saw Mohammed with his precious P2 camera – it was one of those big ones.

'Why couldn't you just take a smaller camera? We have to run around, you know.' I was irritated that things weren't going in step.

'No, I want only this camera, I'll handle it.'

Fine, if that's the way it's going to be, I thought sourly. We were starting our 180km journey to Bharatpur and here I was already picking fights with the crew.

🚌

'Madam, let's have a hasta-khelta journey,' advised Ganga Singh, our fifty-five-year-old driver, sensing the tension in the air. Ganga Singhji was happy with his plum role at NDTV. He was the driver who either drove around the Big Boss to his local appointments, or ferried really, really important guests to and from the studio. He usually didn't sully his hands driving mere reporters around but, Ganga Singhji claimed, he was the only one trustworthy enough to be called in for this venture: 'They told me that only *you* can go.'

We learned very early on that trip that Ganga Singh was a great one for giving unsolicited advice. He was never insolent, at least he never meant to be, but as one of the earliest employees of NDTV, and considerably older than all of us, he thought it his responsibility to dole out the platitudes. 'We have to spend so many days together so we might as well have fun. *Kyon bhai?*'

Before joining the ranks of NDTV drivers Ganga Singhji had been in the army. (He pointed out every place we passed on the journey that looked half impressive, and claimed proudly – 'That is an army area, madam. They always keep their area clean.')

Heeding his advice, I immediately felt the pressure to be immensely social – cracking jokes, talking loudly and generally trying to raise everyone's spirits. 'Guys, can you believe this? We are going to go to Goa and Kerala. Imagine the food!

Oh, so amazing! Do you think the show will be good? Do you? *Do you?*'

'Madam, I have brought my cylinder and utensils,' Ganga Singhji piped up suddenly.

'What? Why?' I was perplexed.

'Ji, madam, in places where we don't get food I will cook for you.' He was quite sweet but I hoped in my heart that we wouldn't need to test his cooking skills.

While I tired myself out with my non-stop babbling, Naghma stayed calm. She felt no pressure to communicate; there was two months to do just that. 'What are we doing for the first show?' she asked finally, hoping, no doubt, to shut me up.

'Okay, I spoke with Sachin Pilot and he told me that he doesn't mind driving down today or tomorrow to Bharatpur for us to record the interview. He told me that once we were about to reach, we should call him.'

I was pretty pleased with myself for organizing this. While the bosses had been very clear that I didn't have to chase after politicians on this show, I knew that no one would complain if I landed an interview with the 'rising star' of the Congress Party, the 'Gen-Next' hero and the urban face of the Gujjar community.

That's because the media loves Pilot and his PLU (People Like Us) image. I felt the PLU factor even more because Pilot was almost the same age as me and we'd both done Bachelor of Arts with Honours at Delhi University, he at the fancy St Stephen's College and me at the less celebrated Jesus and Mary College. I also had a cousin who was his classmate.

I was just amazed that someone who could easily have been my friend or classmate, was actually a politician representing not us, but the Gujjar community! And that part of his job was to rush to Dausa to negotiate whether or not his tribesmen should cut off the limbs of corpses as part of their protest!

In 2008, I had just started covering the Congress Party regularly when a cabinet reshuffle was announced. As usual, senior journalists had been humbled because their sources had told them that Sachin Pilot was becoming a minister and – (shock, horror) – he had not. To be fair, clueless Congress leaders not in sync with Sonia Gandhi had spread these false stories. So the only thing to do then was for all of us to speculate on what had gone wrong for the young Pilot and how it would affect the party.

Embarrassingly, as it turned out, I was the sole reporter who was doing this 'speculation' standing outside Pilot's house. And as it so happened, Pilot watched every bit of the show where I said that this was going to heavily piss off the Gujjar community. It didn't, but I think Sachin Pilot was flattered by the weightage my report gave his exclusion from the prime minister's council of ministers.

I called him now from the car: 'Hi Sachin, so when will you come?' For a long time, I couldn't bring myself to call Sachin by his first name. How can you call a politician by their first name? But Sachinji sounded plain ridiculous and Mr Pilot was way too pompous. Besides, I had to also factor in the point that politicians were now far younger than they used to be. I mean, there were so many now that were younger than *me*. It was depressing.

I continued on the phone: 'It's our first show and we've chosen Bayana and Dausa because that's the location of the only issue that rocked Rajasthan in the last five years. We want you as a young representative to tell us what's the way forward for the Gujjar community. Also, perhaps, you can bring in the element of losing your constituency to delimitation.'

Actually, Sachin Pilot was the perfect person to explain to all of us why a tribal rivalry had spiralled into such a major crisis two summers in a row. It was first in the summer of 2007 that backward-caste Gujjars had organized themselves together demanding an even lower or scheduled-tribe status for themselves, so that they could get reservations in government jobs and educational institutes. They'd blocked highways, sat on rail tracks, and lost 26 people in clashes with the police and the Meenas, members of a rival caste who were opposing their demand. Urban India had been shocked not just at the violence of this agitation, but at the way in which they had paraded their corpses, refusing to cremate them till the government gave in to their demands.

The government didn't give in and thought it had managed to contain them with bureaucratic bullshit but the same drama unfolded again exactly the same time next year. In total, 71 Gujjars lost their lives but at the end of it nothing was resolved. The entire issue was lost in the talks between the central government and the state government. The Gujjar leader, Colonel KM Bainsla had grown too close to the BJP and had lost credibility with his men. So, Sachin Pilot was the only one from the community whom our viewers would relate to, and who, hopefully, would give us some idea about which way the community was voting and whether they would continue to fight for scheduled tribe status.

'Tell me frankly, Sunetra, how long is this interview going to be?' asked Sachin when I phoned him. 'I mean, is it going to be worth it for me to drive down for it?'

I immediately sensed trouble. 'Three or four minutes,' I said biting my lip, wishing I had lied as I spoke.

'Okay, let me think about it and give you a call.'

We all knew what that meant; he wasn't going to call again.

'Do you think we should have done ten minutes of our half-hour show with him?' I asked Naghma. But I knew we couldn't have given him that much time. The Hindi channel did not want so much talk, they wanted the colour of elections. And we couldn't start a show that was about the voters and then assign most of the time to a Delhi politician!

So, we were left without the only thing that was promising to boost our ratings for the first show.

We were starting our journey by arriving in Bharatpur without a bus, and without a story.

4

The Feisty Women of Gujjarland

We were without the bus and we were without the main attraction of our first show – Sachin Pilot. The mood, as we TV people love to describe it, was far from 'buoyant'.

Once in the Bharatpur hotel, having I think given up on me, Naghma started making some calls herself. I was bringing myself around to accepting that instead of a 30-year old PLU like Sachin Pilot, I might have to settle for a 50-something has-been like Colonel Bainsla – Colonel Bainsla who had already talked himself to inanity on TV; Colonel Bainsla who was now discredited even by his own community of Gujjars for going to the Bhartiya Janata Party; Colonel Bainsla who could – maybe – add something to my show but it definitely wasn't going to be the X-factor.

'Don't worry, Sunitra' (that's how they pronounce my name in the boondocks) Colonel Bainsla had said to me. 'I'll come to Bharatpur by ten in the morning.'

Just the thought of doing the Bainsla story was pissing me off; but you get more irritated when someone voices what you've known inside all along. 'You know, everyone gets Colonel Bainsla. He's been heard so many times before,' said Naghma.

'So has Sachin Pilot!' I snapped. I was sulking. Even more so, because I couldn't drown out what she was saying by turning on a television. I looked around the hotel room. Why wouldn't a decent hotel in India provide a TV? It's like those pretentious boutique hotels that charge you the earth but don't put TVs in the room. Why would they do that? If someone didn't want to watch TV – because they were cutting off from the world and connecting with their partners or whatever – couldn't they just leave the damn thing turned off? As far as I'm concerned, I'm pro-choice and I *always* choose to watch TV.

While I was sulking, Naghma organized a local journalist to come over and give us the lowdown on Bharatpur. Sadly, we weren't even going to take a stroll through the bird sanctuary, even though I'd tried my damndest to hard-sell some connection between the sanctuary and elections. 'What if, Naghma, it is a big issue for people here that the sanctuary is not being looked after properly?' I'd demanded.

'Are there reports that it is neglected?' she'd asked.

'Not really, but people are always dissatisfied with the way government runs things. I'm sure we can find some people for whom it could be an issue. You know, it would be a great story for TV – birds and animals are always great visually.'

I think I actually had her convinced. (If not a PLU, then why not a PLU-issue like environment?)

But the bureaucrats manning the gates of Bharatpur wanted to see letters from the Ministry of Environment before they let us anywhere near the sanctuary. We could only curse them and kiss our bird story goodbye.

Naghma's contact, a local journalist, finally showed up. He was a skinny young boy who worked for a local cable channel. He gave us the lowdown on Bharatpur. How it was a prestige issue for Maharaja Vishvendra Singh – a former royal who like all other royals across the country was still referred to as Raja. Vishvendra Singh had won the constituency for the Bhartiya Janata Party lots of times but when the other royal Vasundhara Raje Scindia fought with him over party candidates, he switched to the Congress Party. Unfortunately, he couldn't contest from his fiefdom. Like Sachin Pilot's Dausa had become reserved for a scheduled-tribe candidate, Bharatpur too had become reserved for a scheduled-caste candidate. And even though he'd won parliamentary elections twice from the BJP, he'd lost assembly elections in 2008 on the Congress ticket.

So was he set to regain his lost prestige in the Lok Sabha elections?

'Do you think he'll invite us to his palace?' Naghma asked me uncertainly.

I wasn't really interested in doing a story on the Raja. Our brief had been to do more people-based stories really, but since one interview had fallen through, I saw a slot. 'If he invites us over to his palace, then maybe we should go for it. It'll make a nice colour piece and we'll shoot him with his group of supporters.'

Naghma spoke to the Maharaja for a long time. The first call was always tedious. One had to explain the show. The buzzwords were bus, roadshow, elections, first show. 'He says he wants to come to our hotel,' she announced after finally putting the phone down.

'I don't want to do it here! It'll be boring in our hotel. We don't want just a bite!'

'Let's chuck it then,' Naghma agreed readily. 'I haven't told him what time, anyway. Do you think he'll still come?'

'He's a Raja. Why would he come without us calling again?'

We were quite satisfied that the Raja couldn't be a story unless he allowed us an inside look at the lives of the rich and famous. We were interested in doing the full-colours-of-royalty story – the Raja resplendent in his turban with his bejewelled wife in an ornate sari by his side, strolling through their massive palace as we spoke. We wanted to do the story so that viewers who couldn't be bothered about the caste equation in Bharatpur, or the Raja's strategies for defeating the rival Rani, could simply admire the luxury of his beautiful home. (We later realized that we kept looking for the royal colour throughout our journey and we never quite found it.)

Anyway, on that Saturday evening, with just a visit to the Gujjar village lined up, we had precious little to fill our show.

'Let's try and find young voters,' suggested Naghma.

Actually, if there had been one clear-cut instruction that we'd got from our editors in Delhi, it was to get into the mind of Young India. Estimates said that about a quarter of the electorate were young voters and while we got to hear plenty from the youth of Delhi, Mumbai and other metros, we just didn't hear enough from the youth in smaller cities and towns. Naghma and I were eager to bridge this gap. We turned to our journalist friend: 'Where do we find them?'

'The mandir in town. That's where all young people hang out in the evening.'

So that's where we headed.

Our bulky four-wheel drive somehow made its way to the mandir and yes, it was packed with young people even though it was nine in the evening. Now, the format of our show was to shoot at one go, so that less editing was required. I would do a little bit of a walk-and-talk commentary about the local site, speak to a few people, show the place a little more, speak to a couple of people again, make my point, and wrap.

After spending some time there figuring out who my subjects were going to be, I approached three girls on their cycles waiting to eat chaat at the food stall. In my introduction, I wanted to talk about how we, in Delhi, have coffee shops, lounge bars, book shops, malls, parks – all kinds of places to hang out – but in small towns the most 'happening' place is the temple. Most don't even step into the temple, preferring to hang around outside where there is enough food and enough of a crowd for no one to pay much attention to what you are doing, or whom you are talking to.

I wasn't really sure what I wanted to ask the girls. I suppose I wanted to know if they were happy with what they had in Bharatpur. Did they like meeting here at the temple or did they too want shiny malls and coffee shops? The girls were out at this time of the evening, so did they feel safe in Bharatpur? Things like that, really.

The girls were keen to be on TV so I didn't have any problem convincing them to talk to me, but I wanted to just do a little walk-around first. That became impossible. I had hoped to show viewers what the city looked like, to give them a taste of the food street in Bharatpur and a glimpse of the life there, but I couldn't. All they would have seen would have been me speaking to the camera, with the frame filled to capacity with all sorts of people falling on top of me, blocking my cameraman's view, talking and jeering rudely. 'Madam, why don't you speak to us,' they said to me. 'Ji, ask me my views as well,' another leered.

I turned around to see Naghma lost in a little mob of her own. Was it worse for her because they understood every word she was saying in Hindi and reacted loudly to everything she said? (When, for instance, Naghma said, 'Bharatpur has traditionally voted with the BJP' a storm of protest ensued: 'Madam, how can you say that?' 'Madam, that's not true!' 'Congress Party ki Jai, Congress Party ki Jai!' And before you knew it there was total chaos.)

Or was I the worse off?

In most villages that I went to, the crowds couldn't understand what I was saying because I spoke in English. But in Bharatpur, many young people could understand me but were frustrated because they couldn't carry out a dialogue with me. They had all gone to schools in the area, some of them even to English-medium schools, but this hadn't equipped them with the requisite language skills and that, I found, made them angry.

'Does anybody speak English here?' I asked. A group of boys started teasing each other and one of them pointed to a boy in the group. 'Do you speak English?' I asked, trying very hard not to sound menacing because I was irritated by the elbow that someone was thrusting into my back.

'A little.'

'Okay, what party do you vote for?'

He shook his head and gave up. I felt bad. In any other place, I would have conducted the interviews in Hindi in any case but the crowd was getting uncontrollable. I returned to the car and sat there waiting for Naghma to finish filming.

'I did it,' she said triumphantly getting in.

'How did you manage? They behaved like animals,' I said.

Naghma laughed her head off at the thought of me being intimidated by a group of boys. After all, I was hardly new to this sort of thing.

'Yes, I could have finished my piece if I tried,' I conceded. 'But what's the point? This piece was meant to be an introduction to Bharatpur's nightlife, not its wildlife!'

We woke up to the phone ringing around 11pm.

'The bus is here.'

We all trooped out of the hotel in our pyjamas to have a look at our office-cum-residence for the next two months. Curious hotel employees came out with us to see this big red thing.

'What took you guys so long?' we asked Sumit, the engineer, and Jiggy and Thomas, the two bus drivers, who would take turns to drive it.

'It came back only by afternoon and then we did a puja.'

But of course. We would need all the divine intervention we could muster to complete this mega assignment.

As soon as we climbed into the bus, a lot of the angst that had been building up through the day dissipated. It was great! Just the way we had visualized it. The bright red exterior with the NDTV flag on top was slick, but the inside was even better. It was fitted with five brand new La-Z-Boy look-alikes for us to sprawl in when we travelled, a cute little fridge that we soon stocked high with lassi (to the disappointment of some who thought it should have beer) and on its wall, prominently displayed, was the big map of India I had purchased. We sat on the seats to try them out and stared at the map.

'Can you imagine? We are going to go around the entire country in this,' I said to Naghma.

'I know. We must do a piece around the bus, yaar.'

Though I didn't get a chance to see it then, on our two months on the road, after I came back I saw CNN's election bus on YouTube. It was a thousand times better equipped than ours with multiple satellite links (we had just one), a huge crew working inside the bus, a huge technical team, many plasma screens, a kitchen and a toilet. But, then and even now, I have a sense of wonder and amazement at just what we were setting out to do with the smallest crew possible. And I knew that we could beat the hell out of CNN with our energy and enthusiasm. That night I dreamt only of the red bus and all the brilliant things that I'd have in the first episode of our show.

In the morning it became disconcertingly clear that the stories were only happening in my dream.

'Sunitra,' Colonel Bainsla said, killing my name as usual. 'I am a little stuck in Gurgaon, why don't you come here?'

'But, Colonel Bainsla, I told you that the bus reached Bharatpur yesterday.'

'Oh, acchha. Okay, doesn't matter, I will finish and come down tomorrow morning.'

Colonel Bainsla's interview was supposed to be in Bayana near Bharatpur but since he was stuck, and it was the day before the show, we had to come up with Plan B. So we decided to head for Dausa and find our own stories.

Dausa – the worst-affected area during the Gujjar agitation – was an hour's drive away, about 50 kilometres from Jaipur. I had a contact there who wanted to explain to me why the Gujjars were demanding reservations. He wanted to take me on a poverty tour – to visit the poorest, most dilapidated house in his village so that he could say, 'Look this is what they have reduced us to,' and from there to the enemy area – that is where the Meena tribes live – to show me the roads, and the palatial houses, to impress on me how privileged the Meenas were and how they didn't need reservations anymore. I would have gone along with that story, perhaps, but when we got to Dausa, I had some other ideas.

'How far are the Meena houses in the village from the Gujjar ones?' I asked. My contact told me that they weren't far at all. In fact, some lived right next to each other. I wanted to meet a Gujjar and Meena family who lived side by side, to understand the agitation through their eyes.

Driving the dirt road into a Rajasthani village – led by my contact riding ahead on his motorcycle with a girl and her puppy on the pillion – through miles and miles of fields, it was the first time that I got a sense of what we were going to be doing for the next couple of months. Because we were in a big vehicle, people would just stop and smile at us – Rajasthani women in bright coloured dupattas and lehengas, children with runny noses, and old men squatting languidly around.

Ganga Singhji had an eclectic collection of music CDs, ranging from Bengali devotional songs about trekking to Badrinath, to really bad Garhwali music, and one CD of Indian Ocean. Obviously, we all rooted for Indian Ocean, only agreeing to switch to something else when Ganga Singhji urgently needed a Garhwali number to combat his driving fatigue. But that day, as we drove into the Gujjar–Meena village in Dausa, *Jhini* was playing in the background.

'Is this where they stay?' I asked my contact.

'Yes, yes, but let's have something to eat first.' The little girl with the puppy disappeared into the crowd that had instantly gathered around us – she had been despatched to get rotis prepared for us.

'No, no, we need to finish our work first' – a statement that was usually ignored in rural India. When you walk into a village to meet people in India, they like a little foreplay before talking shop. They want you to have tea, break bread, shoot the breeze and only then are you permitted to figure out how to do your story. But this was a social ritual we simply hadn't the time for. So the bargaining started: 'Sirji, please, we really have to meet lots of people. We'll come next time and eat lunch.' *Please sir, please.*

After much pleading we were finally led towards the houses. One, we were told, belonged to a Gujjar family and the one adjacent to it, to the Meenas. The houses were in front of their patch of wheat fields and the women were out working on them. The men, as far as I could see, were not doing much, except following us around. 'Can you call them,' I asked my contact. He said yes but didn't budge. I finally figured out that he couldn't address the women, and neither could any of the other men, but they felt too shy to say that to an outsider. So, I walked down to the women accompanied by the little girl and her pup.

'Erm, can I speak to you for a second?' I asked the woman closest to me. She giggled from behind her long ghunghat and moved away. 'Hello, I've come from Delhi to speak to you.' More giggles but no one was coming any closer to me, they kept chattering to each other in their dialect. Naghma, standing behind me, looked amused too. I was about to just go and grab the woman's arm till I looked back and realized that I had a gang of men behind me.

'Will you please go away? I think the women aren't talking to me because all of you are standing around.'

The men were very upset about missing out on all the amusement but they stepped back a few paces. While we were waiting for the men to clear off, Naghma said, 'These women have such great bodies, yaar.' We took a minute to just admire them. They had probably all had children but you couldn't tell that from their flat, bare midriffs. That morning I had got up and done several Surya Namaskars but I knew that however many I did, I would never look as fit as these women. I'd probably have to take up working in the fields for that. 'And look at the shirts they are wearing, how nicely cut they are.' We stood there, taking in the blues and pinks and greens that swirled in the field around us while the women giggled.

I walked up to the one who was giggling the most. 'Listen, I need to speak to you,' I was a bit more firm this time.

'Tell me,' she said, pulling back her ghunghat. She was smiling with the pearliest whites I had ever seen.

'What's your name?'

'Suntra (as in orange) Meena.'

I knew she was cracking a few jokes at my expense as she spoke to me because she said something in her dialect that made the other women throw back their heads with laughter. Braving the laughs, I told her we wanted to speak to her and her Gujjar neighbour. She pointed to a woman who was less boisterous and who looked at me shyly. My contact had earlier told me that the Gujjar woman's husband had been killed in the agitation against the Meenas. I thought it would be interesting to speak to the women together, to find out what it was like to work and live side by side when the clash between the communities had cost one woman her husband. I wanted to know if Suntra felt guilty; I wanted to know if the widow blamed Suntra or her husband in any way. I wanted to know how they viewed this entire agitation. I told her what a long way I had come just to meet her.

'Fine, I'll talk, but I'm busy cutting the wheat,' said Suntra. 'And they are also busy. It's a lot of work for us. Why don't you cut some for us?' she added mischievously.

She brandished her sickle and all the women turned to look expectantly at me.

'Is that all? Sure.'

I was quite amused as well. Obviously Suntra wasn't *that* busy if she had time to play such games with me. I picked up the sickle.

My contact came running. 'Madam, please be careful.'

My attitude was – Yeah, yeah, no sweat, I've done this before. They all laughed as I grabbed a handful of wheat and brought the sickle down on it. Mohammed suddenly saw an opportunity for TV and started rolling his camera. 'Say a line to explain what you're doing,' he instructed me. I spoke a line to the camera and tried to simultaneously cut the wheat when I realized how inept I was at it! The women were rolling with laughter. Hearing them laugh the men came back to gawp at me making an ass of myself.

I stopped trying to cut the wheat after a couple of attempts. 'No, do more, do more,' Suntra ordered, only letting me off after I'd gamely gone on at it for a bit. 'See, this is how it's done,' she said, clearing a patch of wheat in one clean swipe.

I bowed my head to her in admiration. 'Can we sit down and talk now?'

She smiled and nodded. Again, we waited for the men to back off. This time they were even more reluctant to leave, thinking they would miss out on more clowning on my part. Finally we got them to move and began to film the backyard – the buffaloes, the charpoys, the village house, all making a scenic rustic frame.

'Sit on the charpoy,' Mohammed instructed Suntra and her neighbour, Keshula Gujjar, the widow's sister-in-law. But they squatted on the ground. I thought they didn't understand what he was saying so I patted the charpoy, but still they remained where they were. I looked accusingly at the men thinking their presence was making them shy and again asked my contact to make them disappear.

'Madam, we will move but the women will not sit on the charpoy.'

It was an exalted place, only for the men, apparently. I was just about to go all feminist when Mohammed said, 'It's fine, it'll make this frame look better.'

Finally, we were ready to roll and the two women, with the ghunghats off their faces, talked to us about their relationship on camera. If I was expecting a heavy Oprah moment – which I always look forward to since I'm such a fan – I wasn't going to get one.

Keshula Gujjar said she had lost her brother-in-law in the agitation for reservations. 'I think he had been drinking so when they had the rally, he also went with all the men,' said Keshula in the most matter-of-fact way. His widow was quiet, she couldn't speak Hindi at all but her face betrayed no emotion. Keshula explained that his death had nothing to do with the demand for special tribal status that would get them a better shot at government jobs or an education. Her husband's brother was foolish and he'd got drunk and got killed; ideology had nothing to do with it. Suntra said – 'We have nothing to do with what is happening outside. For years we have been working in the fields together and we'll continue to do so.'

Mohammed gave me the thumbs up. Our first story was wrapped.

After we had finished shooting, Keshula beckoned me once again. I was a little scared and braced myself for a second round of slavery in the fields. 'We have listened to you, now come and have chai with us,' she said grabbing Naghma and me by the hand and dragging us to the house.

'We love your shirts, where do you get them tailored?' said Naghma, thrilling Keshula to bits.

'Shall I call the tailor?' she offered immediately.

We followed our hosts into the kitchen. It was behind the concrete main house building – where the family men sat in the courtyard. We took off our shoes and went inside. The first thing that struck me was the presence of a bed in the room.

More women crowded in behind us and sat on the floor.

Inside, it was a different world! The women threw off their ghunghats, revealing numerous babies who were proudly paraded about. 'This is my room,' said Keshula, pointing to the bed. It was a bit weird to have a bedroom as a kitchen but I could see that she felt free in this space, free from all the male relatives. I wanted to ask her if her husband slept with her in the kitchen but thought it was a bit impolite to ask that so soon after we'd met.

'Are you married? Do you have children?' They wanted to know from us. When I said we were married, they wanted to know how we'd talked our men into letting us gallivant around like this.

'Our mother-in-law wouldn't let us out, as she'd have to do all the work then,' they laughed. The mother-in-law was also quite a good sport, allowing jokes at her expense. 'She got us so that she could have an easy life,' they giggled. I couldn't figure out where they found the energy to cook and look after their children after working the whole day in the fields. I thought of my life in Delhi – doing no manual labour at all, and yet, feeling too darn lazy to come back home and cook; inflicting our cook Savitri's insipid dal and half-cooked bhindi on poor Sudeep every day.

The thing is, it would have been easy for me to assume that the women were exploited. But they didn't look exploited. They were laughing, they were feisty and if they had got their way with me, I'm sure they got their way with their men too. I'm glad we spared some time for chai and lots of photographs before we said good bye.

🚌

'Rajaji had come,' one of the hotel employees informed us as soon we landed in the hotel.

'What?'

'Rajaji came and he walked around the lawns while waiting for you,' he said accusingly.

Oh dear! Vishvendra Singh had turned up after all! The Raja had come to meet the Delhi reporters – without any entourage, without any supporters, without any women – and they had stood him up.

'How was I supposed to know that he would just turn up like that?' Naghma said unhappily.

'You know that he will never give us an interview again, right?' I said to Naghma. It wasn't entirely our fault. 'What if Vishvendra Singh complains about us?' I was always scared about things like that so I thought, let me just grovel my way out of this. 'I'll tell him to come over for our show and we can maybe fit him into a one-minute live.'

What would the King think if he heard us trying to make amends by offering a minute on our precious rundown? We knew that a minute is a lot of time. As anchors we have often been instructed to distil complex ideas and arguments into minute-long stories for evening bulletins, but it's something interviewees have never understood. They always look offended when you tell them about the one-minute show.

So I was kind of glad that the Maharaja chose not to take my call.

5

5,4,3,2,1... Cue – You're on Air

Just two days on the road, and I had figured out that Ganga Singhji was going to be a godsend on this trip – he was going to be our saviour, our Mr Fix-it. In just two days, he had won us all over. When any of us got really hungry in the car he'd whip out his special mixture of peanuts and gram to tide us over till the next pit stop. If we went to a dhaba with some loutish types hanging around, he'd gallantly say, 'Madam, why don't you just stay here, I'll get the food sent to the car.' He was willing to share his cigarettes with Mohammed and he never shirked any work, never acted lazy even though he was the oldest member of our team, and was always, always keen to be helpful.

That Monday afternoon, just four hours before airtime, we needed helpful people around. Ganga Singhji had realized we weren't going to have time to go to a restaurant so he'd brought us food – spicy dal, shahi paneer and roti. Mohammed and I had uplinked all our footage and stories so we were both on the floor, eating. I was sitting on the floor of the bus because the plastic plate I was eating out of was so flimsy that the dal was making it crumple. I laid it on the floor so that the dal wouldn't spill. The food, as it hadn't come from a fine dining restaurant, was all in polythene bags. When we opened one we had to either pour it all out on to a flimsy plate or eat with one hand while the other clutched the bag with the food in it. To step up the challenge, we didn't have any cutlery either and the Bharatpur heat was giving our air-conditioners a run for their money.

Of course this was nothing compared to the time during the 2007 Gujarat elections when we were stationed outside Narendra Modi's house. Modi had just swept the elections but unlike other politicians, he didn't believe in spreading the joy to the waiting media crews outside his home. So, after standing in front of the camera all day long, my colleagues and I, dressed in formal wear, had squatted on the road – the actual road, mind, not the pavement – to eat. We ate in the presence of a full audience of Gujarati onlookers watching our butts get toasted on the tar road; the day their illusion of TV glamour was blown to smithereens.

'The food is good, madamji,' said Ganga Singhji, pre-empting any irritation on my part. 'I directed him to cook it specially.'

But food wasn't the real crisis. 'Forget about the food, Ganga Singhji, please can you do some shopping?'

My list was simple – disposable cutlery, a few plates, a dustbin – and a mirror.

'A *mirror?*'

I'm sure he thought, how vain *is* this woman?

'Ganga Singhji, I don't care where you get it from. I have to have a mirror.'

Naghma and Nishant were trying to figure out the edit on one of their pieces. But she immediately looked up at the mention of a mirror. 'Yeah, that's a *great* idea,' Naghma said fervently.

Believe me, we weren't being vain. It's just that the last thing anyone needs on a TV show is bad hair and bad make-up. When I was a TV reporting virgin, fresh from the high-brow environment of a newspaper and journalism school, I was naive enough to believe that all I needed was a diary full of contacts to ensure me good stories. Sure, that goes a long way; trouble is, no one *comes* that long way with you if you look like you've just climbed out of bed. I was told – and now I believe it too – that if your hair is a mess and you are standing and delivering the biggest scoop in TV journalism no one will hear anything you say; they'll keep looking at your hair and asking themselves – How did they *let* someone like that on TV?

For the longest time, I got the worst kind of feedback when I presented the news. I spent lots of time thinking of clever things to say, writing it out in the most lucid language with clever captions, only surrendering myself to the mercy of a make-up person with fifteen minutes to go. The results were evident from viewers' letters – and here I am quoting actual feedback, this one from a Sanjay, dated August 2005:

> *Why do your anchors have so much make-up on? Look at Sunetra Chowdhury.... BLUE EYE SHADOW... she looks ghastly. i thnk (sic), you need to change your make-up artist and need to do a subtle job for news make-up.*

these aren't your page 3 reporters you know.. also, please give them a lesson or two in dressing sense and what pendants to wear with what clothes.

And this was one of the milder letters that I've received. How about this from another lovely gent:

Sunetra Choudhury: Apart from the fact that she is a biological enigma (because she speaks in a manner and tone of voice which makes one believe, particularly if one is not looking at the box, that it's a male newscaster reading) has she been issued specific instructions that her lips and cheek movements have to ape a particularly repulsive variety of serpent found in WILD AMAZONIA show? I believe the creature in question is found in the Brazilian rain forests. She gives the impression of frantically SUCKING on a straw to MILK the last drops from a Frooti tetra pack.

It was so insulting! I wasn't even sure I understood the intensity of this insult but there was nothing obscure about other mails:

Silver eye shadow, Shimmering lip gloss and she herself falling all over the table with drooping eyes like on some late night news show or something. STOP! For heaven's sake.

These weren't the words of some unforgiving TV critic. These were regular viewers who were so allergic to the way I looked, they had to do something about it. Thankfully, as time went by, along with acquiring a habit for the hair dryer I acquired a thicker skin. It wasn't the nasty emails that made me pay greater attention to my appearance (*that* would have made me go the other way entirely; maybe I would have grown a moustache!). No, what made me change my attitude was an honest exchange with my boss, Sonia.

Sonia explained very clearly that not caring about my appearance was simply not an option. I had to make sure my hair was in place and my face was fixed not because it would make up for the shortcomings in my story, but so people weren't distracted *away* from my story.

'As anchors at NDTV, we expect you not to be just newsreaders,' said Sonia. 'Because if you aren't happy with the way you look, the viewers won't be either.' I respected Sonia and so I gave in – I spent more time on my appearance and I surrendered my hair to the office stylist. (The vicious emails didn't disappear altogether, but they found other objects for their ire.)

So the plastic, green-framed mirror from the Bharatpur Bazaar that Ganga Singhji bought was placed right at the entrance of the bus, next to the big India map. We would have to get ready right here on the bus for our show, as we'd checked out of our hotel that morning, ready to move to our next destination.

Pity we couldn't ask Ganga Singhji to also shop for a mobile loo for us.

The hunt for loos was going to be a recurrent theme throughout the trip but it was one of those horrors of road travel that Naghma and I had surrendered ourselves to.

It wasn't topmost in our minds that afternoon though, when we had far bigger worries – like our apparent rudeness to the Maharaja of Bharatpur. Anyway, karma always has a way of evening things out: if we had left Vishvendra Singh waiting, Colonel Bainsla had stood us up.

He kept us hanging for a few hours by saying, 'I am running a little fever, Sunitra, but don't worry, I am coming,' each time I called. Then he changed it to: 'I am coming but I'm coming a little late.' At 1pm he stopped taking my calls altogether.

Still, we did have the introductory piece about the show; a piece featuring our journey, the bus and the crew – many of whom, like Jigmender the bus driver – ('Madam, just call me Jiggy') – turned out to be natural stars.

Because of their abundant waistlines, the drivers Jiggy and Thomas were also affectionately referred to as 'Sumos' by the rest of the crew. But that was the only thing they had in common. Thomas was shy and hardly spoke, while Jiggy really played to the cameras, talking easily and at length about the capacity of the bus and his ability to take on the dangers ahead. Engineer Sumit, at 24, was the youngest in our team, and he lapped up the gaze of the cameras, telling everyone how no village was too small, no road too narrow for the NDTV election bus to visit and beam live from! Mohammed and Nishant demonstrated the luxuries that the bus offered in the form of the fridge and the La-Z-Boy look-alikes.

That morning, while driving into location at the Bharatpur town centre, we'd seen people suddenly switching to slow motion when they saw our red bus go by – cyclists forgetting to look ahead and falling off their cycles, children shouting and running after us, and roadside idlers forgetting what they were saying. We felt their excitement and their obvious enthusiasm inspired a four-minute piece dedicated to the bus.

It became a constant segment that we would call 'Bus and Us' – a segment suggested by NDTV veteran Vinod Dua. Before we'd left, Mr Dua had told us, 'The bus should be a constant character in your piece, I think you should have a name for it.' He seemed to be in love with the bus himself.

In previous elections, Mr Dua had mapped the country by train. Once, he'd even met voters by going around in an autorickshaw, but I'd got the feeling that what he really wanted was to get on our bus. 'Once you and Naghma have finished with it, give it to me, I'll take it out,' Vinod Dua had said, gazing wistfully at it.

Apart from the piece introducing the show we'd also done a piece at the Dausa post-graduate college. The college had just one Gujjar teacher: Rajendra Singh Gujjar, who told us how he'd been very lucky to get an education in his community. He could speak English but he wanted to be rid of his unique status; he wanted more people from his community to be able to speak the language. Unlike the violent Gujjar faces we were used to seeing on television, Rajendra Singh had no intention of lying down on the railway tracks or blackmailing the government using the dead bodies of his community members. Nonetheless, Rajendra Singh was an activist. He wasn't afraid to say that reservation was the only way out for a backward community like the Gujjars; a way out for his students who were now stuck working in the fields despite being educated. Some of the boys told us that they had spent the morning before the exam cutting wheat and were going right back there, once the exam was over. When I asked them what kind of jobs they aspired to, they all said the same thing – they wanted to be teachers.

'No, it's not because I am very popular,' Rajendra Singh laughed at my suggestion. 'It's the only job they feel is within their reach.'

Political power wasn't within their reach in Dausa, just yet. They were simply a tenth of the community there, while the Meenas made up a third. Only a person from a scheduled tribe could contest elections in Dausa and the Gujjars hadn't got that title yet. But, they were getting a Kashmiri Gujjar to come down to the desert to fight elections. Qamar Rabbani Chechi was to be their candidate because, in our complicated democracy, the Gujjars were considered a scheduled tribe in Jammu and Kashmir. But when I called for an interview with him, Chechi was still stuck in the hills, sorting out his scheduled tribe status certificate to file his nomination.

I had enough stories, but I was worried about whether there was fair representation in the rundown. Was I giving equal space to the Gujjars and the Meenas? Was meeting and profiling a doctor family of the Meenas enough to tell the truth about these parts or was I expressing some innate bias? What about the common people of Bharatpur – shouldn't I have spoken to some of them? I quickly set up a mock voters' booth outside the bus where locals could make their demands to their MPs. (They made demands like: fix the drain outside my house, I am getting too many mosquito bites; I have written many songs and poems, I want my MP to help me market them, etc.) I knew that these stories were physically possible to do, but they had to have some rationale behind them. But by 5.30 that evening, all rationale went out of the window.

Apparently, the feed we sent via satellite to Delhi had glitches.

Sumit informed me that we would have to uplink it all over again.

'What do you mean the feed has glitches? And why are you telling me this now and not four hours ago when we uplinked it in the first place? I don't understand. Why? *Why?*'

I wasn't shouting. I simply failed to understand why these things happened to me. Then Naghma and my 'at-peace' factor got strained a bit: 'Sunetra, they haven't edited any of my bits so can I just send mine first?'

'I don't think they'll be able to handle all of your pieces at one go. Why don't you send one of yours and then I send one of mine?'

Just when we'd brokered a delicate agreement, Mohammed reared his head — 'Guys, stop all this and let's start setting up our lights.'

That was the cue for Nishant, Thomas, Jiggy and Ganga Singhji to drop everything that they were doing and to grab the lights, the equipment, and the cable and to stand by waiting for Mohammed's instructions.

Mohammed kept taking drags from his cigarette, playing the creative director to the hilt, looking at various angles for inspiration; it was his turn to play diva so neither Naghma nor I could take any of his team members away for other work.

Finally Naghma popped out of the bus and said, 'So, what's the frame going to be like today, Mohammed?'

'Don't worry, I've got it all sorted out.'

Of course, things weren't fully sorted as I came off the bus and took position in front of the camera. Apparently, the power connection to the lights was a bit dodgy; they weren't working. 'Sumit, yaar, what the hell,' Mohammed said, mad at the thought of doing the first show in unflattering camera light.

I paid no attention. This was my show, and I was going to wow them all with how good I was, even if it meant they had to shine a torch on my face.

The lights, the big bus and the 'powdered-lipsticked' girls in front of the camera, had proven irresistible for the cream of Bharatpur rowdies, who were crowded around threatening to ruin my piece.

'Sunetra, can you hear us?' The Delhi Production Control Room (PCR) crackled.

'Yes, yes, I can hear you.'

'Where are you?'

And just when I was going to start bitching about the lousy lights, I must have appeared lit on their screen. 'The bus looks good, yaar,' said someone in Delhi. I smiled and then remembered the rowdies crowding outside. I turned to them: 'Bhaiyya, if you want to watch the show, you are welcome to do so but please, keep it down.' I didn't want a repeat of our first night in Bharatpur, but before I knew it the cameras were rolling:

'Stand by, Sunetra, 40 seconds.'

We were on air.

'Good evening and welcome to the very first episode of an amazing journey. The *Election Express* has set out to meet voters across the country before the elections. Whether you live in a city or a village, we're coming to meet you to find out what matters to you...' I had jotted down a few lines before going on air as an articulate intro to our first show, but the crowds and the tension of our first episode, made me forget all the words. I just went along and said a lot of 'amazings', a lot of 'adventures', a lot of 'journeys'.

During a commercial break, the PCR asked if I wanted to do a quick chat with someone from the crowd. 'They don't speak English here,' I said out loud.

'Madam, how can you say that?'

I turned around to look at a boy, barely out of his teens. 'You never asked us.'

'I'm sorry, I thought I did,' I was totally on the defensive here. 'Are you old enough to vote?'

'Yes, madam, I am going to vote for the first time.' So we took the boy on air for about 40 seconds. He said the usual stuff about how politicians should do more for young people like him; how they should inspire confidence, etc. but when he finished his mini-speech in English, the entire crowd of rowdies burst into applause. They were so proud that one of them had given it back to me: 'So you thought we couldn't speak English, huh? Take this.'

Sudeep was the first to call when the show ended. (I'd warned him he'd be walking on very thin ice if he didn't watch the first show!) 'Good show, babu,' he said. Oh happiness. 'But you have got to stop saying, "There you have it" at the end of every package.'

'I know. But otherwise?'

'Otherwise it was good.'

Sudeep was a tough one to please. I wondered if I'd get any feedback from the bosses; whether they'd had the time to watch the show at all. I didn't have to wait long. Both Barkha and Sonia sent me text messages and the Big Boss thought it was a great start. I exhaled and smiled.

Things didn't go so well for Naghma, though.

'I can't believe what happened, yaar,' Naghma said when she came back into the bus after finishing her show. 'I couldn't hear a thing!' She was really upset. Apparently, she couldn't hear the cues so there were awkward pauses and the show suffered for no fault of hers. Nishant had been working the phones; Naghma had been screaming out loud; and I saw how easily things could get messed up.

Naghma was upset about all that had gone wrong with her show, and the glow from the compliments I received for the English programme wore thin as we left the bus and bundled into the SUV to get to Agra, which was only 55 kilometres away. The road was the antithesis of the road to Bharatpur – full of potholes, mindless construction and mismanaged traffic. The nasty bumps were a bit of a reality check.

One email from a colleague at work said: *Really liked the show, folks – looked good and fresh. Now the challenge will be to keep the momentum going. Good Luck.*

Talk about stating the obvious.

When I worked for a newspaper I was repeatedly told I was only as good as my last byline. I was told that my story, however big it was, was fated to be forgotten the next day, and become bin-liner. I might get a few words of praise when I spun an exclusive but I would only be allowed to strut around for a few hours as the next morning the editor would inevitably ask: 'What have you got for us today?'

All my working life this has been my existential angst, but it has multiplied exponentially since I joined TV. Here, my blood, sweat, toil and tears are compressed into a few minutes of airtime that can dissipate into nothing if the telly isn't on. And, unlike in the newspapers, you can't go back and look up your story, your work, the child of your labour. Your editor will say: 'Haven't seen any story from you lately.'

That's because they only telecast it at 6am and you're not watching at that time, you might want to retaliate. To which the boss could well riposte, 'It probably didn't deserve to get played more. You better get your act together.'

Aah, the existential angst of a television reporter! I tried to snap out of it and forced myself to concentrate on the show ahead. After being let down by Sachin Pilot and Colonel Bainsla – and letting down HRH Raja Vishvendra Singh – I really needed a recognizable face on the show.

🚌

'Naghma, will you call Raj Babbar and see what time he is meeting us?

Member of Parliament and erstwhile film star Raj Babbar was contesting from the brand new constituency of Fatehpur Sikri, adjacent to his existing constituency of Agra.

Naghma got him on the line: 'Ji, Ji adaab. We were hoping to do the show using the backdrop of the lovely Buland Darwaza. Ji, ji, we think it would look nice with you there. Yes, yes, what time? We'll just take half an hour. Ji, okay, adab.' Naghma turned off her cell phone and turned to me: 'It's done. He'll meet us at 11am and he says it's no problem filming there.'

Sitting in the front seat of the SUV, Mohammed said, 'I am telling you, I have a feeling that this show is going to be a hit.'

Then Ganga Singhji added: 'Madam, people have already started recognizing our bus...'

Trust Ganga Singhji to come up with this exaggeration to make us feel good about ourselves. We all burst out laughing as strains of *Jhini* filled the air.

🚌

We started from our hotel at 8.30am the next morning despite Mohammed gunning to leave at 7am so that he would have more time to shoot. We were all aware that today's show was going to be the real test: shooting, editing and airing on the same day. But I just couldn't go to bed after midnight and be expected to wake up before seven; we had to work hard, sure, but I really wanted to last out for the two months.

'It's okay, Mohammed,' I'd said lamely as I crawled into the bus. 'There aren't many people who want to be interviewed at 7.30 in the morning.'

And, quite honestly, Yusuf Khan, the owner of Agra's only call centre really wasn't ready to receive a TV crew even at 8.30am. The 31-year old entrepreneur was busy gathering together his scattered team of young executives – who would have been part of a nascent BPO sector in Agra if the city hadn't beat them down. After Yusuf Khan had been forced to scale down operations in Agra, he told us, his team had to look for work elsewhere. The lucky ones got jobs in the BPO sector in places like Noida, but others had resorted to other occupations – like 29-year-old Gurwinder Singh who was now a tourist guide in the Taj Mahal. As young voters and as young people trying to make a living in India, I wanted to know how Yusuf Khan and Gurwinder Singh felt about the political leadership.

We went to the house from where Yusuf ran his BPO business. It looked like a backyard operation: two rooms in somebody's ground floor home with a couple of computers. Yusuf said that even with this limited investment, he had managed to generate considerable business till he had been forced to shut down. He said, 'Can you believe that I had to shut shop because of a bad internet connection?'

I am not much of a business journalist but I really thought that India was the hub of the BPO business in the world. I mean, come on, 'Bangalored' was coined on our outsourcing business, the terror of employees across the world. I knew that the road to the Taj Mahal was the worst in the world, with holes the size of craters, but surely the access to the virtual world should be better?

'It's just not good enough for business,' said Yusuf. 'Besides, who can work with such killer power-cuts?'

Nor was that the end of Yusuf's problems: his partner in the business, an older gentleman called RK Gupta, said, 'I used to run a leather factory but I wanted to do something else after the Supreme Court cracked down on pollution.' He was referring to the 1996 apex court ruling that ordered all factories operating near the Taj to switch to natural gas or relocate. 'I thought that I would be part of this call centre because it was a new industry but I didn't know that it was going to be like this.' He recalled how they were harassed by policemen when office cars would go to drop female employees late at night. 'In Delhi, everyone understands this industry; they understand that people have to work with different time zones but here these policemen would abuse us and say that we are running a call girl racket,' said Gupta. Yusuf said that initially, it was a problem getting the parents of the girls on board but they eventually understood. The people who didn't understand, he said, were the authorities. When it became too hard to work against these impossible odds, Yusuf just decided to scale down operations and move out.

He moved his business to Noida but Gurwinder couldn't move there.

Gurwinder Singh had to stay on in Agra with his family but he didn't look too unhappy either. 'I am now working as a guide,' he said in his carefully cultivated BPO-trained Indo-American accent. Wasn't the money better in the BPO sector? I could tell from his smile that showing people around the Taj Mahal wasn't that bad a prospect, either. 'I am not unhappy but I just wish that we had as many career choices as everyone else in the country.'

His words echoed in my ears all day. He had just gone from being a potential Bill Gates-like businessman to a smart but conventional tour guide and the transition wasn't making him unhappy at all; what he *didn't* like was that the option of the BPO trainer was no longer open to him.

Or consider the stance of the young voters, like the ones we met at a fashion school in Agra. We had made an appointment with a fashion school because we'd heard that if there was a boom in one sector in Agra, it was in the schools of fashion. The city was full of new institutes, and consequently new boutiques opened by fresh fashion graduates.

When we reached the institute we found the students waiting to meet us dressed in some of their own creations. One girl wore an asymmetrical dress whose right side dipped to her calves while the left side finished around her thighs. Another wore an off-the-shoulder top made of lace and satin while a third was clad in an evening gown. They didn't look like Agra girls at all.

'Are you sure you want to interview them?' Naghma whispered, taking me aside.

'Yeah, why?'

'Look at those outfits. Do you think that we'll be making fun of them?' Naghma was really concerned.

It's true that the designs were not exactly haute couture and the chances of one of them attaining Sabyasachi fame or becoming the toast of Lakme Fashion Week were remote, but when we started speaking to them the girls were so sassy there was no way that anyone could make fun of them. When I asked them whom they looked up to, expecting some political name since we were doing a political show, one said, 'Rakhi Sawant.'

When I asked why, she replied, 'Because she is so sexy!' and the other girls squealed with delight.

Rakhi Sawant, the reality-TV star, with her brazen behaviour and her audacious fashion sense, had grabbed the country's attention, but I couldn't get over the fact that what I thought of as much more conventional small-town India, had embraced her so wholeheartedly.

I was just beginning to understand that even though I had been a reporter for a decade, that even though my job was just to speak to people across the country, to find out what was going on in their lives, even though I thought I was a good reporter, I really had no idea what the people thought or what they wanted.

When we came out of the institute and headed towards the old city to film some shots, we got a taste of the old world. We were walking through the narrow lanes of the city looking for shops that sold political fliers and flags. We wanted to see how their business was doing now that election panels had become strict about the use of campaign material. I was still thinking about Gurwinder and the girls and how they could have been anywhere in Delhi, when I realized I'd been pushed right off the road! A herd of buffalo was passing slowly by and till it passed we couldn't get through. For five very long minutes, we just stood and watched the animals lumber past.

There was no point hurrying, there was no point worrying about deadlines, because this is how things worked over here – buffalo jams with BPO dreams, and Rakhi Sawant as the poster girl.

When we met Raj Babbar, later on that day, I couldn't get all these people out of my head. I kept thinking about what Gurwinder and Yusuf had said and how, despite all the problems they faced in the city, they still liked their MP, Raj Babbar. They thought he was a good man, and they probably echoed the thoughts of many others as he had won twice from Agra and was now contesting for the third time from the same constituency.

I remembered the Abhishek Bachchan–Rani Mukherji film *'Bunty aur Babli'* in which Babbar had played a forbidding small-town father trying to curtail the big dreams of his ambitious son. I asked him why, despite the privilege of two terms in office in Agra, Raj Babbar had nothing to show for it.

'You know, Sunetra, in Uttar Pradesh, people only go by caste equations, I wish they would talk about development, but this talk of vikas (development) doesn't work over here,' he replied.

Then I asked why, despite having the Taj Mahal, Agra chose to punish tourists with the worst roads? I wanted to know whether he even noticed these things. 'You were in that film about small-town dreams, do you think you are helping others realize their small-town dreams, sir?'

'Yes, yes, I think small towns have an energy that big cities lack...'

Either he missed the thrust of my question or, like a typical politician, he just ducked it. But when I watched him doing the same interview with Naghma later, I realized that Raj Babbar was an anachronism in Agra, as out of it as his hennaed hair and the indigo jeans that he wore yanked up almost to his chest.

His constituents were talking of their BPO dreams, and he thought development wasn't an issue!

Maybe, it wasn't Raj Babbar's fault. Maybe, people like him just didn't have access to young voters like Gurwinder who recognized the goodness in their politicians, and recognized their honesty but also were practical enough to know that they needed more than noble intentions to live.

6

'Sir, Are You a Dacoit?'

'....my wishes and prayers to all who have been chosen to take the whole country by this road show called NDTV bus this is something very nice and very helpful to know more about our own leaders in their home town, hats off to NDTV for making this happen and I wish my best in all they do ...my wishes, prayers and safety to the crew of this 'election bus' ... all the best...'

When we'd received emails like this one from Patrick in Hyderabad, and twenty-seven others, by Tuesday evening, we knew that there were at least *some* people, other than our friends, family, bosses, and co-workers who were watching the show.

I wish I could say that we were inundated by emails, text messages, and calls to the NDTV board begging to be on the bus, but that would be a lie. What wasn't a lie was that the *Election Express* had generated more viewer feedback than I'd ever experienced in my career. Mails poured in from Tuticorin, Asansol, Ooty, Darbhanga and many other places I couldn't even place on the map. For the first time, I was experiencing quick feedback, appreciation – and some criticism – directly from the people.

It was all quite overwhelming for someone who had started her career at *The Indian Express*, where letters to the editor were mostly by snotty readers voicing their own lofty opinions. In the three-and-a-half years that I'd worked in the paper, my stories had elicited a grand total of one letter – seeking a clarification on my story instead of appreciating my journalistic effort.

Then, when I moved to TV, the letters or emails increased but as the last chapter illustrated, they were notable for different reasons. I had never experienced people writing in to tell me they were excited about my story, that they felt a part of it, and that, to them, it was a commendable enterprise. Those twenty-seven emails had managed to infuse their energy and amazement directly into me. It's as if they reaffirmed my faith in our project. To make sure we took it all in, I read each one out loud to Naghma and the gang, on the way back to the hotel after the Agra show.

I didn't really expect Naghma to be taken in by all this. After all, unlike me, she was used to a lot of adulation, a lot of fan mail. I remember being totally awestruck the first time we had gone reporting together in Haridwar, where walking down a lane I'd hear people go: 'Naghma madam aa gayi' or smart-alecky types who kept repeating her sign-off: 'From New Delhi, Naghma Sahar for NDTV'. I remember thinking, 'Oh my god, *this* is what it means to be a celebrity.' Of course, Naghma had acted as if there was nothing extraordinary about it.

But, there's nothing ordinary about people thinking they know you, of people actually thinking you're part of their family and chatting you up like an old friend. There's nothing ordinary about featuring in gossip columns, or in reports that the film director Ashutosh Gowarikar had approached you to be in Shah Rukh Khan's next movie.

'Was it true?' I had asked Naghma, all agog. (I needed to know if I was in the company of a potential Bollywood star.)

Naghma had laughed her head off at my wide-eyed curiosity. 'Yes, he did call me,' she'd said laughing at how thrilled I was.

Of course, not all fans were the Bollywood director types. We were eating lunch in Agra, and Naghma was just about to put a bite of roti and sabzi in her mouth when a voice commanded: 'Don't start eating yet!' We turned around to look at this big guy making his way to our table. 'Don't eat, we want a picture with you,' he ordered again.

Are you kidding me? I thought. How about saying please? I expected Naghma to give the guy a tongue-lashing because, frankly, he was just rude. But Naghma politely put her plate aside and posed with the man's wife and kids, who had appeared out of nowhere. Of course Naghma's expression wasn't her happiest. Later, when I asked her why she didn't protest, she shrugged: 'The man wanted to convey to me that he wasn't intimidated by the fact that I'm well known. He also wanted to send me the message that just because his family wanted to take a picture with me, I wasn't necessarily better than him.'

'You've got a lot of mails too, Sunetra,' Naghma teased me. in turn. 'A lot of them from south India.'

Yes, I guess that's what they call 'World Famous in Tuticorin'.

I told the gang the story Sudeep loves to tell about the time when he and I were in Lucknow. Sudeep claims that we were just getting off the elevator when an elderly gent walked towards me saying, 'Excuse me'. Apparently, I impatiently held up my hand and turned up my nose, like someone who'd been disturbed yet again by a desperate fan, and said, 'Yes, yes, NDTV.' And the old man had looked blankly at me and said, 'Do you know where I can find room number 506?'

The SUV lurched to a stop and Ganga Singhji got off.

'What's wrong?'

'Madam, I am just checking.' Ganga Singhji had his head under the bonnet.

'Ganga Singhji, what's happening?'

'Madam, the clutch plate has broken.'

I didn't understand what that meant and neither did Naghma. 'How much time will it take, Ganga Singhji?'

'Madam, I will try to fix it. I'm going to do some jugaad.'

A half-hour went by. It was already 1pm. 'I think I'll have to go get it fixed,' Ganga Singhji finally announced.

'Why couldn't he just figure it out before?' Naghma and I couldn't help but crib, sitting in the car, at least 20 kilometres away from our story.

But Ganga Singhji had been gung-ho: 'It'll just take me half-an-hour to go with this guy and get a pipe which may make it work.'

Our local contact Naseem informed us that getting another car was going to be extremely tough, so we didn't have much choice but to wait. That's when Naghma looked at me, suddenly all chirpy: 'Let's go have sugarcane juice!'

Uh-oh, what was she, nuts? The last time I'd had sugarcane juice was when I was six years old and lived in RK Puram; my dad had left the house armed with a couple of large containers to organize some from the local vendor. After that one time, we had to make do with just the memory of the sweet juice with its distinctive odour. Delhi's civic authorities had soon choked supplies as the courts decreed that sugarcane juice dispensers had notoriously poor hygiene standards. Ma and Papa wasted no time in describing all the diseases we could contract from drinking it, putting the fear of god in me. I had not ventured near a sugarcane juice stall since. Two decades later, Naghma's suggestion brought back that fear: 'But it'll be dirty,' I said weakly, knowing what a chicken I sounded.

'Arrey, don't worry, we'll make them wash the machine,' she said.

We left the guys to tend the broken car and walked down to a nearby juice stand. The walk wasn't exactly pleasant with Agra notching up 40 degrees, and I was glad that I'd brought along a dupatta to cover my head. On seeing us the vendor moved towards the fridge that contained the bottled drinks. 'No, bhaiyya, we want some juice,' said Naghma. 'But first clean the machine.'

If someone had come into my establishment and ordered a thorough cleaning, I'd have told them where to go. In Delhi, many vendors and restaurants will tell you *exactly* where to go for lesser reasons: 'We don't have change, go to hell'; 'We only have masala dosas, go to hell'; 'We only have this table, go to hell.' But this juicewala acted as if asking for a clean up was a routine and legitimate demand.

'Wash it well, okay?' Naghma continued with her directions. 'Now make it without the masala, okay? Just plain.'

I didn't want to reveal my non-gourmet knowledge of the best way to drink sugarcane juice and anyway, Naghma seemed to know what she was doing, so I took the glass of juice sans condiments, the way she had prescribed it. I don't know whether it was because my throat was parched and we were in the middle of nowhere, between Taj Mahal and Buland Darwaza, but the juice tasted like a glass straight from heaven. I couldn't stop raving about it: 'Oh my god, how amazing is this? Isn't it? *Isn't it?*'

Naghma looked pleased with herself – she'd shown an ignoramus from the city one of the pleasures of small-town life. We walked back refreshed and ready to get on with our journey but our SUV was still not moving.

I turned to Naseem imploringly: 'Naseem, what do we do now?' Poor Naseem, our local fixer, hitched a ride back to Buland Darwaza where the cab stand was and returned in a Qualis with no air-conditioning and seats so hard they blistered our buttocks.

'This is not looking good, yaar,' said Naghma, as we bumped along sorely. 'Second day, and we have a breakdown.'

I was more hassled about having to forgo lunch. I'd made a deal with Naseem to stop at his friend's restaurant for Mughlai food, which he'd said was seriously good.

But I was still on a sugar high. I think the juice had kind of seduced me into loving the idea of life on the road. So even though we got back to town all hot and sweaty with only a half-hour to set up the show and even after we were caught in a major traffic jam, and even though we'd panicked and screamed 'Naseem, *do* something!' – we all burst into laughter when like an honourable warrior, Naseem called the local cops: 'Sir, the NDTV team is here, please come and get us out of this jam.'

What did we expect? Special choppers deployed by the police to land, lift us up and take us to our show location? Even though we knew it was totally irrational, we just felt better that Naseem had made some calls. Soon enough, the traffic had eased on its own and we did a happy show. This time Naghma was pleased with all the production work here and in Delhi. She got lots of calls telling her how fabulous and clever it was to have done the show from a roadside dhaba, sipping chai.

The warm fuzzy feeling was still strong the next morning as we headed for Gwalior. We were travelling the 118 kilometres from Agra by bus and the road was just amazing. It was the first time that we had the feeling of journeying on a new road. We'd all done the Delhi–Agra route lots of times before, but even though Gwalior hardly qualified as unchartered territory, none of us had done that route by road before.

'This is where the dacoits used to be, this is the Chambal region,' Naghma announced as we entered a distinctly ravine landscape.

Naghma had figured out that she'd clocked the maximum amount of travel among all of us and so she had assumed the role of guide. What she hadn't prepared herself for was my unbridled enthusiasm; my adrenaline-induced super-enthusiastic high for everything.

'It looks amazing! Wow!' I said every thirty seconds clicking pictures so frantically it would have put a tourist from Tokyo to shame. 'Oh my god, Phoolan Devi would have hung out here...Do you know, I think they actually shot *Bandit Queen* over here...it looks very familiar...Do you think there are still some dacoits there?'

I think my questions were irritating Naghma. She started a phone conversation with her friend and I heard her say, 'Yes, Sunetra is thrilled that we are going through Chambal. She wants to know if dacoits still live here...' And they both had a good laugh over it.

Naghma was still on the phone when I suddenly shouted, 'What the hell?'

It was a scene straight out of a curry Western! There were two men on a motorbike; the man driving the bike was in his forties, the one on the pillion was older. The older man held three big guns, two on one shoulder and one on the other. My scream got everyone's attention, and we all turned back to look and see if they were for real.

'What are those people *doing* riding with guns?'

Naghma was silenced.

Ganga Singhji said, 'Madam, they will just shoot us.'

Would they? Of course not, I thought. 'Ganga Singhji, stop the car! I want to speak with them.' No one was quite sure where I was going with this and I didn't really have the time to explain what I was doing; I wasn't sure either. If I was travelling across the country, I just wanted to know why in god's name people thought it was okay to drive on the highway with lethal weapons slung across their shoulder. Maybe, it wasn't very surprising for many. But, I sure hadn't seen a sight like this, and definitely not in Delhi's Vasant Kunj!

Mohammed took my cue and readied his camera but none of us got off the SUV. 'Ganga Singhji, will you signal for them to stop?'

'They won't stop,' Ganga Singhji said, hoping they wouldn't, but he put his hand out as soon as we caught up with them and they slowed down their bike. To my delight, the older man with the guns got off the bike and came towards our car. Anyway, despite his guns, he was smiling at us. When he came closer, I saw that he had the most benign grandfatherly expression. His wrinkled, bespectacled face didn't look like it'd take offence at anything I'd say, however stupid.

I leant across and lowered the window to look at the old man in his dhoti, kurta, gamcha and guns, using what I like to think of as my special strategy; a strategy I use in some tricky reporting situations where because my questions have the potential to anger the interviewee, I deliberately play dumb. I giggle a lot, laugh loudly and say some silly things so the interviewee indulgently attributes my offensive questioning to my dumbness. With politicians, tricky bureaucrats, police officers, it's always worked. They always respond with mild irritation but oftentimes also divulge prize information thinking that my dumbness wouldn't be able to process the information!

So, in fact, in my mind, *that* was what I was doing again, but of course, for everyone else in the car, it was going down as something else altogether –

'Sir, we are journalists from Delhi and we just saw you with these guns, so we wanted to know what you do,' was my introductory line in Hindi. As soon as I said it, I knew that it was pretty bizarre calling someone here 'sir'; 'bhaisaheb' or 'babaji' or anything else would have been more appropriate but I just wanted to sound polite, servile even.

'Where do you stay, sir?'

'In Morena.'

Then I put my foot in it: 'Are you from a dacoit family, sir?'

Everyone's heart skipped a beat. *Is he going to blow Sunetra's head off now?*

But the old man just laughed. Was it my imagination, or was the strain showing on his forehead? I decided to go for the jugular: 'Sir, are you a dacoit?'

The man couldn't take it anymore. 'I am a Sanskrit teacher,' he said, smiling through gritted teeth.

'You are? Then what are you doing with guns, sir?'

'We are going to hand them over today. It's the last day for that.'

'Are guns necessary to survive in Morena, sir?'

He laughed indulgently at my silliness.

'Do you vote?'

'Yes, we usually vote for the Bhartiya Janata Party around here.'

'What's your name, sir?'

'Radhey Shyam Shastri.'

By this point I felt the man deserved a medal for not blowing my head off for asking such puerile questions, so just to make him happy, I said, 'Your guns are very cool.'

I don't know how Radhey Shyamji knew the meaning of 'cool' but he was well pleased with my compliment.

'Hahahahahaha.'

'It was great to meet you.'

'Jai Shri Ram'.

As soon as he roared away on his bike, everyone burst out laughing. Naghma said, 'Sunetra, only you can do this!

"Sir, you are very cool", "Sir, are you from a Daku family?" How could you *ask* him that?'

'Guys, I had to ask him like that. How else would he have said anything?'

As it turned out, this exchange became the most quoted one on our journey. Whenever things got too stressed, someone would bring up my conversation with Radhey Shyam Shastri. It went beyond the group of course, once it was aired. I had friends calling me up: 'Listen, my colleague said that apparently you asked a guy with guns whether he was a dacoit, please tell me that's not true?'

'Yes, but you have to have been there to understand the context.'

Others were worried: 'Don't ask such questions, yaar, it's not safe.' I knew that this was one Daku encounter I wasn't going to live down!

By the time we reached Gwalior, Naghma had called everyone in Delhi and even instructed her producers to carry my little clip with the Daku in the Hindi show. Everyone hoped that this entertaining piece of television was just a precursor for all the good stuff we had waiting for us in town.

'Yashodhara Raje Scindia is especially coming in from Delhi for our interview,' I announced to the team, pleased to have her on the show but still smarting from the fact that her nephew, Jyotiraditya Scindia, who was the MP from our next destination Shivpuri in Guna, was not going to be able to make it.

I'd gone chopper hopping with him once during the 2008 assembly elections, and it was the most fun that I'd ever had covering a politician. Madhya Pradesh is full of former royals who have become politicians. They all talk the new language of democracy and votes, but when you travel with them, you see people still referring to them as 'Maharaja', still falling flat on the ground to kiss their feet, still getting a lot of mileage because the populace thinks it's their right to rule.

Jyotiraditya Scindia is one of the crop of young MPs-turned-ministers but unlike the others, he has a reputation, among reporters, of being terribly snooty. 'He really has an attitude problem, yaar,' I was told. 'He still thinks he is a Raja.'

As I had no illusions of being friends with any politician, I had no problems with that. He had been polite enough every time I'd met him for a story or a short interview. But when I'd accompanied him on his campaign trail to Madhya Pradesh, it gave me an insight into how a modern day Raja connects with the common man, how many citizens actually prefer them because they think that, coming from royalty and thus already rich, people like Jyotiraditya would not be greedy and corrupt.

I remember that's precisely what I asked Jyotiraditya Scindia when I went with him on the campaign trail in November, 2008. I couldn't claim to share any common ground with him. But over the course of the 24 hours that cameraperson Puja Arya and I were with him, he was very amiable. We were staying at the same hotel and we expected that like for any other minister, Scindia's people would have organized a suite for him at the Tana Bana Hotel in Chanderi. Okay, the Tana Bana did not have a suite, but they would have at least organized the best room for Mantriji. Maybe they had tried but he'd been forced to take a regular room because it was already taken by foreign tourists.

Anyway, during the course of our interview, Jyotiraditya had talked about how he met his wife; accepted that she had looked great in the *Vogue* magazine photo spread she had done, but could never be seen like that in his constituency; how he felt he didn't live up to his ideal of being a father; and how he could perhaps never live up to the image of his father, Madhavrao Scindia.

He also displayed a sense of humour.

'I have to ask you this,' I said. 'When you were in your Ivy League School, did you ever try to pull women by telling them you are a Maharaja?'

'I don't think I needed to tell them that,' he had replied, his nose high up in the air. (The added bonus was that the camera was rolling.)

It's the kind of humour and openness that one expects from young politicians – on how they handle their relationship with their other halves, their children, their colleagues – but it's also the kind that is never seen among edgy Congressmen. They are so caught up with watching their back and so paranoid about a wrong message being sent out that they just don't talk normally.

🚌

Jyotiraditya's aunt, from the rival Bhartiya Janata Party, Yashodhara Scindia was quite unknown to me but I hoped that frankness was a common family trait. I knew that the two sides of the family didn't get along, being divided along party lines, but apart from that Yashodhara was also the Scindia people had heard least about.

'What would you like me to do, Sunetra?' she'd asked me over the phone, 'Tell me, so that I can organize it.'

'Ma'am, it would be great to do the interview with you walking around the palace. And maybe, if we saw you interacting with people as well.'

'You know that he has locked most of the palace, right?' The 'he' referred to her nephew, Jyotiraditya Scindia. 'So I shall show you around the parts I have access to in Rani Mahal.'

Nothing like a bit of palace intrigue and mystery, I thought. Both Yashodhara and Jyotiraditya, even though they represented neighbouring constituencies with overlapping interests, were famous for not saying anything against each other. What if she chose to break that rule with me?

Unfortunately, the other interesting aspect about the interview, a chance to meet her son Akshay Bhansali, had fallen through – he had dropped out at the last minute.

Akshay, who works for MTV in New York, had emailed me earlier to tell me that he would be flying down for my interview with his mother. Akshay had provided the oomph factor in her previous campaign and had also helped counter Jyotiraditya's youth factor for his mother. 'We should see how he asks for votes for his mother in his American accent,' Naghma had said. We had all been gleeful at the prospect of this video jockey type in a village choupal asking for votes – great television.

But – 'Sunetra, he had to go for a shoot somewhere, so unfortunately he will not be able to make it,' his mother informed me.

Bugger, bugger, we'd have to make do with the posh, royal mother then.

Yashodara Scindia's aide was waiting for us at the doorway when we arrived, an hour late: 'She is waiting for you, please go in.' As we made our way through the waiting crowds at

Rani Mahal, I hoped she wouldn't give us hell for being late. I knew it was my fault for coming late, especially when she'd come down all the way from Delhi, but how could I have not stopped to speak to the man carrying the guns?

'Please wait here,' a guard stopped us.

'She'll make us wait now,' predicted Naghma. All politicians loved playing these little power games. Even if they weren't doing anything, even if you had arrived just two minutes off the allotted time, you were made to wait for half an hour just to drive home to you that it's they who have the upper hand. So, we stood around and admired the palace with its massive portraits of her brother, and Jyotiraditya's father, Madhavrao Scindia. 'If they are fighting, then why doesn't she take down his pictures?' We later figured that this was because both she and Jyotiraditya were trying to cash in on Madhavrao's legacy and claiming to be his heir.

'Maharaja is just coming,' said her aide.

'Huh, which Maharaja?'

Apparently, both aunt and nephew were also claiming the title (which was supposed to be obsolete in independent India).

'What do you think will happen if *both* Jyotiraditya and Yashodhara are in town?' Naghma and I were seized by a fit of girly giggles again. 'Who will they call the *real* Maharaja?'

'Arrey, it's like this in these parts,' Naghma explained. 'When I was in Bihar, they would keep calling me sir instead of madam.'

'But what happens if Vasundhara comes to visit as well? Is she also a Maharaja?'

There was a sudden flutter announcing that this Maharaja was coming down the stairs. We stood up, waiting for her along with a local channel journalist. 'She's very haughty,' he warned us. 'She keeps losing her temper.'

Yashodhara walked right past us and the crowds towards the palace courtyard. She was wearing a colourful chiffon sari with the pallu pulled over her head and large designer sunglasses. I wasn't sure whether she had failed to see us or was subjecting us to the silent treatment because we were late. I decided to announce my presence. 'Hi,' I managed the biggest smile I could muster.

She wasn't amused. 'You are late,' she said. 'The women who had come to meet me have all gone. Now I have to go campaigning to the village.'

'Ma'am, what to do, there was so much traffic on the highway. We'll just take two minutes.'

She knew it was a lie, and I knew it was a lie but we were both playing a well-practised routine. She had come to Gwalior only to give me the interview and I was willing to beg, so it depended on how much massaging her ego needed. She decided that there was no point in wasting time so she switched back quickly to her charming self, the self that knew how to make reporters happy. For instance, every time she met me in Parliament, she would say, 'Oh, I love watching your dimples on TV. Yours and Preity Zinta's.' Of course, I would melt every time I heard that.

'Ma'am, this is Naghma, she'll be doing the interview in Hindi.'

'Of course, I remember watching her on Aaj Tak.' Yashodhara gave us her lovely smile.

'You girls must be so tired, right?' she continued. 'After the interview you must go upstairs to get fresh. That's the locals version of "getting fresh", and not how you and I may mean it.'

We laughed, totally taken up by her banter. There is something about PLU or People Like Us politicians. However much I tried, or for however long I covered politics, I was never going to have this kind of comfort level with heartland politicians like Mulayam Singh Yadav. Just as Yashodhara or Jyotiraditya Scindia could get away with cracking these kind of jokes with us and not with other reporters. There were many Delhi politicians who would sometimes think that just because you were from NDTV, you were from their social set. Shiela Dixit referring to us as 'darling' in private conversations was quite endearing but I could never get used to air-kissing a politician.

We decided that the gardens of the Rani Mahal with the palace in the backdrop would be the right place for her interview. 'That part of the palace is all locked up,' Yashodhara said, indicating a section of the palace as we walked towards the gardens.

'What happens when Jyotiraditya is also in town?'

'We make sure our paths don't cross.'

They could afford that luxury because the palace was so huge. Her staff worked for their Maharaja in one wing of the palace and Jyotiraditya's people carried on operations from another. What hurt her, she told us, was that he had limited her to a very small portion of the palace but there wasn't much she could do about it. And yet, local journalists talked about a silent understanding under all that acrimony. An understanding that however much they hated each other, they would ensure that the constituency never left the Scindia family. 'That's why other candidates always lose,' one local reporter told me. 'Jyotiraditya may campaign for her rival but in the end, even his supporters always back her.'

I asked Yashodhara what the deal was. 'We like to maintain the family dignity. In my constituency, I'm now known as bua (aunt), because of him.'

Clearly, no family secrets were about to be revealed on the *Election Express*. How could we have expected a tell-all over a quickie meeting? Still it was interesting to have her on the show, speaking about why she kept a low profile despite being from a high profile family: 'My sister (Vasundhara) has got where she is because of her hard work but that's why she has all the arrows pointing at her,' she said. By the time, we finished with the interview, Naghma and I were both satisfied with the outcome.

Mohammed was very happy as well. Yashodhara Scindia is the type of politician who knows that the cameraman is a power centre. So she obliged him, giving him all the angles he wanted, walking up and down the pathway so he could get the perfect shot. Mohammed was flattered that Her Majesty was sharing a few jokes with him and following his instructions.

'Now, would you girls like to come with me to the villages?'

Naghma and I hesitated because we knew we had to do other stories and not just stories around her. Seeing us dither she said, 'I think you have enough over here, there's no need really.' She understood us so well. 'I cannot offer you lunch but I can offer you some nimbu paani.'

At least she was honest. I remember how once her fellow MP from Madhya Pradesh invited me to a breakfast meeting at his home during the elections. During the filming, he ate vast amounts of toast, hash browns and daliya and didn't even offer me a cup of tea! It wasn't as if I was dying to eat his food but then why invite me for a 'breakfast meeting' in the first place?

Yashodhara hollered for her aide, who came running, cradling a mobile to his ear. 'Get off the phone, Sharma,' she snapped and then told him to show us to her loo upstairs. 'So that you can get fresh,' she winked, as she left.

We didn't mind 'getting fresh' and we waited to be shown upstairs to Yashodhara's toilet. After all that travel, and at the thought of all the hard work that lay ahead, a clean toilet was a godsend. Her aide guided us indoors but took us towards the public area, instead of her private quarters upstairs.

He showed us to a loo in the waiting area.

I was mighty pissed off: 'She told you to take me to *her* toilet.'

'Madam, believe me, this is fine.'

What could I do? I could hardly call Yashodhara and tell her that her aides weren't letting me 'get fresh'.

I braced myself for the stink.

All memories of a bad loo were washed away after spending the night at the beautiful Usha Kiran Palace in Gwalior. So what if the breakfast wasn't paid for, so what if the rates for breakfast would take two days of our allowance to buy? Nor did it matter to me that the first thing we did after checking out of the hotel was to look for a dhaba to have our morning chai; I just loved the fact that we had the softest beds to sleep in. And the nice loo in the morning with its covet-worthy cosmetics had set me up for the day.

The next morning, I was checking out some of the pictures that Naghma had taken of the hotel. I knew that I couldn't afford to come back to the Usha Kiran on my salary and it was wise to keep the memories. 'Did you actually take pictures of the *bathtub*, Naghma?'

'Yes,' admitted Naghma, sheepishly. 'It was *so* nice, wasn't it? How lucky Jyotiraditya Scindia is.'

She pointed to the private homes that had now come up adjacent to the Mahal:

'I'm sure the Scindias don't like the commoners living so close to them. Must be quite a pain, all this democracy. I wouldn't like it. Imagine owning that hotel, imagine just living there! Why would anyone want to bother with politics at all?'

7

Bhuri and Hirendra

Who is responsible when an area is so deprived of resources, they have to bathe on top of charpoys, so that the bath water can be recollected and used as drinking water for the livestock? Or when an area is just 10 kilometres away from a big city but it has never experienced electricity? Is it the area MLA, or the civic corporator who has a smaller area to work on and funds at his or her disposal to fix things? Is it the Member of Parliament who unlike the MLA has more funds and perhaps access to the central government to get water resources going in his area? What happens if the MP's political party is not in power in the state? Does that mean he cannot push through help for his constituents even though he's really trying to? Are they both not responsible, and does the blame then lie with the chief minister or even the prime minister? With whom does the buck stop?

I don't think I'll ever have answers for questions like these. And I didn't get them – not in Shivpuri, MP, nor in Shivgarh,

UP either – but they certainly inundated my mind. These questions weren't really the ones that the *Election Express* was aiming to handle. When you drive into a place one morning, film around the area and talk to the people over a couple of hours, basing stories on that minimal interaction and Google searches on your handheld, you do not expect to do ground-breaking exposés or gritty journalism. You don't even have the time to ask tough questions and then dissect the answers, as you're already moving on to the next destination. In a way, you are fulfilling the very first step of the journalistic process. You get to the area and you listen to as many people as you can and who knows someday, you, or somebody else, might return to get to the bottom of the story and expose the people who have done them wrong.

The people of Shivpuri had a long list of people who'd done them wrong but they'd had no one with whom to register their protest. While doing some initial research on the place, I'd called a local reporter and he'd said flatly: 'There is no development here.'

'There must have been *something* that has happened in the last five years, something the government has built which could have been a bad idea or a good idea?'

'No, madam, nothing like that. They have done *nothing*.'

I was getting exasperated. 'Okay, then can you show me something that represents all the nothingness that the local authorities have not done?'

He didn't know what I was talking about.

'You know, maybe some road which is being built for the last ten years, or an area which is very, very dirty and has caused particular problems for the people, something like that?'

'Can you give me a day or two?'

At that time I wasn't very hopeful. After all, I couldn't remember the last time I had seen a story out of Shivpuri. Now, I had to dish out six or seven stories and they couldn't be boring stuff like no roads, no electricity, etc. I knew that bijli and sadak were important issues – they are issues that can make or break governments – but no one wants to watch a TV programme that shows the same problems every day:

'Hello and welcome, today we are live from Shivpuri where people say they have no development.'

No shit, Sherlock. That's the story of the entire country, isn't it?

I really had to look deeper even in the few hours that I had, to come up with something new within that story, to come up with what many news editors call a 'sexy' angle.

The local journo called back. 'How would you like to do a story on a dam that keeps being inaugurated and has been under construction for the last 34 years?'

Oh yes, yes, *yes*. *That's* what I call a sexy story.

He told me about the Atal Sagar Dam, that had changed names; seen political regimes of both the Congress and the BJP; seen various chief ministers, MPs and different central governments; been the trophy for politicians to beg votes with; but had never provided water. I had to go see this dam that was taking longer than the Taj Mahal to build. I knew it would be easy to do for the format of the show as well. We go to the dam prepared with the research, speak to a few locals and some authorities if they are available, and then ask, 'What next?'

But small towns have their problems. It's scary how you just have to enter into city limits for political types to catch you on their radar.

'Sunetraji, I'm calling from Scindiaji's office. Can I be of any service?'

The first instinct is to feel flattered: *Oooh, I'm so important, I get calls from the MP's office as soon as I ride into town.* 'That's very kind of you but not really, we are here just for a day.'

'Okay, give us a call if you need anything,' he signed off.

'That was the MP's office,' I announced as soon as I got off the phone but no one in the car seemed much impressed.

They weren't paying attention to me because they were all too busy looking out. The drive from Gwalior to Shivpuri had been heart-stoppingly beautiful. The two-hour journey had taken us through an arid terrain that was rugged and yet inviting. Now and then we'd spot a tree with bright red flowers, starkly outlined against a horizon of the bluest sky. 'Mohammed, please take a shot of this,' Naghma would constantly say. 'We should show people this beautiful journey.' And Mohammed, thoroughly enjoying the drive till then, would grudgingly hoist his 15-kilo camera on to his shoulder. (It's not like she meant to be a killjoy, but a huge part of the television show was just capturing our journey, our movement from one place to another, traversing an entirely new landscape every day.)

When the camera rolled, capturing the scenery outside, it also captured so much that we didn't have a story for — the changing features and skin tones of the people, darker here, not so dark a little ahead; the changing scripts on the signboards — sometimes the message on the signboard itself,

'Shashi Uncle's Chainise' proclaimed one roadside eatery; the road itself, dual carriageway here and single-way there; and of course, our fellow travellers.

Like the two lascivious truck drivers we met on the road to Shivpuri.

We had stopped to talk to them because they wouldn't stop staring at the bus. At first, they were quite entertaining on camera: ('Your bus looks *tanatan,*' they said.) But after the highway interviews were over, and we were ready to go, they clung on. ('*Ab to hum pura safar aap ke saath karenge,* hehehehe.') Thank god, we had to get off the highway to get to the dam and we were finally able to shake them off.

As the highway disappeared, so did the veneer of development and modernity. We got a taste of classic Madhya Pradesh road, the sort that gives you a headache because you keep bouncing off the seat and smashing your head against the roof.

'Madam, these are the real roads of Madhya Pradesh,' said the local reporter who was accompanying us to the dam. Till now, we'd obviously only seen the privileged parts of the state, the roads used by the Scindias to travel from their palace in Gwalior to favoured pocket boroughs.

I wasn't totally surprised, actually. I remember once having to drive from Neemuch to Ratlam to catch a train after finishing an assignment. I'd asked people how long it would take to get there. Some said three hours, some said five. It was just a 130 kilometres away and it took me five-and-a-half hours without any traffic! That's because many parts of the road were just dirt tracks.

'Here we are, welcome to the Atal Sagar Dam.' It was beautiful – a large stretch of still blue water, the calmness only interrupted by the incessant sound of construction.

'What are they doing?' I asked the reporter.

'They are building it, I *told* you.'

True, but when he'd said that to me, I'd thought that since they had started building it in the 70's, they would have tired of it by now. I had expected signs of neglect, at most maybe an abandoned crane and a couple of workers with no idea what to do. But work here was going ahead full throttle. There were people scurrying about, some kind of motor drill drowning our voices, and everybody looked busy.

'Can I speak to someone in charge?' I asked at the local office.

'Tell me,' the man behind the desk said self-importantly, without bothering to look up. I've been a journalist long enough to know that people like him can never help. He was obviously not the man in charge, nor did he look like someone who would share the details of the project with me out of the kindness of his heart. But I had to talk to him because his status as gatekeeper had to be indulged.

'I'm a TV reporter from Delhi. We wanted to ask why this project has taken so long.' I wanted to scare him a bit.

'Manager saab is not available now,' he said without batting an eyelid.

Right. The flak-catchers sat far away, in Bhopal or in Delhi. So what was I supposed to do? Forget the story because no one was going to give me any answers over here? An official response would take too long and would probably just drown me in bureaucratese.

Anyway, it was senior Congress leader Arjun Singh who had sanctioned the second phase of the project decades ago, and then Chief Minister Shivraj Singh Chauhan who'd inaugurated it before the state elections a couple of years later. It was they whom I should have been grilling and since they weren't there, I decided to just speak to a local who was familiar with the background. The story goes something like this: the plan to build the dam was initiated by Jyotiraditya's grandmother, Vijayaraje Scindia in 1974. The politicians and the bureaucrats mulled over the proposal for two years and finally laid the foundation of the dam. Till 1978, work on the dam progressed fairly well. When Arjun Singh was chief minister from 1984 to 1985, he got considerable credit for sanctioning some money for the Rs 2002 crore project. It was too much of a goldmine for politicians to resist – a benefit to 453 villages, with irrigation for 162,000 hectares of land, 60 megawatts of electricity production every day, and an unlimited supply of clean Sindhu water for desperate Shivpuri residents. The promise of water from the dam had been the main poll promise in every election since the 70s. Eight lives had been lost just in the last year during clashes in queues for water – water that the villagers collected from their baths, and then used to wash their dishes, before giving to their livestock to drink. The promise of water from the Manikheda Dam – which had been renamed the Atal Sagar Dam in tribute to the BJP's Atal Bihari Vajpayee – had failed to reach the people long after Atal Bihari himself had faded away from politics, long after Vijayaraje Scindia was dead, even though her grandson had got an extra Rs 52 crores for the same project.

Suddenly, the story that had only meant to be a headline-grabber, got me really angry. I couldn't understand it. Were we Indians really stupid? How did we allow politicians to get away with something like this? Shivraj Singh Chauhan was supposed to be the model chief minister. After his victory in the assembly polls, we had celebrated him as the people's chief minister who travelled without any fuss to meet his people and solve their problems. How could he have come and inaugurated a dam that didn't work? You always hear that politics encourages unethical behaviour in seemingly upright people, but when you see an instance of it, it's still a little shocking. And locals said that Jyotiraditya Scindia couldn't do much because the local government was from the rival party and didn't want him to take all the credit.

But why hadn't we asked him if he could do more? When I went to follow his campaign in 2008, why didn't I ask him about this unfinished work in his constituency instead of asking him about his chat-up lines with women? Is it because a reference to the dam does not come up in my Google search on him? Or was it simply because I wanted to keep my interview with him light and frothy and wanted to avoid asking him the tough questions?

But voters are said to be much smarter than journalists. So I asked people around the dam, and around Shivpuri. They all listed unemployment, water scarcity and lack of development as major issues. Then why weren't they voting for change? When Yashodhara Raje Scindia was the local legislator, they voted for her and the BJP out of loyalty to the royal family. In the MP elections, they voted for Jyotiraditya Scindia, again out of loyalty.

'We know him,' Shivpuri residents Sushil and Anita Varma explained to me. 'Jyotiraditya is a good man.' The Varmas were both doctors who may not have had the kind of problems that confronted thirsty villagers near the dam but they were still unhappy about the pace of change. They wanted industry, they wanted less patients with malaria and malnutrition, and they wouldn't have minded some patients who could actually pay their fees. But they insisted that Jyotiraditya Scindia's hands were tied. He was a Congress MP working in a BJP state.

'Do you like living in Shivpuri?' I asked Dr Varma.

'Yes, it's a beautiful place and it has nice people.'

'But it's very small with only 3 lakh people. Did you always want to live here?'

'No, after I finished my MBBS, I wanted to go to Delhi or Bombay but my father made me come back here and take over his practice.'

'Your son is becoming a doctor, will you let him go out now?'

'Why should I? He also has to come back here and handle my practice.' We laughed as we tucked into a lovely home-cooked meal.

Clearly, change wasn't coming to Shivpuri overnight; nor, it seems, was it rushing towards our next destination.

🚌

We'd chosen Jhansi as our next destination because like Shivpuri in MP, it was the most backward region of Uttar Pradesh. And there was no dearth of stories to do there. There was the desperation for water here as well, the demand for a separate state of Bundelkhand, and the rotting state of the Bundelkhand University. I was hoping to pack in as much as I could but one story was of particular interest to us. We wanted to look at dalit voters in Jhansi, a votebank that both Chief Minister Mayawati and Congress leader Rahul Gandhi were fighting for.

'Would you like to go to a village that has no electricity?' our local fixer Vinod asked us. Naghma and I looked at each other. This was a bit tricky. A village without electricity was not a story that's unheard of in India. Uttar Pradesh, particularly, has many such villages that NDTV had covered from time to time, so the novelty factor hardly worked.

'I haven't been to one though,' I admitted. 'I am a bit curious.'

Naghma was willing to indulge me: 'How do we do it? Should we shoot our initial footage in darkness to build the drama before we put the camera light on and suddenly become visible on screen?' It would be dramatic for sure, but was it a bit tacky? I am not what some call a bleeding-heart journalist; on the contrary, a good story is my only priority. I was hesitating not just because I didn't want to trivialize the situation of a community that was without power in the 21st century; I was worried about doing an old story. 'I have seen that been done before,' I said. Unable to make up our minds, we decided to first visit the dalit colony and then take a call.

Unlike Shivpuri, which made up for its lack of modern infrastructure with old-world charm and cleanliness, Jhansi had nothing to redeem itself. The roads overflowed with disorderly traffic and where there were no vehicles, there was dirt. Our big red bus set off a wave of panic on the streets. We'd only gone a kilometre inside the city, when we were stopped by two policemen on a motorbike, one with a handlebar moustache and an open-necked shirt. They both had rifles slung across their shoulders and the word 'COBRA' inscribed on their lapel. We almost surrendered to the assumption that we had broken some Jhansi law about blocking traffic, when I saw the chest-exhibiting cop start redirecting traffic so that we could make our way through it.

'You are mediawallahs?'

We nodded.

'This bus will get stuck in the bridge there so I will show you where you should park.'

Grateful for his help, we asked what 'COBRA' meant.

'You see there used to be lots of petty crime in this area. Lots of BCs,' he said.

(If you want to maintain credibility in front of an Indian policeman, you cannot, I repeat, you cannot ask him what a 'BC' means. It's a term that is widely used in police handouts. The first time I heard it, I naturally assumed it was an acronym of the Hindi expletive. It could easily be used for that, but the technical term is 'Bad Character'. Every police station in the country, has a list of BC's in the area.)

'The BCs would do a lot of chain-snatching and pick-pocketing,' continued the cop. 'So Mayawatiji made a special force called COBRA to tackle them.'

I didn't know then that COBRA stood for Combat Battalion for Resolute Action – a nationally constituted force to combat Naxals. So I was damn impressed, first with a formidable name like COBRA and then with Mayawati's apparent intolerance of petty thieves. 'Damn good, yaar,' I said to Naghma. 'You know this is perhaps why she got a majority in Uttar Pradesh. She realized that people have simple needs – they want to feel safe.'

🚌

But Mayawati's attention had clearly been distracted from the dalit slum colony, Penchmohalla. And from one of her earliest supporters: Durjan Member. His name wasn't the only extraordinary thing about the eighty-year-old man. He used to be a member of the Bahujan Samaj Party when Kanshi Ram headed it. At that time, his neighbours told us, Mayawati used to be a young follower of Kanshi Ram and during special campaigns or visits to Jhansi, they would both stay in Durjan's house. Durjan's house seemed no grander than any other house in the vicinity. It was a small single-storeyed affair. He lived in one room, while his son and his family lived in the rest of the house.

Durjan Member was not home when we reached. 'Madam, he is in a very bad shape,' said the neighbours. 'Mayawatiji doesn't care for him anymore. He doesn't even have money to eat most of the time.'

They told me how his love for his party president went so deep, he'd alienated his entire family. They hadn't liked the fact that he spent his entire day campaigning: 'Brother, press the button for the elephant. We have to make Sister Mayawati win. We have to make her the prime minister.' That was the mantra he kept repeating around Penchmohalla, they said. While other party-workers had moved on to Pajeros, Ford Endeavours or at least Mahindra Boleros, he was as faithful to his bicycle as he was to his leaders. Durjan Member's cries extolling the party were familiar to everyone in the colony but Behenji hadn't given him a hearing in a long time.

His son wasn't happy that we'd come to talk to his father about Mayawati. It was before noon and the man was already drunk. He kept muttering to himself as he watched us set up our filming equipment around the house. A whole bunch of locals had gathered to watch the tamasha. One of them explained that because Durjan had given away all his money and his property to his party chief, his son had been left out in the cold, and couldn't forgive his father. Frustrated, the son had finally tottered up to me: 'Madam, I will tell you what they have done to the old man,' he said, his breath stinking of cheap liquor. 'She has taken everything away from him,' he said referring to Mayawati. His embarrassed wife tried to pull him away. And then out of nowhere the drunken sod said in English, 'Why don't you shut up and fuck me?'

I was shocked, and more scared than I cared to admit. I walked away quickly. 'Did he actually say that?' I asked Naghma. Nishant had heard him too. I don't know why it got me so rattled.

Luckily Durjan came home just then. He was a little hard of hearing but when he heard that Naghma and I had come to meet him because we'd heard that he was one of the oldest members of the party, he started to cry. It was the kind of crying that makes you want to join in as well. Not silent tears, but body-wracking sobs.

'We heard, Babaji, that you are one of the original party loyalists. Do you feel bad that the party has forgotten you?'

'Mayawati is my daughter,' the old man wept. 'Mayawati is our pride. She raises the stature of our community.' He spoke with folded hands. In all my years as a political journalist meeting party-workers I had never met anyone who felt so overwhelmed by his bond to the party. He kept crying, almost as if he was overjoyed to get his feelings across to Mayawati, because he couldn't meet her any other way. Maybe, he was so hard up, and his faith in the party was shaken but by showing up to interview him, he felt that his faith in his party had been redeemed. I don't know. Durjan Member didn't have the vocabulary or the capacity to explain his philosophy to me.

I asked, 'You live so simply, Durjanji, when you see Mayawatiji wearing diamonds, how does it make you feel?'

More tears. 'It makes me feel great. She *deserves* to wear diamonds. She's not wearing illicitly begotten diamonds. She's wearing diamonds that *we* have paid for and they look great on her. Kanshi Ram told us that one major principle of our party is donation, and that's what we've done.'

I knew that he was sincere in what he was saying. Through Durjan Member, BSP's principle finally became clear to me. I could see the Penchmohalla community, living in the filthy armpit of Uttar Pradesh, watching Mayawati, resplendent in her diamonds and her favourite pink salwar kameez on TV, turning an untouchable community into a viable force. They saw powerful bureaucrats fight amongst themselves to feed her cake on her birthday, and they saw her force the crown prince of Indian politics to spend the night in their village. When Mayawati flashed those big diamonds, people like Durjan didn't think that she could have spent that money on a few more tube-wells in Penchmohalla; they were happy that it was their earning, their hard work, that had got Mayawati this far. The Central Bureau of Investigation, while inquiring into her unaccounted wealth, said that they had evidence that her donations weren't really donations. The CBI said that Mayawati's list of donors were people of small means – people like rickshawallahs, sweepers and manual labourers. Everyone was sceptical. 'How can these poor people have contributed to an income that adds up to crores of rupees?'

At that time, we had blindly agreed with the CBI's logic. Now, I wasn't so sure. After all, Durjan was also a slum-dweller but he'd given everything he owned to make sure that Mayawati lived well; far, far away, in a huge bungalow.

I like to think that I'm not a blubberer. My stint as a crime reporter has ensured that even though I cry like a baby when watching films, I am not affected while reporting. I have been initiated by fire – and I mean this literally – in the burns ward, at Lok Nayak Jai Prakash Hospital, to be precise.

In 1999, when the Yamuna Pushta slum went up in flames – as it does quite often, during the summer months – the burns victims were taken there. As it wasn't considered a big story, trainees like me were sent to cover it. In a poor government hospital like LNJP, no one stopped us from entering the burns ward – of course we were also a lot more subtle then, being without a camera. So, we walked in, faced the horror of pain and death head on, and got our story, all in a matter of minutes. I dealt with it pretty well, and without many nightmares. My trick is a childhood habit of closing my eyes when I see something scary. It certainly didn't get in my way of being a crime reporter for a couple of years.

But you can't close your eyes or anticipate the strength of someone's emotion. Maybe, Durjan Member's sobbing just got to me. When we finished the interview, he touched both my hands as if he were blessing me. He was in pain and yet he found it in his heart to bless me, to wish me well.

🚌

Then there was the spontaneity of 11-year old Hirendra, who I met in Penchmohalla as well. We were just waiting around while the boys took a few shots of the village when I saw this cute little boy staring at me. I tried chatting him up even though I knew that my skills at entertaining children were, er, limited. When I asked him his name, Hirendra Singh replied in English.

'Where did you learn to speak such good English?' I asked.

And Hirendra replied, 'My friend and I speak. There is no playground in our school. So we study.'

It was that simple. Here, in a dalit settlement in backward Jhansi, two little boys had, by themselves, channelled their hopelessness to their advantage. They had used their time to equip themselves with a skill that everyone in town wanted, and from what I could make out, very few people had.

'I want to be doctor,' Hirendra continued.

'Why?'

'Because it is my dream.'

'You seem to be really bright, what do you think of politics?'

'Mayawati is our great leader. She has done a lot of improvement in the country. She has made roads and tube-wells.'

Behind my cheap and mercifully huge sunglasses, I started to cry. I had no idea why. Maybe, out of despair at a system that fails to encourage talent like Hirendra's.

Maybe, because I knew that even with all his talent, chances were that the system would push Hirendra to grow up to be like Durjan's drunken, frustrated son, shouting: 'Shut up and fuck me!'

Whatever his plight, Hirendra had more of a chance of escaping Penchmohalla than little Bhuri from Shivgarh.

Shivgarh was a village eight kilometres away from Jhansi that had never known electricity. We'd decided we'd do the show from Shivgarh, so by 4.30pm we'd driven through fields and reasonably good roads to arrive there. It was a medium-sized settlement with a hundred houses and unlike Jhansi, it was super, super clean. No longer in a mood to decide on TV frames, I left the decision of how best to convey the wretchedness of the villagers to Mohammed. 'You decide,' I said getting out of the car. 'I want some tea.'

Pressing against the car door, was a group of children. They weren't saying anything, just staring at us in silent fascination.

'Nobody ever comes here, that's why they are looking,' said an old man seated nearby. I thought maybe I had inadvertently looked irritated. Wanting to instantly make amends, I took out my camera and took a few pictures to show the kids. It worked, as always. They were thrilled and I felt better too.

'Look at how they all have light eyes,' said Naghma. Those beautiful light eyes couldn't get any wider, trying to take in all the people who had landed up at their village.

I walked into the courtyard of the nearest house, followed faithfully by my young posse. Walking up to a young woman there I said, 'I'm from Delhi and I just wanted to come and meet you.' The young woman smiled encouragingly so I went on, 'I wanted to understand what it's like to live without electricity.'

By that time, other women, curious neighbours, also turned up to size us up. They all laughed, throwing their heads back. 'Sit and we shall tell you.'

They pulled out a charpoy for me, made some tea and then continued to stare at me. Staring the hardest was one of the little girls with light eyes I'd met outside. 'What beautiful eyes she has,' I said.

'Her name is Bhuri, after the colour of her eyes.'

A skinny young man walked out from one of the rooms. He was carrying a cell phone. He was a little taken aback when I asked him about it, but was reassured when he saw the rows of smiling women sitting there. 'We all have cell phones,' he said proudly.

'But how is it possible? You don't have electricity?'

'We also have TV.'

Get out of here, I wanted to say. 'Show me.'

I followed the man and he showed me a TV set of a vintage make, but a proper TV set, nonetheless. 'How do you run it?'

'Battery,' he smiled. They were all thrilled that they'd surprised me.

'Tell me how!'

Apparently it was the oldest trick in the book. They ran all their appliances on their tractor batteries! So after a hard day in the field, they took the battery out of the tractor and turned on the TV with it. Of course, they weren't stupid enough to run individual TVs even though they all had one of their own. They took turns to run a show. Enterprising local businessmen recharged the batteries for a flat fee and that service, along with the service of recharging cell phones, came for an apparently affordable fee of 50 rupees a month.

'So you all watch TV and movies?'

'We cannot watch cable but we watch movies on CD.'

'No wonder you all look so happy!' (I felt like a rock star comedienne; they were rolling on the floor with everything I said.)

'Is there any reason you miss having electricity?' I asked, thinking perhaps that this community, like the ultra-rich in south Delhi, had dispensed with government support. They were finding their own solutions to very serious problems.

'There are huge mosquitoes here. Their number would be reduced if we had electric fans.'

'It is very difficult for our children to study. Their education would be a lot more easier if they could study at night.'

I looked at Bhuri. Her eyes hadn't moved from my face. She was truly, truly beautiful, despite the aching sadness in her eyes.

'Didi, why don't you take her?' one of the women suggested suddenly.

'What?'

'Didi, her mother has died and her father is hardly there for her,' said the owner of the house. 'Take her and make her like you.'

'Yes, didi, what will happen if she stays here? If she goes outside, you can make her like you.'

I was horrified: 'Don't say that. She's fine here.' My tone had changed, the women sensed that. 'How will she feel? She belongs here and you are trying to give her away.' I didn't even have my sunglasses on to hide my horror and my voice had taken the tone of an ugly sob.

'Arrey, didi, we are just kidding,' one them said quickly. 'Do you think we give away our girls? Of course, we won't give her away, we were just teasing you.'

Throughout this exchange, Bhuri kept staring at me. She was old enough to understand what was happening. I tried to gauge what was going through her mind. Was it my imagination, or was she trying to look her best for me? Was she willing me to like her? Was she silently beseeching me to take her away?

When you are in TV, I think it's essential to have a sense of humour. Not because it makes you a better presenter, though, sure, I wouldn't mind being like CNN's Jeanie Mose who always knows how to inject wit into boring political scripts.

What I'm talking about here is a sense of humour for the sake of sanity, for peace of mind, for survival. In just 24 hours, there were two instances where I was tempted to resort to another childhood habit – lying on the floor, flailing my limbs about, and screaming out loud. The reason I didn't is because over the last six years I have consciously cultivated a sense of humour about my work, where I try and channel my frustration into a funny anecdote for the future.

Also, I realized that, unlike when I was younger, throwing a tantrum like that would only get me some *very* funny looks.

But, imagine being in my shoes: You've worked 16 hours non-stop every day despite the 40-something heat; you've given up snoozing while travelling because you're busy lining up interviews for your next destination; you wake up every day at 6am, hoping and praying that your roommate i.e. Naghma will decide to go to the loo first so that you can get an extra half-hour to sleep and every day, you are let down; you realize that your no-carbohydrates-after-sundown diet cannot survive on the road so you spend five minutes in the toilet every day just staring at your tummy in the mirror to figure out if it's slowly ballooning and *willing* it to stop; you go crazy trying to figure where and how and when to launder your 'dainties' so you don't have to carry damp underwear from city to city because you haven't spent more than one night in a place; you realize that the perfume bottle that you put in your travel bag is almost finished so the rest of the trip has to be endured without smelling nice (unless your tastes are of the Yardley and Charlie variety); your husband and friends aren't too sympathetic about your situation because they think you're having a bloody good time; they've also become less enthusiastic about your phone calls when all you can say is, 'I was thinking of doing this story, what do *you* think?'

Hell, you go through all that for just *one* reason – that at the end of it all, you'll at least have *30 minutes* of air time.

That your blood, sweat, toil and tears are going to amount to a show every evening; that you'd have something to show for all the torture you've undergone.

But as they say in the best circles, it's in the nature of the beast to have something spoil your plans.

And it would have probably upset the probability of good TV performances to have a week full of perfect shows.

My Friday night show was the chosen one.

🚌

It was the show meant for the big reveal.

We had decided that since everyone in Shivgarh village had cell phones and DVD players despite not having electricity, we would focus on that aspect instead of the no electricity angle. We would do a happy show about how people made the most of circumstances, and how they were to be admired for their innovative spirit instead of being pitied.

Mohammed had organized an elaborate set-up. For the opening shot, I was supposed to walk through a huge group of villagers watching TV and induce the drama through my introductory lines:

'*Good evening. For this edition of the* Election Express, *we are coming to you live from a village in Uttar Pradesh, a village*

*that is yet to be introduced to electricity. The light that enables
you to see me this evening is actually from our bus. Never before
has Shivgarh seen artificial light. But, this show is not going
to be a sad story. Over the next 30 minutes, we'll tell you how
Shivgarh residents stay happy, how they are able to watch TV
(camera pans to the crowds glued to a set) and what they really
need from the government...'*

Till that point it looked grand. I was thrilled that I'd been
able to take the clichéd poor-Indian-village-without-electricity
story and give it a positive spin. I had lined up some chirpy
village women to talk to on the show and they had carried
their smiles to their on-air appearance as well. Actually,
what really blew me away was the make-up that the women
wore for the show. While chatting with me earlier – as they
cooked the evening meal and milked their buffaloes – their
faces had been quite unmade-up, but when I asked them to
join my show in the evening, they all came expertly made-up
with powder, kajal and bright red lipstick. In a way, it really
narrowed the divide between me as an urban working woman
from Delhi and them, housewives from a village near Jhansi.
Both of us, no matter how good or bad our day, had to put
on some make-up to face the world. And so what if it was
too dark or there were no lights in the evening, you couldn't
be caught looking like a minger in candlelight.

'Did you also grow up in a village without electricity?' I
asked the women in my live interview.

'Oh no. We always had electricity in our parents' homes.'

'Then why did you ever agree to come live here after
marriage?'

They were all laughing now: 'I didn't realize it then,' said
one. 'They had brought in so many generators that the road
to this village was lit up like Diwali.'

Alas, in the midst of this live report which, if I may say so myself, was engaging and enlightening, I heard an ominous crackle in my talk-back: 'Sunetra, this is just to warn you, there may be breaking news from Obama, so we might have to cut live to it in the middle of your show,' Delhi PCR said.

That killed the show for me.

I couldn't concentrate on the interviews anymore because all I could think was what would happen to the many stories that I had done from Jhansi, what would happen to the story about COBRA, Durjan Member and Penchmohalla? And, it's not like I could go to Udaipur and show people what I'd found in Jhansi, could I? Hadn't they had enough of Barack Obama? What the hell was the attention-seeking American President saying now?

I found out soon enough.

When they came out of commercial breaks, the news went straight to Washington. I was left spluttering without an audience: 'Will you ask them how long they will stay on it?' I queried Delhi.

Silence.

'Will you ask them when they'll return?'

No response.

'What about *my* stories, you guys?'

The minutes ticked away, quickly approaching 7.30, the outer limit for my show. Three of my stories looked like they would never be aired. Barack Obama droned on about his policy for Afghanistan and Pakistan – not one of his most inspiring speeches, if you ask me. But our channel couldn't bear to tear itself away. Wasn't it basic journalism that distance determined news value? So for instance, if a murder took place in south Delhi, it was far more important to us than if ten people died in Jhumritalaiya. (Hey, it sounds cruel, but I didn't make those rules.)

At 7.23 pm, Mohammed approached me to prepare for Naghma's show, seven minutes later. 'Erm, Sunetra, the talk-back?'

I wouldn't part with it because I still thought I had a chance to go on air.

'You poor thing, they dropped your show?' Naghma was sympathetic but she wanted me to move away from the camera, as it was her turn. 'Thank god Hindi is not that interested in it.'

Obama's voice droned on in my ear. There's no reason why English should have been so interested as to cut live either, I thought, but who cared about my opinion. I relinquished the camera and sat glumly in the bus, just wanting to leave.

🚌

I got off the bus and waited for pack-up with Bhuri and the other children crowding around us. As evening set in the children's faces were becoming difficult to see. Mohammed and the gang were packing up one light kit after another, and we had started our descent into darkness.

'Do you feel the mosquitoes?' Naghma said, slapping her arm.

'You know, I always think that mosquitoes bite me more. I'm dying, man.'

'Maybe we should go inside the bus,' said Naghma. 'But these kids are so cute. And you know what that woman was telling me?' Naghma continued: 'She said that no one ever comes to their village, nobody, no politicians, no officials, nobody. So they are thrilled we came because they had a good time-pass today.'

I thought of my colleague, the fantastic cameraperson Puja Arya. On outstation assignments Puja would always buy toffees at every stop. Initially I thought she bought them for an emergency glucose hit, which was sorely needed sometimes because of all the physical exertion we were required to do. But she'd said, 'No, you know, when you go to villages, it's nice to give something to the kids.'

I really wished I had some chocolates or something with me but there were no shops nearby. I wanted to give the children something, or to give something to Bhuri at least. Earlier in the evening, when Naghma and I were in dire need of a loo, she had led us to a shack, shooed away all the onlookers, and signalled for us to go in. 'But doesn't someone live here?' I had asked in Hindi. 'They are not here,' she had grinned in reply, standing guard while Naghma and I took turns defiling someone's private space.

I thought of what I had in my bag that would make a present for Bhuri. My mother, whenever she made a trip or was on holiday, was always on the lookout for good luck charms for me. They always stayed with me in my bag but I knew she wouldn't mind if I gave Bhuri the little red bracelet with the evil-eye beads she'd got for me from Darjeeling. I wanted Bhuri to know that I thought she was really special, even though her village women made it seem that I wasn't interested in taking her with me; I wanted her to know that I would remember her forever.

Naghma had noticed the 'Sania Mirza' t-shirt Bhuri was wearing so she gave her one of her own. Bhuri clutched it with her bracelet-clad arm. As the bus revved to life, the headlights of the bus shone on the children. We pulled away, watching the children run behind our bus for a very short while before their village disappeared completely, swallowed by the overwhelming darkness.

🚌

'Where are we going to stay?' I said quickly, feeling that familiar welling-up sensation in my eyes and desperate to talk about something else.

'Orchha is just 16 kilometres away, and the hotels are decent so I've booked us there,' said Nishant.

'No way! Seriously?' I said, remembering someone raving about how beautiful Orchha was. Maybe, after a heart-wrenchingly awful day, things were finally going to look up.

The good thing was that all we had to do over the weekend was a 500 km journey to Udaipur in Rajasthan. So, at least for Saturday, we could afford to sit back and sleep our way to the next destination. We could finally put the luxury seats on the bus to good use.

I focused on the fact that we were going to stay at the fabulous Lake Palace in Udaipur, with its extra-fabulous views of the city. I imagined myself eating at one of Udaipur's many fine restaurants, and pictured myself having a lazy lie-in on Sunday morning. I had planned to call my editors in Delhi to crib about my lost stories, but the thought of the weekend ahead was already making me feel better.

'You are being very calm about this,' said Naghma as we drove towards Orchha.

'That's fine, yaar, I'll get them to put the unused stories in the "Best of the Week" show for tomorrow,' I said. 'Truth is, I can't believe we are going to be at the Lake Palace tomorrow night! Ganga Singhji, how long will you take to get us there?'

'Madam, I have spoken to some people. If we leave early morning, then we will be there by evening. I will get you there, don't worry,' Ganga Singhji reassured me confidently.

'Yes, but Ganga Singhji, we won't fly too much because we have to take the bus and do a show tomorrow as well.'

'Arrey, you don't worry, madamji, I'll get you there.'

Ganga Singhji put on our favourite (by default) CD. As strains of *Jhini* filled the bus, Ganga Singhji said, 'Aur madamji, I am also going to cook for you tomorrow. I will catch a desi chicken and cook it.'

'Yes, I saw you eyeing them in the village, Ganga Singhji,' teased Mohammed.

'I want some fish, I really want some fish,' I said. I think my Bengali roots only kicked in when I left home. In Delhi, I could go for months without eating the damn thing.

By the time we reached Orchha we were starving. The hotel, located on the banks of the Betwa river, had an amazing view of one of the many palaces around. We all sighed and headed straight for the balcony restaurant. A little girl with fake long hair danced around in circles. Nishant and I ordered beer, Mohammed ordered whisky for Ganga Singhji and Naghma went and sat down with the local musicians to take pictures of the little dancing girl. We ordered everything on the menu, the comfort food being chilli chicken, fish fry, paneer and rice.

We toasted one week down; seven more to go.

8

The 500 km Detour

'Madamji, you've made us late.' Ganga Singhji said accusingly. Both he and his car were ready and shining and raring to go when I finally emerged from my room. 'I wanted you to be there by sundown.'

All my good intentions of waking up in the morning to walk to the chattris or mahals had come to nought. At 8am, I was still drooling on my pillow when my phone had rung: 'Listen, Sunetra, we really should get going. You have to do a live intro to the highlights of your show, don't you?'

Bloody hell, yes. The stories would be taken from the week's programmes, but I still had to introduce it live which meant the bus would move very slowly.

'What to do, Ganga Singhji, I was really tired,' I said, apologizing profusely.

'Doesn't matter, madamji, I'll have you in Udaipur by seven or so.'

'Which way are we going?'

'Madamji, I've found out the best route; we have to go via Agra.'

I remembered our local fixer Vinod also telling us the same thing, but my internet search had shown a distance of 500-odd kilometres. I was quite impressed that we'd be there by sundown. 'You know, there's this dining place there with tables overlooking the lake,' I said. 'We should head there for dinner. I'm taking everyone out.'

'You've got me all excited about Lake Palace as well now,' said Naghma. 'Usually, I don't care about fancy hotels.'

'How can you not? It totally takes away all the exhaustion,' I said and then teased her: 'You are this hippie chick, like those firangs who want authentic Indian stuff even if it is a bit dirty.'

Naghma laughed.

'It's true, isn't it? You want that backpacker-like atmosphere, and all that folksy-music? Like last night even when they were singing really badly? Boss, I'm telling you, when you've been in dirt all day, it's nice to clean up in a decent, well-equipped loo – even if it lacks character!'

Naghma kept laughing and didn't protest. I think we'd had this same conversation during the Mumbai serial train blasts in 2006. A colleague of ours had forgotten something in her hotel room and had gone back to find a hotel guy crapping in her loo. She had been so shocked she couldn't focus on her story the entire day!

'I think you are right,' Naghma smiled. 'I think I can make do with a terrible hotel room for one night, but not on an extended trip like this one. Sunetra, even I am becoming like you now.'

Of course, most people just assumed that we slept in the bus. They'd send us touching emails about taking care of ourselves, about staying safe and also offering us hospitality. Like Gajendra Asutkar:

> *Sunetra & team, When are you and your team expected in Nagpur? I know on this Marathon tour you are missing Ghar ka khana, My Family Invites you for Lunch at my home when your team is in Nagpur. Hope you accept my invitation to dinner.*

Or Parvesh Babu of Alwar:

> *My hats off to NDTV...really appreciate you...hope to see you in Alwar also. My pleasure if I can provide hospitality to NDTV*

And many homesick NRIs who were following our journey, like Manish Tiwari in London:

> *While you clock up the miles, and check the pre-election voter pulse, you do have an environment impact, hope your firm would offset carbon emission through carbon neutral points. Despite simplicity and ease of reporting that appears to us, you have navigated through some of the tough regions of the country in short span. Not sure if you are spending any nights in an actual village where there is no electricity, clean water or even toilets in homes. I do like to watch despite glooming economy in UK and pressures of investment banking job.*

'What if we really had to live in the bus?' asked Naghma.

'*Eyugh!*' It was a thought too scary to imagine.

Two girls and six men, with varying hygiene standards, sharing a cramped space together for eight weeks. *Gross!* Imagine the state of the loo, if there had been a loo on board. Maybe I would have done it if I knew that at the end of it I'd get some sort of medal.

Maybe, not even then.

It was a little after Agra, when we stopped for lunch at a dhaba, that the first warning bells went off. Having finished his food before us, Ganga Singhji thought it an appropriate time to ask for directions.

Two minutes later he approached me gingerly: 'Madamji, I don't think that the 500 kilometres that you've written is right...'

'What?' I was taking the lead in this conversation and getting more stressed than the others because, obviously, I had mapped the route. How could mapsofindia.com be so wrong?

'Madamji, they are saying Jaipur is quite far from here and then Udaipur is an extra 6-7 hours after that.'

I didn't understand what he was saying, and my big map of India was in the bus which was travelling at its own pace. 'Ganga Singhji, have we come the wrong way?'

'No, madamji, this is the only way to go, everyone has told me that but we have done 250 kilometres since morning and Jaipur is still 200 kilometres away, so Udaipur cannot be 500 kilometres away!'

I was thoroughly confused and irritated. 'Ganga Singhji, what time can you get us there?'

'Madamji, I will get you there as soon as possible but madamji, it is quite far.'

I was flummoxed. But there was nothing I could do so we decided to just follow the path. 'Are you sure we have to go via Jaipur, Ganga Singhji?'

'Madamji, I have asked, from here there is no other route to go to Udaipur.'

We set off but I was hugely worried. All our plans of going out for dinner now looked distinctly improbable; the carefree, light-hearted mood inside the car had vanished.

'Maybe that distance was as the crow flies,' suggested Naghma.

Maybe, and maybe, that distance was over un-motorable roads. Who knows? I hadn't done this journey before and apparently, no one I knew had been crazy enough to do it either. I was feeling very bad because I now remembered my producer asking me: 'Are you *sure* you want to go to Udaipur from Jhansi? Isn't that going back up instead of coming down?'

At that time, I'd told her it was the best way to get into Gujarat.

At about 6pm, we stopped 60 kilometres short of Jaipur to do our weekend-show live. As soon as I got onto the bus, I went straight for the map. And then it hit me. We'd taken the wrong route and made a 500 km detour! Our big mistake had been to come via Agra. We should have just taken National Highway 76 which goes via Shivpuri, to Kota, Chittorgarh and to Udaipur. *That* route was about 500 kilometres.

'Ganga Singhji come here!' I was livid. 'Who told you to come via Agra, Ganga Singhji? Look, this is where we are, and that is where we should have been. We've come the opposite way.'

Ganga Singhji stared at the map, muttering now and then, that he had asked people. When I asked who, he could only name our local fixer. I remembered then that it was he who had first put the 'via Agra' idea in our head. 'But Ganga Singhji, why did you just go by what he was saying? Why didn't you ask someone else before we left?'

'I did, madamji – in Agra.'

'That was too late, Ganga Singhji,' I screamed, no longer able to control my temper. I was also angry because maybe it was not just Ganga Singhji's mistake; it was the entire team's fault. I had been working like crazy planning the whole thing for everyone, I thought, why couldn't they share some of the planning now? Wasn't it enough that I was thinking of stories and executing them? Were the logistics to be my problem as well? Obviously, I couldn't say all of this out loud, but keeping a cool face wasn't lessening my resentment.

That's the problem with long trips with a group of people in intense situations. If I'd had some time-out from them, I'd probably have been able to regain my composure, but when you are surrounded by the same people, day in day out, it brings out the worst in you.

My show that evening was also not the best.

As I stood to do my links, a drunken man, possibly a political worker from the Meena community, got enraged by the word 'Election' on our bus. Perhaps, some local channel somewhere had said something nasty about his favourite leader or party, and he now wished to avenge this insult.

I looked positively cross-eyed during the entire show because I had one eye on the man who, every now and then, lurched forward to pick up a big stone that he was threatening to lob at me.

Nishant tried to talk him out of it but he couldn't be too aggressive because we were clearly outnumbered. We couldn't move to another location because there was simply no time and I was live. So, I did all my happy intros looking terrified as hell, afraid of the projectile that could come my way any moment. I was especially scared because it would hardly be a glamorous injury. It wasn't like a shrapnel injury while covering a bomb blast which would then go into my reporting memoirs.

'How did you get hurt?'

'A drunk threw a stone at me.'

At best, a live shot of me being taken a pot-shot at while doing my link would make it to the year-end bloopers' package. Fortunately, the drunk man left by the end of the show, hurling only an expletive.

Hot and sweaty from the Rajasthan heat and completely frustrated with the Travel Gods who had so messed with my plans, I called Sudeep to complain. He laughed when I told him about the detour. 'Babu, it's okay. What can anyone do? This happens when you are travelling. Now get on with it.'

So I decided to give it a rest with Ganga Singhji. I could see that he was hurting and that his pride had taken a major hit. He was silent through the trip and drove with renewed zeal. At Jaipur, he stopped and tersely told the team: 'Eat up because I'm not stopping after this.'

'We were supposed to eat in a lake-view restaurant, instead we are here,' moaned Naghma.

'Here' was one of those sad restaurants that dot the highway. We had to take the lift to go up to it and when we walked in it was totally empty. The waiter took a long time to take our order and by the time it came, we had reached the end of our patience. The food looked so pathetic, I couldn't eat and I wanted to tell everyone to get going, but then again, you have to go along with everyone when you're travelling. By the time we started on the road again, it was 10pm. We could only expect to reach the Lake Palace by about 4 in the morning.

Ganga Singh ate nothing. Maybe because he feared it would make him sleepy, but I felt immediately guilty. He wasn't sulking, I realized. The best thing about Ganga Singhji was that he just wanted to set his wrong right. As soon as the meal was over we set off. Ganga Singhji had tied his handkerchief around his forehead like a warrior. Mohammed sat on the passenger seat next to him to keep him awake, and promptly fell asleep.

'I'm worried about him, yaar,' Naghma whispered to me. 'He'll feel sleepy as well.' I didn't say anything because I too was not a late-night person and felt really sleepy while travelling.

So between Naghma and Nishant, they kept up the effort of keeping Ganga Singhji awake. At his age, it wasn't easy for Ganga Singhji. He pushed himself to stay awake with pinches of tobacco.

I didn't have the confidence to drive on the highway but I could see that after driving for fourteen hours at a stretch, Ganga Singhji was exhausted. Nishant finally offered to drive. Ganga Singhji started to snore the minute he sat on the passenger seat.

'Poor thing, I hope he doesn't fall ill, yaar,' Naghma said.

This was a pretty scary prospect considering that Nishant was the worst kind of driver possible. He drove like an 18-year old who couldn't believe that his father had actually let him take the car out!

Looking back, I wonder why we never thought of staying in Jaipur for the night. I think there were several reasons for this. One, we feared they might charge us for changing our bookings at the last minute. Also, we didn't want to spend another day just travelling. And, greedy reporter that I was, I wanted to get started on a story in Udaipur by afternoon. So we soldiered on, and it was only by 4am that four cranky journalists from NDTV drove up to the foyer of the Lake Palace in Udaipur.

'Thank you, Ganga Singhji,' I said gratefully. 'And please rest tomorrow, we will drive ourselves around the city.'

I was wishing I could say that to myself so that we could kick around the Lake Palace on Sunday. We could see the Lake Palace shimmering in the water and by the time we sat on the boat, half our exhaustion was over. 'This almost makes up for what we've been through,' I said, even gathering the energy to take pictures of us gliding towards the hotel.

'No. We have to get ourselves head massages and pedicures to really get over it,' said Naghma.

I couldn't agree more.

9

Indulgences and Consequences in Udaipur

I wiggled my toes, inspecting my feet after the pedicure, which, combined with a head massage, had set me back by 4000 rupees. I had promised myself that I wouldn't be my usual stingy self. That I needed a little indulgence after a traumatic week and a very hot Sunday in Udaipur, but I guess it's hard to quieten middle-class sensibilities. My neighbourhood parlour just charged a couple of hundred rupees to repair the toll that reporting took on my feet every month. The hotel was perhaps a little nicer, but was it 4000 rupees nicer?

I don't think so.

The poor girl who actually had to touch my dirty feet had tried her best, but it's hard to wash away grime encrusted over a couple of thousand kilometres. At least four white towels had turned black and still my soles were stained. I had two light bands from my sandal straps on my feet to show how much I'd tanned.

'Madam, you have deep tanning, we will try to reduce that,' the girl had promised valiantly before we'd started off, but I wasn't holding my breath.

I turned to Naghma in the seat next to me: 'What do you think the boys are doing?' I asked. She didn't reply; she'd dozed off as her ministering angel worked her upper shoulders.

It hadn't been the team's best day.

'Guys, are you ready?' I'd called up the boys at 11am.

'We'll just take a little longer.' The boys sounded like they'd just been woken up. Even though it was a Sunday, even though we all deserved a break, it was still a bit irritating to be ready on time and then wait for the others.

'It's not fair, yaar.' I'd complained to Naghma. 'We also went to bed at 4.30 or 5, but we woke up at 9.30, didn't we?'

But then, just because we were hyper about our stories, there's no reason why the entire team had to be that way. The problem with a touristy place like Udaipur is that there weren't any obvious political stories. So Naghma and I were antsy about work on Sunday morning; we were worried we'd be unable to fill our half-hour slot.

'Mohammed was sleeping in the car as well, so why should he be tired?'

'It's their show as well, isn't it?'

We carped on like two old biddies. We were hungry as well. The abundant hotel breakfast spread was way beyond our means, and a dhaba meant crossing the lake. So we spent time bitching about everything till the guys arrived. Apparently, the bus had only reached at 6am. Their sleep had been more disturbed than ours as they had to wait up to let in the engineer, Sumit. Then, the hotel people had taken ages to get an extra bed. I instantly felt a little bad because their night had clearly been worse than ours but I was too low on energy myself to revive the spirits of the gang. Everyone was just too sleepy, too tired and too hot to be bothered with civilities.

So, the jibes continued on both sides. If we gave the men a rude, unsympathetic awakening, they got their own back. We were driving out sullenly with Nishant at the wheel, when Naghma said, 'Maybe, we should stop and grab something to eat.' Udaipur was so hot that the sun's rays actually felt like they would burn a hole in one's skin. I just wanted to stay inside the air-conditioned car; I'd been hungry so long that I didn't even feel hunger anymore. But Naghma had spotted a food cart. 'Look, I think they have puris. Let's at least check it out.'

Nishant stopped the car and got off to check out the food. The cart was a little way off, so we thought that Nishant was going to do a quick recce of what was going and maybe place orders for us. Usually, these carts have no place to sit, so the vendor carries the food to the waiting cars. Mohammed got off to have a smoke.

'What's taking Nishant so long to check things out?' I wondered aloud after a while, popping my head out of the car – and saw that the two men had sat down and were busy eating! 'Naghma, they're just eating there!' I said. 'They have forgotten about us.'

Naghma got off and walked over to them. When she returned in a couple of minutes, she said, 'You know, they hadn't even ordered for us. I've told that guy now to bring us our food here.'

'But why wouldn't they have ordered?' I said, a bit hurt, really. 'They knew we were so hungry.'

Maybe, the guys were even hungrier, maybe they thought it was all too greasy for our taste and decided to wait till healthier options were available; I'm sure there were many perfectly good explanations for their behaviour, but at that moment the team was firmly divided into us versus them – the girls versus the boys – and nope, we definitely didn't feel the love.

It got worse when we were shooting with Bhil tribals outside Udaipur. We were filming a group of tribals who were using music and songs to encourage the community to vote. Filming them was a time-consuming process because the singers first wanted us to hear the songs they had written for their campaign before we chose which ones to film. They were also camera-shy, and it took them some time to loosen up and follow Mohammed's directions.

So, we thought it might be a good idea for Nishant to go up ahead to the settlement and get some footage of the way the Bhils lived. When Nishant asked where the settlement was he was told by a local that it was right around the corner. He wasn't very happy about going without us, but we pushed him: 'Go on, we'll just finish with this and do the interviews there,' we said.

By the time we finished, it was perhaps 43 degrees. The sun was reflecting off the stone-covered hills and irritating our skins. We were all drenched in sweat but the villagers had gathered around, determined to make us walk right to the top and then further on, behind some hills to the settlement. They had never before met outsiders who were remotely interested in their lives, so they weren't going to let this opportunity go easily. We started walking with them but when our local guide saw our sorry pace, he offered someone's car.

'This car is small, why don't you guys go ahead in this? We will walk quickly and come.'

There was no hesitation as Naghma, Mohammed and I quickly jumped in. It's amazing how, when it's a matter of survival, you lose your manners. We didn't care that the owners of the car would now have to walk through the heat while we enjoyed the comfort of being driven. We just knew that if we didn't sit down immediately, we would faint. The air-conditioning wasn't effective but as long as we were away from the direct glare of the sunlight, we were okay.

Perhaps to teach us a lesson for our rudeness, the car gave up halfway up the hill.

'Bloody hell, yaar, what do we do now?'

We looked up to where some villagers stood waiting for us. We could see Nishant's silhouette among them.

'Forget it. Let some of them come down here for the interview. We've already got the shots of their houses.'

That was true. Besides, we were standing at the spot where the villagers were due to start work on a road to their settlement. It was part of an employment-guarantee scheme that paid them a daily wage from the government in return for helping with public projects. The villagers had wanted to talk to us about how the employment-guarantee scheme had promised them 100 rupees per day, but due to rampant local corruption they were only getting about 60 or 70 rupees.

'Yes, I think, visually as well, it makes sense to record interviews here.'

It was decided. We started flailing our arms about. 'Come down, come down.'

The villagers on the top of the hill were all a little confused at first but they finally realized that the three of us weren't budging from where we stood. When they all made their way down again and queried us on this change of location we didn't admit that it was because we were too hot and tired to climb up.

'This is a better location,' we told our fixer and somehow we managed to finish our interviews.

'Where's Nishant?' I asked as we were getting ready to pile back into the car that would take us to our car on the main road.

'There he is,' pointed Mohammed. He told us that Nishant had decided to walk back as well. 'I think he's a little upset that we made him walk, while we took the car,' said Mohammed. Nishant had obviously said something to him.

'But we didn't know, did we?' protested Naghma.

'Apparently, it was a really long way that the villagers took him by,' said Mohammed.

'These locals, yaar,' said Naghma. 'They are always overenthusiastic. Why couldn't they have all come down where we did the interviews? What was the point of them trying to take us all the way up?'

By the time we got back, Nishant had already arrived and was silently washing his face. It seems he'd had a nose bleed. We felt bad for him but we didn't know what to do. Besides, our next appointment was waiting.

🚌

'We have to go to the Maharana's palace now,' I said to Nishant but he didn't reply. Nishant was only 25 years old and of the entire team, he had the least amount of experience with such shoots. His usual work assignments revolved around *Raftaar*, a show that reviewed cars and motorbikes. He had been sent with us because the bosses thought it would tie in with his sense of adventure, but maybe it was all proving a bit too much for him. He didn't join us for the shoot at the Maharana's palace.

So Mohammed, Naghma and I went without Nishant to meet the man who owned all the impressive buildings of Udaipur. Maharana Arvind Singh Mewar, or Shreeji as he's popularly called, had granted us an 'audience' at his palace.

I'd tried to wrangle a lunch for the *Election Express* team, after watching Shreeji personally cook a meat dish and throw a party for Anthony Bourdain, and host another party for Ian Wright and many others on Discovery Channel. I'd figured, if those correspondents had got a meal, surely India's best, NDTV, warranted a lunch?

Our intentions were not merely to appease our hungry stomachs. Shreeji's son, the young prince, had campaigned for the first time and could influence poll results. I thought our cameras could feast on his colourful, antique-filled palace while we washed Shreeji's words down with some royal cuisine.

No such luck.

His media advisor Jyoti Jasol totally ignored that part of my email and gave us an appointment for a post-lunch slot, at 4pm.

By the time, we got to Shreeji's palace, we could have really done with some lunch. He was very nice to us but royalty can also be a bit stubborn.

'Sir, we wanted to walk around the palace and do the interview.'

'No, no, no, let's sit over here.'

He wanted to sit in his living room and give me a boring single frame. However much I pleaded with him that it would look nice on TV to show off the palace a bit and do the interview in different parts of the palace, all he wanted was to sit on his sofa. I had to give up my pleading when he finally lost his patience and thundered, 'Look, I am no Amitabh Bachchan.' He also casually threw in the fact that he knew all the top people at NDTV, and was flying off soon to meet them in Delhi for another show. Naghma, clearly, charmed him more than I did, because he conceded to walk a few steps with her during her interview.

'Jyoti, give them some tea or something,' he said after talking to us for a while, indicating that it was the end of our audience. Pure survival instincts kicked in as we quickly accepted Jyoti's invitation to get something to eat. It may not have been made by the Maharana himself – we were obviously not being treated as well as Discovery Channel! – but then, at that time, there was no space for pride.

As we sat in the restaurant of the hotel wing of Maharana's palace, looking at the sun setting over Pichola lake and wolfing down pakoras and sandwiches, we felt our spirits rise for the first time that day. In a way it was a relief that the day was over; sundown meant no more shooting. I wondered how far I'd push us all, if it were possible to work through the night.

'Call Nishant,' I said to Mohammed. I was ready to make amends and I hadn't forgotten my promise: 'Do you guys want to go for dinner? I know some really nice places here in Udaipur.'

'I just want to go back to the hotel and go to sleep,' said Mohammed. I nodded, understanding the strain that he had to bear carrying the huge P2 camera. 'You guys carry on,' he suggested.

'No, no, we'll go when we are all ready to go.'

So while Naghma and I napped on our massage beds, Nishant explored the bar at Lake Palace. He dragged the engineer Sumit, who like Mohammed, didn't drink, but was at least not averse to sitting with him at the bar. I would have killed for a drink as well. But, one, I wasn't invited and two, Nishant and I hadn't really developed the kind of rapport to unwind together now and then with a drink. And there was no way I was going to risk my reputation by asking Ganga Singhji to buy me couple of bottles of beer. Even though I'm sure Ganga Singhji was not judgemental, it would be like asking a venerable old uncle at home to buy me a bottle – not acceptable at all.

'Let's order something really nice from room service,' suggested Naghma.

'You are so bad, Naghma, you are making me spend so much money,' I said.

'What else are we earning for, yaar? Let's get something nice.'

'But not something Indian, okay?' Dhaba food had meant an incessant barrage of paneer, dal, roti, rice and occasionally, some vegetables. I wanted something different. I'd been dreaming of having a smoothie and sandwiches at Udaipur's German bakery but was just too tired to go out.

'How about we share a Caesar salad and then have Thai red curry and rice?'

We were so gleeful at the thought of having a fancy meal that we didn't care that it would take three days of our allowance just to pay for it.

I didn't know it then, but the heavy price I paid was not just in terms of cold cash.

We'd checked out early from the hotel, after finishing the rest of our filming, and had spent the morning speaking to local groups who'd blamed the former chief minister, Vasundhara Scindia, for allowing encroachment all around the lake. 'If it was up to us, the citizens of Udaipur,' an activist told me, 'we'd vote for a Congress government because they've cared more for the lake.' I'd never met a community that was so obsessed with its lakes, but with a lake as beautiful as the one in Udaipur, I really couldn't blame them.

Vadodara was at least five hours away from Udaipur. We needed to leave Udaipur by 3pm so that even if we stopped to do our show at 6pm, we would have a three hour head-start. And after that, even if we left by 9pm, we could be in Vadodara latest by midnight.

'But we have to have lunch at Udaipur and then go,' I insisted. 'I want to eat Laal Maas.' Now, commonsense should have told me that it was just too hot to stomach a dish that was basically mutton cooked in red chillies. But I was determined to maintain the fun part of this India road trip and to experience all the delicacies the road show promised.

In Rajasthan that meant Laal Maas to me.

The men didn't care either way. Mohammed was a skinny man who ate just enough to get the strength to lift his camera, and Nishant, who was not so skinny, wasn't really talking too much to me at the time. To get Naghma on my side, all I had to say were the magic words: 'authentic' and 'local delight'. So, we sent the bus ahead and went to a local haveli packed with white tourists. The hotel overlooked the lake, and it was only from the shade of where we sat, that we could appreciate how beautiful it was.

'Laal Maas and rotis, please.'

The dish, when it arrived, turned out to be the most succulent mutton dish I'd ever tasted. It was hot enough to make your eyes water, but, god, it was glorious. 'Should we order some more?' I looked around hopefully.

'Sure,' said Naghma and we waited like greedy pigs for the second serving to arrive. We were sweating. It was so hot, but that mutton was *sooo* good. I was behaving like one of those desperate people who didn't know when she'd get her next square meal. 'The food in Gujarat is superb too,' I said stuffing my face with Laal Maas as everyone else's eyes just glazed over. 'Some people think that it is too sweet but I think that no one makes sophisticated vegetarian food like the Gujjus do.' Like a true Bengali, I was already making future plans – not story but food-wise. I'm sure everyone thought that I was a right gas-bag because I kept going on and on, talking about the next meal even as I wiped up this one.

And then my stomach started to cramp.

I was still sitting at the table with some pieces of mutton left on my plate when I recognized the classic symptoms of overeating. I would have to use the loo soon or there would be a *very* embarrassing situation on my hands. I went towards the loo, pretending I just needed to wash up, and thought about what Nishant and Mohammed would think if they got to know of my predicament:

'Sunetra was so greedy, that she had to go and crap *straight* from her lunch table!'

It was the kind of hilarious college story that I'd heard from Sudeep and other male relatives. They'd go to a buffet, and eat so much that they'd have to take a toilet break in between. Obviously, my greed had surpassed my body's limitations.

I peeked into the toilet. It wasn't the dirtiest of toilets that I'd seen but I still didn't want to use it. I quickly reviewed my options. We had checked out of our hotel and since it was in the middle of a lake, I couldn't go back to it without revealing the truth. Did I have to use this loo or did I have an option? I remembered, suddenly, that a contact of mine had a brother-in-law who had a hotel somewhere, and it was a simple but a very clean hotel. And it was probably on our way out of the city.

'Listen guys, I need to stop and say hello to a contact. I'll just take two minutes.' I saw that Naghma was curious but I could not afford to reveal all to her. I was too embarrassed, and besides the men were listening in. I was a little undecided about my strategy. Should I wait to meet my friend's brother-in-law and confess all to him? Or should I pretend to be there for journalistic work and then say, 'By the way, can I use your restroom?'

As we drew up to that hotel, I really didn't know. I left Naghma and the guys in the car and ran in.

'Saheb hain?' I asked the man at the reception.

'Saheb has just gone home.'

Phew. I was quite relieved; it was better to keep the pleasantries to a minimum. 'I'm a journalist from Delhi and I knew his brother in Bikaner and he told me to come and see him,' I said importantly.

He dialled a number. 'Sir, this madam has come from NDTV,' he chatted with him for a long time before he hung up.

'Saheb is saying he'll be back here by 5pm if you want to come back.'

'That's fine, I'll do that,' I said with relief. 'Can I please use your loo before that?' I prayed hard and strong: *Please god, let him not take me to the dirty staff loo. Please* god, let him show me to a loo that is usable, and Hallelujah, he did. I used it as quickly as possible and after mumbling a word of thanks, I went back into the car. They were sitting in air-conditioned comfort and hadn't suspected anything at all. I kept thanking god for the close escape that I'd had. What if I'd been on the highway when my stomach had started to cramp? What if I hadn't known about this hotel?

When I'd signed up for journalism school, I knew that the most exciting part of my job was the uncertainty of never knowing what we were going to be doing the next day. What hadn't been made clear was that we'd also have to grapple with the uncertainty of never knowing *where* we'd be doing our job, on the job!

The quest for a clean loo was a perpetual one. Of course, I'd had enough practice finding clean loos even in Delhi. For years, we would drive very confidently to five-star hotels and use the facilities. Maybe the doorman guessed what you had been up to when you came out of the hotel just five minutes after you went in, but there were far too many people at a hotel for anyone to really notice. Wherever our assignment was taking us for the day, and if it was too far from office, we could be assured a clean bowl at a five-star hotel. But since the unfortunate attacks of 26/11, the bloody terrorists robbed us of that pleasure too.

Now, entering a five-star hotel is like entering a fortress. There are endless checks with pesky guards asking you where you are headed. You can lie at that point, but if you are seen wavering in the lobby, you could be gunned down by security. And if you're not, someone is sure to be watching, and whispering into their walky-talky – 'False alarm, another of those freeloaders for our clean loos.'

No, I would definitely have to keep my greed in check, or like Naghma, be greedy for the right things. Naghma would lust after fresh fruits and juices. Whenever she'd see a vendor she'd scream at Ganga Singhji – 'Stop, stop, let's have some cucumber or something.' She was very careful about avoiding dehydration and would always pick healthy food options. So I promised myself that like her, I would keep away from the meat, at least for a little while.

But that very evening, I had to make an exception.

We'd stopped to do our show from the highway near Godhra in Gujarat. It was a fantastic road but it lacked character so we'd driven a little off the national highway till we'd found a nice hut to act as a backdrop for our live links.

'How was it?' I'd asked my very young producer Priyanka Khaneja in Delhi after the show. I was a little worried because we'd had a couple of good stories but there was no story in my half-hour that day that had blown my mind away or which could qualify as a good piece of journalism. Our show ender had been an item on the guides of Udaipur. It was like a homage to the classic Dev Anand film, *Guide*, which had been shot in Udaipur. The real life guides had a ready supply of one-liners in various foreign languages and in a fun way, they told us what they wanted from politicians.

'The lake looked *so* beautiful,' said Priyanka.

Right. When you don't have a big story, look for good looking locations.

Naghma had just finished her show and I thought we were wrapping up for the day, but then I heard Ganga Singhji shout for me: 'Madamji, please come and eat.'

Ganga Singhji stood over a tiny stove, stirring vigorously into a pressure cooker. He had cooked chicken for everyone.

'But how?' I was amazed.

'I just did it, madamji.'

Apparently, while Naghma and I'd been putting up our show, Ganga Singhji had gone hunting. Even though we weren't exactly living in the wild, even though we could see a dhaba just a little distance away, Ganga Singhji had decided that what the team needed was to be ministered his tender cooking skills.

'And the rotis?'

He reluctantly revealed that he had obtained the rotis and the spices for the chicken from the dhaba across the road. But we were still impressed. Mohammed and Nishant teased him the most. 'Ganga Singhji, you had to do this because you knew that it would be vegetarian food in Gujarat, didn't you?'

'Let's film this,' I said to Mohammed. 'We should get the entire team in. Nishant, will you get the other camera so that Mohammed is also in the shot?'

After a long time, we all felt relaxed and like a team again. The boys loved the attention of being on screen, even though Mohammed protested and said he didn't much care to be on TV.

'You should, because your family will get to see you that way,' I said and he easily gave in.

Jiggy and Sumit, of course didn't need any convincing. Jiggy always came alive in front of the camera, and Sumit didn't need any cues at all. As the cameras rolled, they all moved in purposefully towards Ganga Singhji by the stove, making very good TV comments:

'Wow, it smells good.' (Jiggy and Sumit were both strict vegetarians but they made the dish appear really appetizing on TV, coming close and smelling it appreciatively and patting Ganga Singhji on his back.)

'This is really good,' said Naghma later, as we sat down on some rocks to eat the thick rotis and Ganga Singhji's chicken. 'I like involving the whole team in our shoot.'

No one brought up the fact that the rotis were too hard and the masala in the chicken wasn't cooked through. Because we were happy that our differences were resolved and we were a team again. And because none of us could remember the last time a 55-year old man had cooked for us, in excruciating heat, after driving a few hundred kilometres.

We felt pretty lucky and pretty blessed.

10

The Pathans of Modiland

'You know what would be amazing? If we could speak to Irfan Pathan and his family,' said Naghma as we bumped along on our way to Vadodara.

But of course. Why didn't *I* think of them?

Probably because I had never been able to force myself to sit down and watch an entire cricket match. I'd been told a thousand times that I shouldn't even dream of being a journalist in India if I didn't follow cricket. And I'd really tried but it was difficult. I got the politics behind the game; I got the fact that it was the one story that mattered to most of my audience and that it was a story full of drama and human emotion. But I could never even sit through an over, let alone an entire match.

To cover my ignorance, I'd read only those bits of the sports news that made it to the front page. I figured, if it wasn't there, we probably didn't need to know about it.

Not the smartest strategy, I admit, but no one's perfect.

'Yeah, didn't Modi harass them in some way? I can't remember exactly but weren't they affected in the riots?'

'Yeah, something like that, it would be great to talk to them.'

Eight years have gone by, but journalists like me were still finding it difficult to move on from the story of the persecution of Muslims in Gujarat. The people of Gujarat had moved on with their lives, even the minority community wanted to move on, but we, in the press, had had no closure. However much Narendra Modi wanted to talk about Gujarat's development, the media wanted him to explain, to admit, to break down and confess all about the 2002 riots.

He never did, and we never tired either.

I scrolled down vigorously on Naghma's Blackberry. (Mine was a heavy, antiquated model that could not cope with the pressure of my compulsive jabbing.) 'Yes, here it is. When the Twenty20 team won the World Cup in 2007, all state governments rewarded their players. But Modi took a long time.'

'I thought he didn't reward them at all?'

'No, he did but he rewarded them much, much later – after everyone started giving him flak.'

Narendra Modi had given the Pathan brothers five lakh rupees each, many days after all other state governments had announced cash rewards for their players, many of them, like Maharashtra, giving much more money too.

'It would be amazing, no, to have the Pathan family talk about living in Modi-land?'

'They won't, though, I've never heard them talk about it.'

'Okay, doing *anything* with them will be amazing for this show.'

We both had that crazed newshound gleam in our eyes as we called Nilesh Thakkar, our local stringer. Journalistically speaking, getting Irfan Pathan or Yusuf Pathan wasn't really intrinsic to a show on the elections. But they were local heroes, they were cute boys, one more than the other, and people loved to hear them talk. I remembered this small interview that Irfan Pathan had done with my colleague Afsha Anjum, where he talked about his brother Yusuf becoming popular with the ladies – it had aired over and over on our channel. Even a non sports-fan like myself couldn't help being charmed by them. They were just endearingly regular lads dealing with an unimaginable degree of fame. I wanted to know if that fame, that power of having so many followers across the country, made their lives different from that of other Muslims in Gujarat. I wanted to know whether, despite having so much, they still felt insecure in Gujarat and if they did not, had they always felt that way.

I like to think that I'm not obsessed with Gujarat and the story about Muslim persecution. In fact, when I went there to cover the December 2007 local elections, I told myself the issue was old, and spent the first ten days deliberately avoiding any kind of post-riots story. I concentrated on first-time voters, the Gujarati's pride in being one of the most economically successful states in the country, and their hero, Chief Minister Narendra Modi. Even the young Muslim voter whom I'd interviewed looked on Narendra Modi as an icon, as someone who'd taken his state to new heights. I think I disappointed some NGO workers who, while acknowledging that my story was based on fact, said that they feared that

I was making a hero out of Narendra Modi, a man they considered solely responsible for the deaths of more than 1000 people in the post-Godhra riots of 2002. They didn't like the shades of grey within my story, they wanted me to paint him an emphatic black. I didn't want to be an instrument of somebody's agenda. If most people celebrated Narendra Modi because they thought he was a good politician, who was I to block out their views? My job as an objective reporter was to highlight every point of view.

But my attitude changed in a short time. I don't quite know what it was. Maybe, it was the blatant discrimination that hits you as an outsider. For instance, the billboards that brazenly proclaimed, 'This is a Hindu Land'.

When I did that story, a couple of local reporters instantly objected: 'Boss, this isn't new. These signs came up around the time of the riots in 2002.' My point was that the signboards had still not been taken down. In an hour of driving around Ahmedabad, I easily counted five. And then, here's the best bit, when I went to ask the local BJP corporator why he allowed the signboards, he gave me this classic explanation: 'When you have garbage lying around anywhere, people complain and we get it removed. No one has complained about these boards, so I don't think there's any grounds for removing them.' He didn't even bother making excuses, or saying that the administration wasn't aware of them or that 'they would look into it'. I tried to imagine myself as an ordinary Muslim living in Ahmedabad, these boards a constant reminder that I was viewed as a second-class citizen by the state. I couldn't fathom how the state could openly display discrimination, and the more I thought about it, the more obsessed I got.

In fact, after that incident, this became the underlying theme, the underlying question in all my stories. It was as if I could see nothing else. The story of the taxi-drivers in Gujarat who changed their names and displayed posters of Hindu gods to protect themselves; the story of Juhapura where rich and poor Muslims shared the apathy of years of neglect; the story of riot-burnt houses turning into urinals for uncaring men – these were the kind of stories I did in the run-up to the Gujarat elections 2007; the type of stories that Narendra Modi dismissed as the English media's 'obsession', stories that apparently endeared him more to the Gujarati *manoos*.

There's an infamous anecdote going back to the first elections after the riots, in December 2002. The national media was outraged at what it saw as a state-sponsored pogrom personally choreographed by Narendra Modi. So, on polling day, they were driving this point home by beaming live from voting booths in Muslim areas and reporting how Muslims were coming out in large numbers to register their protest against the Modi government, how women in burqas were also lining up because they wanted change. Apparently, this got Gujarat's middle-class so incensed, that after lunch, these people who had never bothered to vote before, started coming out in droves. An insipid turnout was suddenly fired up, and because of the bad press Narendra Modi won hands-down.

The *Election Express* of course had no such agenda. We just wanted to speak to different kinds of people, to explore the impact of recession in Vadodara and to tap the source of the famous Gujarati *asmita* or pride. But the thought of meeting the Pathan family brought back memories.

'Nilesh is saying that the family will not meet us and Irfan and Yusuf are not even here,' said Naghma as she got off the phone. 'But their father will meet us.'

So we made our way towards the old city in Vadodara, towards the Juma Masjid where Mr Pathan once worked.

'They used to live there before but now they have a nice new place,' Nilesh said. I love to hear stories of success dramatically changing lives and even though the Pathans hadn't exactly been in rags earlier, their life had totally turned around after their sons' cricketing careers took off.

The Juma Masjid was not a very grand looking mosque. It was located right in the middle of a busy market square and housed in a dilapidated building, with a small courtyard at its entrance. Irfan and Yusuf had grown up in a one-room tenement facing the courtyard. Mr Pathan used to be the muezzin of the mosque but was removed because once, when he was travelling abroad, watching county cricket, rainwater had seeped in and damaged the holy Koran. He may have lost his job as the muezzin, which was passed on to him by his father, but he was still fighting eviction proceedings. Every aspect of their life, including this fight, including their move to a new house, was reported as news. The Pathans seemed to accept this invasion of their privacy, letting curious reporters like Nilesh and us into their lives every day. They saw it as a necessary fall-out of their sons' achievements.

'Uncle comes here every day, na, so we usually meet him here,' said Nilesh. 'But Irfan's mother rarely gives interviews, she's in purdah.'

Hoping that seeing two female journalists would make her change her mind, we followed him into a tiny little room crammed with cricket memorabilia: cricket bats, awards, and prizes, and lots and lots of pictures, mostly of Irfan. The Pathans had moved out, but it was obvious that this space had been maintained for the benefit of fans and journalists who wanted to know where the boys had grown up; I had never watched their game, I wasn't a fan, but just being in this cramped space that had nurtured two heroes of the Indian cricket team, made me all gooey inside.

Mr Pathan walked in and greeted us with: 'I don't like meeting too many journalists but Nilesh said that Naghma wanted to meet, so I thought why not?'

I winked at Naghma who as usual seemed unaffected by the fact that the first family of Vadodara was also a fan of hers. She just seemed quietly determined to get us our interview: 'We are going all over the country, and when we were in your town, we thought we must come and meet you all, meet Irfan and Yusuf to see if they vote,' said Naghma.

'They left just yesterday,' said Mr Pathan. 'IPL is about to begin, na, so they've gone to Delhi.'

'We heard, but we thought we'll meet their ammi and sister and you and talk to you.'

'You are welcome,' said Mr Pathan. 'But, she doesn't usually talk.' As he said this, he picked up the phone and dialled his wife: 'Arrey, Naghma has come from Delhi, she says she wants to meet you.' We were hopeful because Mr Pathan seemed totally bowled over by Naghma. He gave the phone to her: 'Here talk to her.'

Naghma took the phone and turned her back to me because I was going crazy trying to signal messages to her with my eyes, no doubt looking a little mental doing it. Mr Pathan, meanwhile, was guiding Nishant and Mohammed's cameras to the pictures: 'Here's when we went for Haj, here's when he went for that tour, here's the first trophy that he won.'

'Salam alaikum, ji, I'm fine,' – I was straining to listen in on Naghma's conversation – 'Yes, yes, so should we come over? Yes, yes, hmmm, okay, let us come and then we can eat lunch with you.'

I couldn't believe it! Not only did Naghma get the reticent family to meet us, she had also wrangled a lunch invitation for us!

Mr Pathan was mighty pleased to have Naghma coming over and announced that he'd be accompanying us in our vehicle to their new home. As he locked up their room in the mosque, he told us how some in the mosque were jealous of his sons' achievements, which is why they were trying to throw him out. 'My father worked for this mosque all his life, and so have I, I will not give it up,' he said. I found it amazing that even though Irfan and Yusuf were obviously taking care of their parents, that even though Mr Pathan could afford to retire, he didn't want to give up his right to work, or that tiny quarter.

'In this corridor, they would constantly play cricket, he would practise his bowling,' Mr Pathan said. 'I would keep shouting at them telling them to keep it down, but they would keep practising.'

On the way out, he waved to a juice vendor: 'Even now Irfan comes here to get juice,' he said. 'He is mad. When he came this time, he said, "Abba, I want to buy a cycle", so we went and bought a cycle. So many children recognize me also. When I walk down the street, they say, "Look it's Irfan Pathan's father."'

We drew up to a bungalow in what looked like a nice part of town. There was nothing about it that said 'celebrity home' but compared to the mosque quarter, it was a palace. We spotted a goat and a hen as we entered. 'Yusuf's pets,' explained Mr Pathan. 'Every time he's in town, he gets one of those. You'll see his cat inside.'

We didn't have to wait long. A Persian cat descended on Naghma and me, (the boys had been asked to wait outside) as soon as we entered the house and sat on the sofa. It rubbed itself against us. It was the only luxurious looking thing in an otherwise middle-class home. Neither of us had any special affinity for cats so we were desperate to have the family control the touchy-feely feline.

'Yusuf obviously has eclectic tastes,' I whispered to Naghma as Mr Pathan went in to fetch the missus. 'From goats and hens to Persian cats.'

A kit bag along with a huge suitcase lay on the floor but for the life of me I couldn't remember where the team had just returned from. 'It is a bit strange, no,' I said to Naghma, 'when they are on tour cricketers like Irfan look like they are playing the field, that they are having fun with so many girls, but you visit them at home and they are living with their mommy and daddy.'

Naghma wasn't moved by my observation but I was fascinated because I was sure that Irfan's mum still did his laundry for him. And just as I thought that, she walked in, smiling at both of us.

Mrs Pathan was the spitting image of her son Irfan with the same light eyes. I remember thinking that she was so very young. She stared hard at Naghma. 'We keep watching you on TV,' she said. 'Why have you lost so much weight?'

I looked at Naghma too and empathized with Mrs Pathan's sense of awe. When you see someone on TV every day, sharing the news of the world with you, you feel like you know them but when that distance closes in and you see them in flesh and blood, they can be quite different. For many uncool people like me, it can also lead to embarrassing howlers. For instance, at a Diwali party at my former editor Shekhar Gupta's house that had attracted quite a few well-known faces – but not enough from Bollywood as it turned out – I couldn't handle coming face to face with the singer Adnan Sami. Shekhar had herded him towards me, thinking that I, a poised TV anchor, would chat civilly with him for a few minutes. But as soon as I was introduced, I screamed: 'Oh my god, oh my god!' The poor man struggled to maintain his polite smile. 'Oh my god, you've lost so much weight, you look great!' I continued to scream till Shekhar decided enough was enough and pushed Sami out of my reach.

Mrs Pathan was much more composed than that. She'd been followed in by her daughter Shagufta and some other female relatives. 'We just saw pictures of you at the mosque,' I piped up, more to register my presence than anything else.

'I hope you didn't allow your cameramen to take photos of my pictures,' she replied. 'Because I'm in purdah, and if you did, you have to promise you won't use them.' She turned to her husband: 'He never stops anyone but I don't like it.'

'Of course we won't use them,' said Naghma. 'But you have to give us an interview.'

'About what?'

'Elections are coming, na, so we want to know what you want from them.'

Mrs Pathan just stared at her. 'I don't do interviews, ask him,' she said pointing to Mr Pathan.

'Arrey, Naghma has come all the way, are you going to disappoint her?' Mr Pathan said as he punched a number on his cell phone, 'Hello, Guddu? Yes, Naghma has come. Here talk to her.' He thrust the phone at Naghma while Naghma silently mouthed 'Who's Guddu?' to me.

It turned out to be Irfan Pathan. While Naghma chatted with him, I tried to reassure Mrs Pathan about the interview. She just smiled vaguely at me and kept looking at Naghma. 'Okay, good to speak with you,' said Naghma finally and handed the phone back to Mr Pathan. Then she turned and whispered to me, 'Irfan is a bit wary. He asked me what we were doing there. I just told him that we wanted to meet his parents and he was like, alright then. He must have been worried about what we were going to ask his parents.'

Perhaps Irfan gave his parents the green signal, or perhaps Naghma's persuasive skills worked, because Mrs Pathan and Shagufta finally went in to get changed. And as a special concession to us, they were going to let our cameraman into the house to film the interview.

We were so grateful. Even though it was difficult to tell the mother from the sister after they put their burkhas on, we knew that they'd gone all out for us.

'The city has a lovely atmosphere about it, we love it here,' said Mrs Pathan on television.

'There are great sports facilities and we give credit to the authorities for helping bring out Irfan and Yusuf's talent,' said Mr Pathan.

They were both very careful not to offend Gujarat's Big Brother and I didn't put them in a spot.

'We always vote, the boys always vote but there is one problem,' said Mrs Pathan. 'Whenever we have guests over, we are embarrassed by the state of the road leading to our house. They say, how can your celebrity son live in a place that has such bad roads! I would like the politicians to fix the road.'

So, as it turned out, the Pathans of Vadodara had a very basic demand from the elections. They didn't ask for anything dramatic like justice for those who had been burnt alive in a city bakery during the riots. They didn't ask for Narendra Modi's downfall on behalf of the Muslim community. All they wanted, like any other citizen in this country, was a decent road that led to their house.

After the interview, Mrs Pathan apparently took Naghma aside to ask: 'In your line, are they fair to our community?' Naghma assured her that she got by just fine.

When Naghma told me later what Mrs Pathan had asked, I figured that one of the reasons that Mrs Pathan and many other Muslim women like her looked up to Naghma was because they identified with her. So what if Naghma was something of a denim babe, so what if she was more independent than me, travelling alone more than I did, she was also a Muslim who had reached the top in an aspirational space like television. Other women, who had never left home without the burkha, who had to depend on their sons or husbands to go out, would watch Naghma on TV, grilling male politicians, challenging power figures – and think that life could serve up possibilities.

At least that's what I liked to think. It's entirely possible they really only admired her incredibly long hair.

'What about lunch?' Mrs Pathan had asked as we got up to leave. It was a tempting thought, but for once we declined;

they'd already fed us a lot and we'd taken up way too much of their time.

Actually the lunch thing was a programme segment we had worked out. The idea behind that slot was that we would eat with a local family in every destination, which would give us an opportunity to not just explore India's diversity through its food but that the dining table would also serve as an informal backdrop to get people talking; it's always fun to ask people their political preferences as they tear into their phulkas.

For the team members, of course, it was also a good survival strategy. The meal took care of our craving for home-cooked food.

'Make sure you don't demand to be fed by a poor family,' Sonia had instructed us before we'd set out. She imagined that desperate reporters like me would stride into a poor village hut and demand a portion of their meagre food just to show TV viewers what they lived like – I have often wondered what it is about me that made her imagine that I could do that.

The casual ease with which Naghma had brought up the prospect of lunch with the Pathans had actually been cultivated over the course of our journey. When we had first started out, it was a total disaster. We would ask our local fixers to find willing hosts for this segment, innovatively called 'The Lunch Stop'. The fixer or stringer's initial reaction would be to assume that we were hunting for a free lunch. That wasn't far from the truth but we were very keen to convince them of our journalistic intentions. It was hard enough explaining it to the fixers but we realized very soon, that it wasn't getting through to our hosts either.

In Dausa for instance, a family of doctors, the Meenas, was hosting us. 'Madam, they are very fine people,' said

Avtar, our stringer. 'You don't worry, you will be very happy.'

As soon as we entered their home, Mohammed and Nishant started scoping the place out for lights and possible angles. The Meenas scrambled around in the kitchen and laid out glasses of Coke and some aloo bhujia. We thought that this was their idea of a starter. So we hurriedly drank down our drinks and kept up the small talk. The Meenas were a little impatient, as if they didn't want to converse with us off camera. It was like they were waiting for things to roll. When they left the room, leaving their retired father in the room, we huddled together and asked Avtar: 'Are you *sure* they know we have come for lunch?'

'Yes, yes, no problem,' he replied.

We kept expecting them to start laying the table, and they were getting impatient waiting for us to start filming.

'What would you like us to do?' Dr Meena finally asked.

Mohammed answered with a question. 'Where do you have lunch?'

Dr Meena took him to the dining room, and Mohammed after checking out the natural light over there, started dragging in his light equipment into that room, making Dr Meena even more nervous.

Finally Naghma realized that she would just have to say it like it is. 'Whatever you're having for lunch, if you put it on the table, we'll all sit and eat and shoot it like that.'

The Meenas finally got it. We weren't there for an interview over Coca Cola, we wanted a meal. So, they hit the panic button. And while we sat glaring at Avtar, they hurriedly sent their help to the local restaurant to pick up some food.

When the lunch table was finally laid out, we were forced to describe the mass-produced, red-curried, paneer makhni as a special Rajasthani delight for our cameras. The rotis were the only things that were home-cooked – and we had lots of those. Once the cameras had stopped rolling, and the interviews were over, we thanked our kind hosts.

'Sorry for piling on like this,' we apologized profusely while Avtar, happily oblivious, continued to stuff his face, dipping his roti in the red paneer makhni swimming in oil.

That experience would have caused some faint-hearted souls to abandon The Lunch Stop altogether but we were made of sterner stuff; we just worked a lot more on our plan.

First, we'd check with our stringers about our hosts' preparedness well in advance. So, in Gwalior, the Mehtas had the food laid out when we arrived, and in Shivpuri, the Varmas had moved the dining table to their courtyard, to enable natural light. We would pretend to eat and talk for three minutes, which was the length of the interview, and then all of us, including the crew, would dig into the food. I would love, love, *love* it! Our hosts would regale us with local stories about their politics and their lives, and they'd ask us questions about the media and our lives. We'd feel grateful for a home-cooked meal, they'd feel embarrassed and amused by our gushing praise. Feeding so many people wasn't easy but whenever people would hear how long we'd been out on the road, they'd always say, 'Why don't you come back for dinner as well?'

For me the best part was tasting dishes I'd never eaten before. Most people would have let us in even if we hadn't called them in advance. If anything, it was the fervour of their generosity that was the problem. 'They feed you too much,' complained Mohammed. (In one house he had to run out and hide in the car, because they wouldn't let him leave without eating dessert!)

He wasn't complaining though when we ate with a Gandhian family in Surat. I had spent six weeks in Gujarat before, but I have never eaten a meal like the one they served. The Chokhawala family had fascinating things to say about voting for Narendra Modi despite being Centrist in their leanings, but all I could focus on during the interview was the tantalizing aroma of the puris and the varied dals that wafted up from the table.

Then there was the community meal we had in Daman. I say 'community' because it was produced by a group of Portuguese neighbours.

We'd set out from Delhi and had reached the coast, but still there was no cool breeze to make us feel better. It was hot and sticky. Daman from one end to the other may have only been 10 odd kilometres, but we were certainly feeling stretched. And as soon as we walked in, we had a bit of a culture shock. Lying on the table, next to the green coloured raita, pork and beef roast, were bottles of Peter Scott whiskey and sparkling wine.

'You drink whiskey at lunch?' I exclaimed. I was fascinated. We all knew that Daman was *the* liquor destination, especially for the drink-deprived of Gujarat. But, I couldn't believe that such diverse communities lived in close proximity – one that looked on alcohol as sinful, and one that had whiskey for lunch.

'Yes, we do sometimes, and definitely when we have guests. See, we are used to drinking this much,' they explained, pouring me a generous helping of the sparkling wine. 'But when others come here just to drink and behave badly after getting drunk... that's not nice.'

I nodded looking at Naghma who hadn't had the heart to turn them down. She was also making an exception to her rule of eating only vegetarian food on the road. (It was the safer thing to do in the heat.) But Mohammed and Nishant struggled at the table. It wasn't easy for Mohammed to find pork so close to his plate. They moved around the food on their plate for a while and finally got up. 'I want subzi and roti,' Nishant said when our hosts were out of hearing.

'It's a bit difficult when you're travelling, you have to eat local food, that's what's good for you,' I told him.

Mohammed looked unconvinced.

'Seriously, like when I first when to Tamil Nadu, I wouldn't want to eat so much rice for lunch so one day I asked for roti and subzi. Do you know what happened?' Mohammed still looked blank and disinterested. 'The roti sat in my stomach like a piece of stone. And I realized that the only way to survive was to eat rice.'

'I can't, boss, I need roti,' said Mohammed. We were obviously not going to see each other's point.

So he left, in search of rotis, while I burped, satisfied.

'Office is thinking that we are having a great time with so much food and alcohol on the table,' said Naghma.

'They should wait to see us in Nashik,' I said. 'We'll be drinking wine fresh from the fields.'

11

Louis Vuitton and Seedless Pawars

'I'll only give you guys an interview if you spend the night over here.'

This was our introduction to Daman's generation-next politician, 34-year old Ketan Patel, the son of the sitting Congress MP Dayabhai Patel and the head of the Congress Party in Daman and Diu. We had driven out of Daman after doing a live report for the 9 o'clock news. Essentially, we'd only spent a few hours there — we'd driven in from Surat that morning and weren't even spending the night. We'd only called Ketan Patel because we'd heard that he was one of Rahul Gandhi's bright young guns.

Apparently, there had been this huge tussle because Ketan Patel thought that his time had come. He had really tried to use his so-called influence with the Congress Prince to get the ticket to contest the elections instead of his father. But, after a lot of wrangling, the Congress Party had decided to go with the grey hair. And like many father-son struggles in history, this one had unfolded in the public eye. There were whispers that Ketan was now out to get his father.

Even though we'd never heard of Ketan Patel before, we'd heard about his flamboyant lifestyle. Like many other politicians in Daman, Ketan Patel, it was rumoured, was involved in the gambling business. He was also building a casino, we were told, the likes of which India had never seen before.

After trying his number all morning, and being told that Ketan Patel was out campaigning for elections, we thought we'd have to leave without meeting the young star. Then, just an hour before showtime we received a call: 'Where have you been? Ketan Patel has been trying to get in touch with you for ages,' said his breathless assistant.

'I don't know. I think the phone connectivity in Daman isn't very good,' I replied.

'That's not possible,' he dismissed my answer outright, as if Ketan Patel had cell phone towers at his beck and call. 'Anyway, where are you now?'

'Our bus is parked at the port.'

'Hold on right there, we are coming.'

'Why is he coming now?' asked Naghma when I put down the phone. 'Isn't it a bit late?'

'I want to move the bus to location and see if we can light up the water behind you,' said Mohammed. 'Don't do anymore interviews, yaar.'

'I know, but what can I do?' I said. 'He just said he's coming over here.'

'Okay, then you guys do the interview,' said Mohammed, nodding towards Nishant. 'And I'll go set up on location.'

'What should we ask him?' said Naghma.

'Maybe, we can compare him and his father to Farooq and Omar Abdullah.' The father-son duo from Kashmir had just resolved their race for chief ministership so it was fresh on my mind. 'He may just be an interesting person to meet.'

As if on cue, we heard a cavalcade of cars screeching to a stop outside. Ketan Patel obviously believed in travelling with his entourage. I hastily emptied the last of the channa masala packet into my mouth. (That was all that the Daman seaside had to offer – channa masala and some dodgy ice-cream.) I was wiping the masala from next to my mouth, when Ketan Patel and a hanger-on barged in to the seating area of the bus. He sat down and gave us the once over.

'So, are you guys from Delhi or Bombay?' He wasn't much taller than me.

'Delhi,' we said, as we checked him out ourselves. Naghma was so much better than me in adopting that we-don't-really-care-about-you air. She let me do the talking as she toyed with her phone. 'We were doing an election show in town, so we thought we'd interview you as well,' I explained.

He just checked us out again. 'Where are you staying over here?'

'We aren't. We'll be leaving after the show for Nashik.'

'You can't do that,' he said calmly. 'I'll only give you guys an interview if you spend the night over here.'

'No, we have to go tonight. So if you're willing, we'll do the interview right now.'

Ketan Patel took a few more seconds to quietly size us up. He was wearing the traditional white kurta pajama of the Congress Party but he'd also thrown in a few designer elements. One of these was some make of designer sunglasses perched on the top of his head, and the other was his loafers.

Now, I know very little about designer wear, which is why I had no idea whether his shades were Armani or Dolce and Gabbana but his footwear was unmistakable, even for the fashion-challenged like me. There, on top of his shiny black shoes were two big letters LV or Louis Vuitton. Didn't he just say that he'd been campaigning all day? How was he romping around rural Daman in those Louis Vuitton shoes? How was he meeting fishermen to ask for their votes? I'd not gone to that many places to meet voters but my 100-rupee chappals from Lajpat Nagar were already muddy.

'Okay, let's do it.' The temptation to be on TV was much more seductive than any other conditions he had hoped to impose. 'Let's go to this bridge that we have and record it there.'

All we wanted was to get the interview done with nice and quick. We clambered out of the bus and were surrounded by his supporters. 'Oh my god!' whispered Naghma in my ear. 'It's like the luccha brigade.'

We were speechless. We knew that many politicians had an entourage. Even in villages, the entourage comprised groups of men in cars, others on cycles and rickshaws carrying posters and flags, musicians with drums and women on foot. But Ketan's pack looked straight out of Bollywood. For one, there was no one dressed like a political worker, meaning there was no one in dhoti, pajamas, mundu or anything remotely Indian, apart from Ketan Patel, that is. They all looked like extras from a song sequence in a Karan Johar film. Men with long hair, in tight t-shirts and red pants. I was so confused I grabbed the first car door that I saw.

'Yes, yes, please come with us,' said Ketan Patel.

I recoiled: 'No, no, we'll follow in our own car.'

We finally found our car and clambered in. Looking back from our car we watched the ten-vehicle motorcade.

'Can you imagine? Are all of them political workers, Anand?' Naghma asked our local fixer.

'They are all Ketan's supporters,' he said.

In his interview, Ketan Patel like so many dynastic claimants in India, said that he wanted the ticket because he represented the youth of India, that he was their voice and the people wanted change. 'But I've now withdrawn and given my support to my father in writing,' he said. His vision for Daman – 'To make it a gaming (not gambling or casino) capital like Goa.'

'What happens in the next elections? Will you ask your father to step down?'

'Yes, I will.' Maybe he had not really meant the support which he had put down in writing. Or maybe the people of Daman saw that Ketan Patel couldn't walk the talk in his Louis Vuitton loafers. He certainly hadn't campaigned that day for the dominant tribe in Daman – the fishing community of Tandels – which is why those loafers were squeaky clean and shiny. Whatever the reason, the Congress Party lost from Daman in these elections.

'I should have asked him how much difference a couple of lakhs – which those Louis Vuitton shoes must have cost – would have made to the life of a fisherman,' I thought, as we made our way through the ghats to Nashik, but like an appropriate rejoinder to his come-ons, those words remained unsaid.

After the two-hour drive to Daman, Nashik was another five hours away. 'I wish we could have spent the night in Daman, after all,' said Naghma.

'Don't worry, we'll be there soon,' I said. 'Nishant have you booked us in a good hotel in town?'

'It's a suite at the Sai Palace,' he replied. 'The fixer made me cancel White Lilies and book this other place.'

Hmmm. A toss-up between 'White Lilies' and 'Sai Palace'. We tried to analyse what the names said about the hotels.

'Our chain of hotels is there but they are renovating,' said Nishant. 'They only recommended White Lilies. But the fixer was convinced that we'd like Sai Palace better.'

'It sounds weird – Sai Palace,' I said. But then 'White Lilies' didn't inspire much confidence either.

'You know, if it is run by some Sai devotees' society then it might be very nice,' said the ever-optimistic Naghma. 'They are usually very organized about these things.'

Anyway, I could hardly start calling up contacts in the middle of the night asking them which hotel they recommended so we just left it to the fixer's choice.

At the Sai Palace, we were greeted by a stone statue of the Shirdi Sai. It emanated a kind of red light that gave the room that the hotel owners intended to be a lobby, an eerie aura.

'Looks like they've all gone to sleep,' I said as we waited for someone to help us with our bags. It took a good ten minutes for the staff to start stirring. After collecting our keys, we made our way up to our rooms but there was no one to show us where to go. When we finally found our door, we found it had no keyhole. 'What the hell, yaar, how do you open this thing?'

'Boss, I'm not going all the way down now, what kind of door is this?'

We stood sulking for some time till Naghma walked to the other end of the corridor. 'Oye, there's another door here. This one's got the keyhole.'

By now, we knew that this wasn't going to be a luxury hotel experience, so we braced ourselves as we entered the room.

'Please, Naghma, will you peep into the loo?' Naghma giggled because by now she was getting used to my oddities. I couldn't bear to be taken by surprise by a stained loo, or infinitely worse, stray floaters in the pot. And because I agreed to wake up half an hour early in the morning and use the loo first, she usually went in to check it for me.

I held my breath till she completed her assessment. 'It's not very nice but it'll do,' she reported and I exhaled. A bad loo would have meant that I spent the next two nights in agony. But the source of agony in this hotel was yet to be revealed.

'What is this?' said Naghma, exploring our extra room that came as part of 'the suite'. I walked in to find a bare room with two wooden chairs in it. 'What are we meant to do here? Even the TV is in the bedroom!'

'We're meant to sit and chat.'

We were giggling now because the place was quite ridiculous. The piece de resistance was a painting on the top of our bed. It had a woman in a ghaghra choli lost in the woods, her choli was so short that her bosom spilled out from beneath.

We kept giggling: '*This* is what they put in the Sai Palace? I thought you said that it was going to be made by the temple people?' I took a picture of Naghma looking at the painting. It was really gross but we went to sleep at night in good humour, despite the fact that we could hear rats in the fake ceiling above our heads. They sounded like really big, fat rats because they made a lot of ruckus but we told ourselves they weren't *inside* our room and fell asleep reminding ourselves that this was what travelling was all about – finding strange things in strange places.

But there was nothing funny about it in the morning. I was taking a shower in the dirty green bathtub and wondering why places like this, which have questionable cleaning standards, have bathtubs in the first place. As I was drying myself, I heard a really loud noise, as if someone had jumped through the roof and landed in the bathtub! As if an army of rats had landed in the loo with me!

'Aaarghhh! Oh my god,' I shrieked and ran out of the loo in my towel, screaming my head off. 'Those bloody rats have invaded the loo!'

Naghma went in to check. 'They've become even noisier,' she reported calmly, 'but they are above the ceiling.'

When I called the hotel reception I was almost in tears.

'Madam, we are sending somebody up right now,' they assured me.

A few minutes later I opened the door to a boy armed with no rat-removing equipment whatsoever, staring vacantly at me. He walked into the loo and announced that the rats weren't inside the loo, but safe 'upstairs', above the ceiling.

I lost it: 'What do you mean they are upstairs? What do you *mean*? Do you know what it feels like to have big rats running on top of your head? Do you?' I think everyone in the hotel heard me shriek that day. And I don't know if there was rat genocide at Sai Palace after we left, but they were a much more subdued lot when we returned that night.

🚌

I maintained my screaming banshee form throughout the day, especially when I finally got a look at the White Lilies Hotel across the parking lot. 'He made us change to this for *that*!' The pristine white building looked like the Taj Mahal from where we stood.

'He insisted, you know, he *insisted* I change the bookings,' said Nishant quickly so that I wouldn't start screaming at him. 'Boss, he obviously got a cut, or the Sai Palace owners are his friends and he wanted to do them a favour.'

'Maybe his sensibilities are different from ours, Sunetra. Maybe, according to his taste, Sai Palace *is* better,' said Naghma peacably.

I normally respected how she always thought the best of everyone but sometimes it was just plain irritating. 'Are you kidding me? Just look at this dump! What kind of sensibility appreciates rats?'

I was so angry I wanted to shake the fixer by his neck as soon as we met him. Naghma was convinced that it was just his bad taste that had made him put us up in this hotel from hell. I didn't want to be a villain, so all I said to him when we met him was: 'The hotel is *not* good.'

He looked at me with wide innocent eyes.

'There are humongous rats in it.'

He continued to stare at me blankly for a few seconds. Then he asked, 'Where is the Luxury?'

'Sorry?' I spluttered. 'Luxury? Luxury?' We couldn't figure out what in god's name he was saying.

'Luxury bus,' he finally said.

We soon figured out that the 'Luxury' was the only thing our fixer was interested in. By this time we'd been on the road for two weeks and the bus had become the clear star of the show. Once, just for laughs, we called it 'Sonu (that's me) aur Naghma di Gaddi (Sunetra and Naghma's Vehicle), after which some viewers had started referring to it in that way. Our fixer's nomenclature, however, was pretty unique.

'Luxury will come later,' I said. 'How about we go for our story now?'

'I thought I would help it park.'

How about you help plan our show, you moron?

It became very clear through the day that all our fixer was interested in, and the reason he'd put himself up for this job, was a fascination for our 'Luxury' bus. He didn't care much for any other aspect of the show. For instance, the only big story we'd planned in Nashik was an interview with Nationalist Congress Party leader Samir Bhujbal. He was party hotshot Chhagan Bhujbal's nephew, and he was contesting for the very first time in a polarized community.

Nashik had been at the epicentre of a right-wing campaign to throw out all non-Marathi workers. Many areas in Nashik had been abandoned at the height of this campaign which had seen serious clashes across Maharashtra. We thought it might be interesting to see what a young leader like Bhujbal saw as the future for Nashik.

But our fixer messed it up big time.

'He's already left the place, we'll catch him at the next destination,' said the fixer after hanging up on his conversation with Samir Bhujbal. He'd said the same thing at the last two spots as well. 'Don't worry we'll catch up with him soon.' That 'soon' extended to the next destination, and the one after that, till we were climbing hills up a dirt track.

'Madamji, I don't think he knows what he's doing,' said Ganga Singhji, fed up of what was becoming a wild goose chase. 'Our car will get stuck over here.'

We had strayed at least an hour out of Nashik and were now being led even further out, without the assurance of an interview.

'How long do we have to travel on this dirt track?' Naghma said, finally taking charge, as she looked at the hill path that curved ahead.

'Seven or eight kilometres,' said the fixer.

'Madam, that will take us an hour on this road,' said Ganga Singhji.

'Okay, then just turn the car around. We can't keep going on like this, we'll miss our show,' Naghma decided. I was quiet, and very disappointed to miss out on that interview but I really thanked god that Naghma had taken that decision for us. I wasn't grateful for our fixer though. He didn't look at all apologetic about having wasted our time.

This was a problem that we had faced on many stops. Even though, before we arrived, we'd tell our stringers and fixers a hundred times that we were stressed for time, most never understood just how much. They didn't understand our sort of guerrilla journalism, where we stormed in, and *wham!* finished one story, and moved on to the next.

🚌

'Let's just move to the vineyards.'

We were going to drown our sorrows in the wine belt of our country and we were hoping the fixer would at least get that right. I'd once read that Nashik farmers were now drinking wine with their rotis, truly merging their product with their lifestyle.

'Madam, there is nothing like that.'

'But I read it in a newspaper.'

'Madam, you know how they sometimes embellish the truth?'

The trip to meet the small grape-growers wasn't entirely a waste, though. Once the interviews were over, the farmers insisted that we taste their produce. We declined but suddenly Mohammed stepped in and said, 'I will accept one bottle.'

Before we could ask whether the workload had driven the teetotaller Mohammed to the bottle, he said: 'I want it for Ganga Singh.'

Ganga Singhji could not stop beaming. He readily accepted the gift and carried a couple of bottles to the boot of the car. Naghma and I looked on greedily but couldn't gather the courage to claim one for ourselves. 'Madam, the Sula people are also calling us,' said our fixer.

Why not? we thought. We'd met the small business farmers of Nashik, we could meet the big boys.

Sula was obviously doing great business. We visited their beautiful vineyards not far from Nashik. I have never been to vineyards in France or Italy so I don't really have anything to compare them with but they were truly impressive. The office building housed a restaurant called 'Little Italy' that Naghma and I wistfully eyed – it'd been so long since we'd had a nice, urban meal. I mean, we loved our fresh rotis, sugarcane juice and fruits from the villages but, sigh, we could have really done with a nice bowl of pasta.

As we sat waiting for the manager, we saw lots of foreign clients book the restaurant for a post-vineyard-walk meal. We watched them longingly as we trudged off to the fields to do some interviews. 'Let's finish this off and have something to drink,' said the manager, a jovial looking guy with a tendency to throw his head back and laugh. This time, Naghma and I didn't protest at all and after we quickly finished the interviews, we ignored Mohammed's disapproving glances and headed to the bar. It was post-lunchtime and the sun was shining hot. I know and have read that drinking increases dehydration but I didn't give a damn.

As the wine seeped into my insides I felt my anger against the fixer dissipate. I felt a little more confident about our show in the evening and I realized that this – sitting in the middle of a vineyard and looking out onto the fields – was also part of my job. Loosening up over the drink, the manager was telling me the politics of the wine industry in the country. How older ideas of prohibition were now being relaxed to take economic advantage of a growing interest in wine. How farmers who had never left their village before were now training in France to learn to grow wine.

In my wine-induced nirvana moment, I realized that I should not waste this journey frantically trying to meet deadlines and stories. If I really wanted to learn, I had to take time out to appreciate things, to appreciate people. Even those like my fixer, even though he really irritated me by butting into my interviews in Marathi. And even though we had to spend another night at the rat-infested Sai Palace overlooking the pristine White Lilies.

When it was all over, and we were saying our goodbyes our fixer said, 'Madam, I learnt a lot from you, madam.'

I instantly felt bad. I had just been this screaming monster who'd shouted at him the entire day. Who shouted at him, even though he'd arranged for policemen to ensure that riots didn't break out at the Nashik ghat where the 'Luxury' was parked. 'I was just angry because this hotel is very bad,' I said. 'Please don't make anyone else stay there again.'

He looked at me and flashed that vacuous smile of his one last time.

🚌

We were heading to Goa over the weekend.

'Ganga Singhji, please do not make the same mistake again.'

'Arrey, madamji, how can you say that?' He plucked out two pieces of paper from his chest pocket. 'See, I have it all written down.'

We were all obviously getting better at this. If I was learning to let my hair down a bit, Ganga Singhji was also getting over his habit of driving without directions. We were going to spend the night in Kolhapur after visiting Baramati and then, by Sunday, we'd head for the beach.

'What's the shooting plan?' asked Mohamammed warily. He'd been let down far too many times after being promised some free time on Sundays.

'Oh you poor thing,' I said. 'Look, we'll shoot in Baramati but once we reach Goa, we'll take the day off.'

'Are you sure?' said Nishant. 'Are you sure, sure?'

'Yes, I am.'

'Then, we are going to pack the camera on Sunday and not touch it at all.'

'Yes, baba, even we need a day off.'

Naghma had filled my head with the idea of a massage on the beach but frankly by then, all I could think and fantasize about was a nap in my room.

'What do we shoot in Baramati today?'

I wasn't too sure, actually. We just wanted to have a look at the town that had been a wasteland till a few decades ago, but had now been transformed into a town that could easily pass off as a super city. We'd heard so much about Nationalist Congress Party leader Sharad Pawar's work in Baramati – the kind of work that had guaranteed him victory election after election – and had catapulted him from a regional leader to aspire for prime minister. I also wanted to meet his daughter Supriya Sule; she was contesting for the first time in her father's constituency. She was one of those young politicians who wasn't overexposed. She wasn't always on TV channels expressing her views on everything. Even though I had asked to meet her in Baramati a month before the elections, she had made it clear that she had prior commitments to do with the elections.

'She's very polite but she says she's very busy.'

'Then we'll just take a look around,' said Naghma. 'Sharad Pawar is supposed to be the farmer king so let's find out what he's done.'

I'd found a local journalist called Milind Sangai to get some contacts in Baramati. He turned out to be the exact opposite of our Nashik fixer.

Milind had no reason to give up a lazy Saturday and help us out. But, just as a reminder of how hospitable people outside big cities can be, Milind went out of his way to help us. He didn't just give us the number of the farmers' institute, he fixed an appointment with the director Dr Kaderbhai on a weekend, and personally took us there. We wanted to meet someone from the Pawar family so he took us to meet my namesake, Sunetra – Pawar's nephew's wife. Baramati's farmers had come up with a type of grape which they called the 'Seedless Pawar'. Milind hunted the grapes down in the local bazaar for us to film. Of course, not without the silly giggles from us girls about the epithet 'Seedless Pawars'.

'How did Sharad Pawar do this?' we asked Milind. 'I mean, you are an educated guy, what has he done that's made someone like you stay back in this tiny place instead of going to Bombay or Delhi?'

'The town has everything I need,' said Milind. And for once, I could really see that this was true. The roads across Baramati weren't just good, they were fantastic. When we were driving into Baramati from Pune we didn't see much vegetation at first, but as soon as we neared the place, the horizon turned green. The shopping area in the city should have been like the shopping area in Shivpuri, as they were comparable in size. But here, residents didn't think that department stores like 'Big Bazaars' were meant only for the city. The Big Bazaar, in fact, stocked a lot of the local produce including products by women's self-help groups. The local police station was so fancy that when we saw it in passing, we had to turn our car around to take a closer look.

'Oh my god, it has tennis lawns and it has a gym. And it looks like an art gallery,' Naghma said.

'You know, the new fancy police station they've built in Vasant Kunj (my Delhi neighbourhood), looks like a slum-house compared to this. And the cops inside looked so happy, unlike the grouches back home.'

Dr Kaderbhai at the agricultural institute showed us how they ran Internet help-lines for farmers to solve their problems.

'Wait, wait,' I said. 'I know that PC penetration is increasing but surely everyone cannot email you their problems?'

'Sure, but that's why we have an SMS facility as well,' smiled Dr Kaderbhai.

I couldn't counter that because even in the poorest regions we'd visited, we'd seen everyone with cell phones. And how could I forget Shivgarh where they didn't have power but they had phones?

'And, they can also call in themselves if they want.'

It wasn't just that she was showing us equipment priced at just 300 rupees for testing soil in the laboratory, Dr Kaderbhai herself also personified for me the change in attitude in this part of the country: the woman was working on a Saturday evening, and so were many of the other scientists in the lab! When I'd once visited the Indian Agricultural Research Institute in Delhi on a weekday afternoon it had been completely deserted, but here it was a different kind of world.

People like Dr Kaderbhai, a government employee, weren't afraid of persistent if sometimes silly questions by reporters like me because they didn't fear transparency. They had nothing to hide because they were truly delivering on the job that they were employed to do.

'Do you think that the Pawars still have to work hard to win the elections? After all this, does his daughter Supriya Sule have to worry?' I asked Milind.

'Of course. People have become very demanding over here,' he said. 'They respect the Pawars but that's only because they have seen them deliver. For instance, one big issue in Maharashtra is power cuts. The people want less load shedding. If this doesn't get sorted out and if the Pawars do not handle it well, they will vote them out. The politicians here have also figured it out. Even though the seat has been with Sharad Pawar since the sixties, he and his entire extended family, including his nephew and wife, work day and night for his constituents.'

'Can you do a show comparing this place with Dausa?' said Naghma. 'Seriously, I've been to many VIP constituencies, but they just need to come here and figure out what they need to do.'

'I think if Pawar can do this with Baramati, I want him to do this with the entire country,' I said. 'I think I want him as my prime minister.' Shocking words from a political reporter but we just felt so amazed at what he had managed to achieve. 'Yes, yes, we want Pawar as our prime minister.'

If ever I was asked to go and live in a village, I knew that I would choose to live in Baramati.

Baramati also set up the prospect of great food for the next few days; the food of coastal India. As we sat eating the fantastic vegetarian spread – karela, gobi, dal and beans – organized by the marvelous Milind – we fantasized about the meals yet to come.

'You know we are going to get lots of coconut water in Goa. I love that stuff,' said Naghma.

'Are you kidding me?' I said. 'We're going to go to Goa and you're thinking of coconut water? I want prawns. Lots and lots of prawns.'

'Macchi, madam, macchi,' said Ganga Singhji gleefully.

'Oh god, the southies are only going to have rice, yaar,' said Mohammed. 'I need rotis.'

And so we started off again on our little argument about the need to go with the local diet, about why rice was so important and rotis so bad. We were like a married couple. We had started arguing about the same things over and over.

12

Moralists, Madhavi and Mayawati

'Boss, have you heard?' My journalist friend and gossip guru had called in from Delhi: 'Jarnail Singh threw a shoe at Chidambaram!'

'What? Who?'

'Turn on the TV, boss, it's happened just now. I don't know what came over Jarnail Singh.'

We were on our way back to the Goa hotel, before leaving for Mangalore, and had just ended our stay in the beach town with a lunch stop in the house of a local family, the Mirandas; a grand and fitting finale to a weekend of indulgences.

We had managed to ensure that our work didn't interfere too much with pleasure while we were there. The stories were the same old same old. Goan fishermen were up in arms against the government for imposing the unfair coastal regulation zone: Congressman Churchill Alemao was fighting because his young daughter Vallanka was not being allowed to contest the elections and a rich viscount was wearing diamond party symbols to become an MP.

It didn't take us too long to do the stories. In between, we sat in food shacks consuming vast amounts of Goan fish curry and drinking fresh strawberry milkshakes as we gazed out at the Arabian Sea.

'Turn on the telly,' I said to Naghma. We only had 15 minutes to pack and leave as Mangalore was 400 kilometres away. We'd have to stop on the road and do the show live from somewhere and then continue our journey, reaching our destination very late in the night.

My friends Vishnu Som and Prachi Bhuchar were anchoring the news and the surprise was evident in their voices as they commented on the pictures that were programmed to a loop. We saw Home Minister P Chidambaram addressing a routine press conference at the Congress office and ducking suddenly, as out of nowhere, a sneaker whizzed past his head. It was compulsive viewing. And, from what Vishnu and Prachi were saying, apparently it was a member of our fraternity who had dared to throw his shoe at Chidambaram!

'Prachi, a lot of us in the media know Jarnail Singh and it's most unexpected behaviour from him. He's a senior journalist and highly respected,' Vishnu was saying.

I had no clue who Jarnail Singh was. I learnt later that he was a defence correspondent with the *Dainik Jagran*. What apparently made him so angry at the minister was the Congress government's decision to have Sajjan Kumar and Jagdish Tytler fight the elections from Delhi. The two sitting MPs had both been indicted by the Nanavati Commission for their role in the 1984 anti-Sikh riots, but they were yet to be punished by the CBI, by a court, and especially by their party, the Congress.

3000 people had died twenty-five years ago and no one had been punished! It was enough to make anyone's blood boil. But a Sikh journalist venting his personal rage on a minister had shaken the establishment.

'Lead him out, gently,' Minister Chidambaram had instructed his guards. Jarnail Singh had not been charged by any court, but he did lose his job.

That was the first time since we had set out on our journey that something in the national news had caught our attention. We'd gone so micro, so voter-oriented in the last two months, that it seemed as if we could no longer relate to anything that made headlines in Delhi.

Most of the time, all that was on offer, were the shenanigans of Varun Gandhi and how Mayawati, the BJP and the Congress reacted to them.

'You know, we've done so much of the country by now, spoken to so many people, but no one has brought up Varun Gandhi as an issue,' said Naghma as we drove to Karwar and Udupi. 'It's like they don't care what happens to him. He doesn't affect their lives.'

'That's true. I really cannot understand why the Varun Gandhi story is still being discussed in Delhi,' I replied.

The fact is that not one person through all our travels had told us they were going to vote for or against the BJP for standing by as Varun declared himself a Hindu protector against evil Muslim terrorists. And yet, that's *all* that studio discussions had focused on; that's *all* that newspaper columnists wrote about. I knew I too was writing those stories when I was in Delhi, and in a way I could see their rationale.

After all, this Gandhi family scion was allegedly making derogatory remarks against the Muslims and threatening to 'cut their hands' if they laid them on the Hindus. If the media didn't make a noise about this, then who would? If the media didn't ask a national party like the BJP how they could let their candidate get away with prejudiced statements like that, then we'd be party to it.

We were being hell-raisers on Varun Gandhi but we probably didn't have the time to ask ourselves the questions that the Election Commission was asking before they acted against him. 'The public really wants us to take him to task,' said an official of the Election Commission, the government body that runs the country once elections are announced. 'But, we don't want to make a hero out of him. If we send him to jail, won't he get more mileage out of it?'

Many people thought that the media's Varun Gandhi bashing would go the same way that Narendra Modi's did – lead him to certain victory.

🚌

As we went through Karwar, I thought about something one shy onlooker had said to me in Daman. We were switching off the lights, signalling the end of the show, when the man had sidled closer to me and said, 'Do you know today we have achieved some kind of record?'

He had a peculiar manner about him so I wasn't sure how to respond. 'Sorry?'

'Do you know that the last time we saw any media here was in 2003 when the bridge collapsed?'

'Yeah, I vaguely remember that.' 26 people had died when the bridge over the Damanganga river had collapsed. News crews and broadcast vans from Mumbai had rushed there so it hadn't affected us news-wise in Delhi.

'That was the *only* time when reporters came here, and now NDTV has come here...' He looked away in deep thought, leaving me with a huge burden of responsibility. It was as if, just by being there, we had validated a part of their lives; we'd made them feel that their opinion mattered to the country.

His words made me think. 'You know how the desk keeps asking us to get live elements? Maybe we could really do something solid with that,' I said to Naghma and Mohammed as we soldiered on, on our way to Mangalore. Both of them looked a little alarmed at the prospect of another of my hare-brained ideas. 'Let's just stop at random places, places we have never heard of to do our show.'

Naghma nodded, so I went on: 'Even if we can only spare a couple of minutes or even less, it might be nice to let the people there tell the rest of the country what *they're* all about, what is special about them and what they want fixed.'

'That would be great,' said Naghma. I loved how she always backed me up. Even if we couldn't film it later, even if it was the most impractical thing in the world, she made me happy at that time by acknowledging where I was coming from.

So, very consciously that day, we stopped at a place called Honavar in Karnataka. The browser on my handheld wasn't working, so even the limited information about the place on Google wasn't accessible to me. All we knew about it was that it was a port town and it ran along the national highway. The locals told us that the bridge over Sharavati River was the longest in Karnataka. So with that bridge as our backdrop we marked our 5000 km show (actually, by the time we reached Honavar, we'd done 4990 kms). We didn't exactly highlight the problems of the place – we couldn't even find anyone who spoke English or Hindi, apart from a first-time voter who loved the Congress Party and said that he was very happy with his life in Honavar. What we did manage though, was to go live from a place, not because it was disaster struck, but because we, the media, were really interested in what the people of Honavar had to say.

Conversely, it seems Honavar, too, was equally interested in *us*. Naghma and I were dying to go to the loo by the time we reached the town.

'I have to go pee, or I won't be able to do the show,' I told Naghma. So both of us got off the bus – and were greeted by a massive crowd that had come media-spotting! The poor things had never seen strangers in a fancy vehicle drive into their town before so we couldn't really blame them, but our bladders weren't that understanding.

'Let's walk towards the river and pretend as if we are looking around,' said Naghma. Just at the edge of the river some distance off, we spotted a public loo. I hate, hate, *hate* public loos and I could smell this particular one from a kilometre away but desperation is a great cure for all kinds of hang-ups.

'I can't wait, Naghma. I'm going to die.'

What was upsetting me even more was that a couple of men were still following us.

'Oh shit, it's bloody locked.' I have no idea why a public loo needs to be locked; having been literally led to it by the nose, we were now feeling very let down.

'Don't worry, let's walk along the river,' Naghma proposed. We were hoping that the river would lead us to a secluded, wooded spot; one a little more discreet than the open grounds filled with cricket-playing boys. But after walking a little more, we realized that the only cover we were going to get was some light shrubbery.

When you're as desperate as I was, all genteel middle-class sensibilities quickly vanish. I remembered a remark my cousin once made about the view from Bombay's local trains. 'These women are crapping next to the train track. You can see their panties but you can't see their faces. *Why?*' We'd laughed at that time but I was now in the same position as them. I simply had nowhere else to go.

'Don't worry, you go behind that bush and I'll stand and stop these two from coming too close,' said Naghma. She stood guard with her hands on her hips as I crouched behind the shrub. I knew it was hardly any cover and whoever bothered to look could see what I was doing as there was enough daylight. But after a point, you simply don't care. And Naghma's aggressive stance finally discouraged our dogged stalkers.

I was back in a couple of minutes, much relieved. 'I think I just flashed some poor schoolboys, they look too traumatized to play now.'

They say that intense experiences like war or shared trauma brings you closer to people. To me, my relationship with Naghma was the equivalent of that. Naghma was my trench companion; she shared the trauma and desperation that I had felt so many times during the journey.

'I actually prefer to go in the fields.' (I had to keep talking about this, till I got over it.) 'It saves you from the stink and from seeing gross things, at least. Do you know that once I was in Chhindwara to cover Kamal Nath. The commode was one of those Indo–Western ones.' (We both grimaced at the thought of those.) 'The flush was leaking so it would never fill up, just have water flowing in it constantly, and the worst part was the dirty water from the commode was also *leaking* onto the floor!'

'Eeeyugh!'

'I didn't crap for two days that I was there! And then, when I finally got out and got to Nagpur, I called the stringer and asked him to organize a loo for me for half an hour. Can you imagine? How will that stringer *ever* take me seriously again?'

Naghma was laughing.

'He was very tactful, though. He called me and said that he'd spoken to the Centre Point Hotel and that I could go there to "get fresh". Oh Lord, I blessed him like I've never blessed anybody before!'

'Why didn't you tell Kamal Nath?'

'What? That I need to crap?'

However painful these loo experiences were, they always make great stories. One of my editors and his wife once met a senior BJP leader from Delhi at a party. The editor's wife recounted a shopping trip to Chandni Chowk and how charming it was but for the lack of facilities. So she asked him for the neta's perspective. Why wasn't building clean loos part of the national agenda? And the politician replied, 'Because men can go anywhere and women just develop the capacity to hold it in.'

I don't want to have superhuman capacity with my bladder, minister sahib, thank you very much. I just want clean loos.

Thank god, not everyone thinks like that Delhi politician. The Rural Development Ministry under Raghuvansh Prasad had kick-started the toilet campaign a few years ago. They aim to stop people from going 'in the open' by the end of 2010. A bit too ambitious, I'd say, but a noble goal none the less. To make sure that this wasn't just a scheme on paper, the government linked it to the Panchayat polls – if you didn't have a toilet in your home, they decreed, you couldn't contest the polls. The greed of ambition, officials hoped, would make people in villages get over their belief that toilets polluted their home.

'Remember that story in Haryana, where they won't marry their girls off to homes without loos? Things are changing,' said Naghma.

'Yes, but also remember that Bhuri took us inside a mud hut to pee on the floor!'

Contradictions were thriving across the country. As reporters, we could only observe and mark these; there was no way we could explain why things were the way they were.

Why, for instance, was a liberal, educated community like Mangalore suddenly under the threat of parties like the Ram Sene? We'd all seen TV images of how the right-wing group had dragged women out by their hair because they dared to go to a pub. Their leader Pramod Muthalik was never punished and national outrage had dissipated after the January 2009 incident. Many people believed that it was a manifestation of the new Hindutva that had brought the BJP into power for the first time in the state. Many thought that it was the result of the gradual polarization between the Hindu and the sizeable Muslim communities in the state. After all, the pub attacks were followed soon after by attacks on young inter-religious couples. These theories were all probably legitimate but we didn't have time to explore them.

What Naghma and I wanted to find out was the lasting impact of the pub assault and whether it had affected the vote or not.

When we put this question to our local fixer, Manju Pal, he said that the bar in question, Amnesia, had shut down.

'Why?'

'Well, the government suspended their liquor licence for a few months and then the owner just shut shop.'

'Can we meet him?'

'I'll find out but he's refused to speak to the media ever since the incident.' When we drove down to the pub we saw that the bar still had its fluorescent sign outside. I recognized the corridor through which the girls had been dragged by their hair and beaten in front of press cameras. As I walked in, I saw employees of a hotel next door looking at us curiously so I thought I'd just chat them up but they hastily withdrew: 'No, please, madam, we cannot talk.'

Three months had gone by and people were still scared that some street-side hooligans might come by to rough them up.

'He doesn't want to speak,' said Manju Pal, of the owner of Amnesia. 'I'm trying to get the number of the person who was the manager. Maybe you can try him.'

'Manju, can we meet some families with grown-up daughters in the house?' I suggested.

Manju was the best fixer we had on the trip. He understood deadlines and he seemed to have everyone on speed dial. But on this even he gave up. 'Sunetra, everyone is saying they are very sorry but they cannot afford to take the risk.'

'But have you told them that it's like a casual lunch format and it's only to find out what it's like living in Mangalore after that pub attack?'

'I did but they don't agree,' said Manju. 'They are saying we are welcome to come for lunch, though.'

I finally got to speak to the former manager of Amnesia. Not on camera but on the phone because the poor man was too scared to talk openly. Even though so many months had gone by, he was still a little unsure about exactly what had triggered off that assault on women on his shift that afternoon.

'It was a Saturday, so it wasn't very busy. I remember that the staff didn't have much to do. There was a group of women who'd come in to celebrate someone's birthday, college students mostly,' he said.

'Were there any boys with them?' I asked.

'No, there were boys in the pub but not with this group of women.'

'Were the girls drinking?'

'Not really. They were all having fun and we were standing around. Suddenly, these people (Ram Sainiks) came in and started attacking the women,' he said.

'They didn't attack the boys?'

'They didn't touch the boys. They just dragged the women outside, pulling them by their hair, the footage you would have seen in the media. I don't know how they knew about our bar because it had opened just a month before, in December. I don't know why they targeted the girls but we were stunned.'

'What happened after that?'

'My owner had a tough time because they suspended his license and finally he had to shut shop.'

'The staff?'

'Some of them have had to go to Bangalore, some have had to look for jobs in other sectors.' It was evident that the manager was yet to get over the shock of what had happened to him that night. He said he liked working in the hotel industry but had been forced to go back to working in a pharmacy. The owner of Amnesia, (who had gone totally off the radar), was a dentist. Now, apparently, it was strictly only cavities and root canals for him.

Mangalore wasn't some mofussil town that frowned on drinking or women going out. But this one incident had made everyone feel unsure about their habits and their identities. I'd heard that business in all bars had slumped after the pub attack so just to find out, I popped in, with the cameras, to another bar next door. It was empty apart from one table which had three men and one woman. The woman was so scared at being spotted there, she ran out.

'Please, please, I hope that you haven't taken her picture,' the men said to us. I felt really guilty for alarming everyone like that. The men didn't look the sort who concealed their drinks but they too hastily hid their beer glasses under the table. 'We are just being careful, you see.'

And that's why so many others in the city had just opted to stay away from the pubs. It was better to do so than to be beaten up in public.

In a nation-wide campaign, many liberals had tried to shame the Ram Sene by sending them pink chaddis (underwear). The campaign may have seemed successful on Facebook but Pramod Muthalik was undeterred saying he would send mangalsutras and saris to every female campaigner in return.

'Can't we meet him, Manju?' I asked, even though I knew that it would only provide him with a platform for his misogyny.

'He's not allowed to be in Mangalore, na?'

Right. I'd forgotten all about his externment — an archaic tradition for an archaic guy that meant that he wasn't allowed to enter city limits after the trouble he had caused.

'What about the elections? Is he putting up some candidates?'

'He's supporting this man called Ram Bhatt, who was with the BJP.'

So we went to meet Ram Bhatt instead. I expected an evil-looking man with no compunctions about accepting endorsements from the likes of Pramod Muthalik, but when I met Ram Bhatt he looked like a harmless old man. His lead campaigners were his two sweet-looking boys, his grandsons, both students in a professional college.

I had only one question for him: 'Sir, you are a two-time MLA, why are you taking support from someone who's attacked women and who's being condemned across the country?'

'I have to win, no?' He was just being honest. 'Even if a murderer endorses me, it is okay.'

What could you possibly say to that?

We had some delish buttermilk in a village on the outskirts of Mangalore and headed home. I noticed that Bhatt's audience, at least at that village, wasn't the sort to ever go into a pub or encourage their daughters to do so. Maybe, that's why he didn't care either way about his association with Muthalik.

In a way, both Goa and Mangalore were facing similar conflicts with outsiders and alien cultures.

Of course, we all know that Goa has no one like Pramod Muthalik and the Ram Sene. Indeed, we'd heard stories in Goa about how Muthalik had wanted to come there, but all its political parties had raised the red flag instantly – the tiny state was at peace with its bars and shacks.

Still, under the apparent carefree attitude of the Goan people, there was some discontent with outsiders. When I had lunch with two lovely ladies there, Kim and Geraldine, they had explained why they weren't too happy that more and more Indians were looking at Goa as their second home.

'They are driving up prices so high, we can't afford them anymore,' they said.

'Do you not want people like us to come here?'

'Come, by all means, but go back after some time. Earlier, when I looked out of my home, I could see the sea. Now, I see ugly builders' apartments.'

That I could sympathize with.

'A lot of Gujaratis are coming here to settle,' said Kim. 'They have made their own societies with high walls around. We never had walls around our houses before.'

'They don't want to learn anything about the local culture, they don't want to mingle with the local community and they even complain about our local rituals – like when we sacrifice piglets for festivals.'

'There is a Goan way of life and they want to change it. They don't want to leave Goa the way it is. How will Goa be beautiful, if they keep dumping garbage on our fields?'

I didn't know what to say. I always thought that Goans only had problems with foreigners and not with their fellow Indians. I knew lots of friends who were investing in properties there, who had no clue about angry citizens like Kim and Geraldine. I could quite understand some of their concerns about retaining old Goa – but I couldn't understand *any* of Muthalik's views.

Manju Pal had figured out the kind of stories we were looking for. 'When you go to Kasargod tomorrow,' said Manju Pal, 'you must meet the BSP candidate. We have a woman candidate there for the first time.'

'Forget women, what is the BSP doing there?'

'Mayawati had said, na, that she will contest from the entire country so this is it,' Naghma reminded me.

Wow. It didn't get more bizarre than this! We all identified Mayawati with Hindi heartland politics and here we were in Kerala, the heart of Leftist country, with Mayawati's mascot flying high.

Kasargod was only 50 kilometres away from Mangalore so it didn't take us much time to get there but we had no local contacts, no local fixers. A journalist friend from Delhi had put me in touch with a local reporter there to get some phone numbers. We didn't have much time because right after our show we had to hit the road again for another arduous drive to our next destination: Mysore.

We only had a few hours for Kerala.

'Her name is KH Madhavi and she's also the first tribal to be given a ticket by Mayawati,' said the local reporter, giving us her number. When we dialled her, it turned out that she was busy campaigning in the interior parts of the country. We simply had no time to go chasing after her so we just told her party-men to bring her back to town.

'We are very rude, yaar, telling her to come back like that,' said Naghma.

'Can't be helped. We also have to do a story on all those Gulf-returned people who've lost their jobs.'

So we went off to do our story while Madhavi was being sped back to town. She reached our bus when we were still away. Mohammed called to tell us that she had arrived and we told him to keep her busy and take some shots of her till we returned.

In that incredibly hot and humid weather, Mohammed made Mayawati's flag-bearer in Kasargod, march up and down. The small, fragile looking woman could speak only Malayalam but she did as her party-men asked and after Mohammed had enough shots of her pretending to campaign at a shopping area near our bus, she patiently waited for us.

'Why do you want to fight for Mayawati?' I asked her through a party-worker who was volunteering as a translator.

'She is the only one who cares for the downtrodden,' said Madhavi, who actually looked very weak and vulnerable herself. 'She is the only one who cares for tribals.'

'Have you met Behenji?'

She hadn't, and had no immediate plans of meeting her either. But when our interview finished, she and her party-men gave us a Malayali rendition of slogans we'd previously heard only in north India: 'Jay, Jay, Benji; Jay, Jay, KunshiRem; Jay, Jay BSP'

It was funny and sad all at the same time.

The party-men didn't have the manpower or the funds to carry out a high-powered campaign but they were carrying out Mayawati's will anyhow. KH Madhavi reminded me a little bit of Durjan Member, from the Dalit colony in Jhansi. Like him, she too was expending all her energy promoting her ward. And much like Durjan, Madhavi too had no hope of ever meeting the honourable chief minister of Uttar Pradesh.

'I wish we hadn't made her wait,' said Naghma after the interview was over. 'She looked so tired.'

We imagined the poor woman whose task it was to take on the strong CPM in its stronghold. How was she going to cope with her handful of followers? What was the point of all this? Even though we had met her for just half an hour and couldn't even speak to her properly, Madhavi's impossible battle stayed on in my mind.

🚌

'Guys, have you seen this?' Mohammed had taken a walk while the bus was refueling and came back waving a newspaper.

'What is it?'

'Our bus is on the front page of the local paper: the *Karnataka Vijay*.'

A prominent boxed column showed a picture of the bus. Locals who translated the piece for us said that the story basically said that the *Election Express* had covered the aftermath of the pub attack in Mangalore. We were thrilled beyond belief. Local papers were now registering our journey!

'I told you that it would be a hit, didn't I?' Mohammed said, looking smug.

Yes, it was official.

There was no denying it now.

The bus was a hit.

13

The 'Fetty' and 'Blekky' of Tirupati

The southern leg of our journey, from Mangalore to Machlipatnam (our last stop before we returned to the Hindi-speaking parts of the country) was an excursion in exotica. Or at least, it was for Naghma and me. After all, we were going to places that our reporting budgets usually didn't allow!

The last time the both of us had ventured south of the Vindhyas was when the tsunami hit Tamil Nadu. That had been the *only* story considered big enough for precious funds to be spent on news crews from Delhi. Otherwise, whether for elections or anything else, south India was handled by the local bureaus.

No one among our troupe knew any of the south Indian languages, and paid interpreters are unheard of in Indian journalism. So we were going to have to depend largely on the kindness of local contacts and some nifty sign language. We knew it wasn't a very accurate mode of reporting; never had been. For instance, during the tsunami, the office's idea of giving me an interpreter was to pack me off with a Tamilian cameraperson, Bala. A fantastic professional, Bala however had limited skills in handling anal and impatient reporters like me. Here's how our conversations usually went:

'Bala, ask him to tell you what happened.'

Bala translates. The interviewee starts speaking, gesticulating wildly, speaking volubly for all of five minutes as Bala nods.

'Bala, what is he saying?'

Bala indicates for me to keep quiet. The interviewee keeps talking.

'Bala, *tell* me!'

Bala looks at me like I'm a belligerent child and says: 'He says he lost his house.'

'And?'

That was *it*. After hearing the man talk non-stop for five minutes, Bala decides that's all it was worth.

I would scream at him, he would scream back, and after ten days and some guesswork-backed stories, I was ready to tear my hair out.

Then again, at least during the tsunami, one of the crew members knew Tamil.

My friend Neeta Sharma and I have followed Ottavio Quattrocchi to Argentina without speaking a word of the language. It was a hard news story with new developments every day. We needed to interact with Interpol officials, with immigration officials, local police and lawyers, and well, sometimes we read their nods and gestures wrong.

Like one time, we thought we'd got a major scoop because we understood that the immigration official indicated that they didn't have records of any Ottavio Quattrocchi passing through their borders. We were ready to even do a story that speculated on whether Quattrocchi had *another* passport which he had used to get in to Argentina. Only when we were checking our facts again did we realize that the official had just been talking about a particular date.

Thank god for the Indian Embassy in Buenos Aires. They were the primary source for most stories on that assignment and thanks to our colonial legacy, they all spoke English.

'I don't know how you all operate without a translator,' a French photographer friend once told me. 'I can speak English but I do not trust my skills enough to even use it to report in India. I always hire someone.'

When I told him how our budgets did not have provisions for a translator, he said, 'Then pay for one yourself; that is what I would do.'

'Easy to say when you're earning in dollars,' I had replied.

It's basically in our DNA to do jugaad. It doesn't matter how impossible the circumstances, we as Indians, and desperate reporters, always find some way to do our story. Not speaking the language was just a minor challenge.

After all, we were sure – at least Naghma was – that there'd be enough villagers, or hangers-on, wherever we went, to do some quick translation work for us, and that too, for free.

For me, and I suspect for Naghma too, going there was a novelty associated with going to new towns, where the people looked different, spoke different, ate different, led totally different lives, but were going to vote in the same elections. We, in Delhi, knew their representatives: characters called Stalin, Karunanidhi, Jayalalitha, Vaiko, Yedurappa, Achuthanandan and YSR, but we hardly knew them.

Naghma and I were like two enthused tourists who'd read each page of *The Lonely Planet* and wanted to cram every experience described in it into 24 hours.

'I want to have the Mangalorean fish curry, and the prawns and the appam!'

'I want to have Gadbad ice-cream, everyone's told me it's amazing!'

'Apparently, the place where the movie *Bombay* was filmed is just 13 kilometres from Kasargod, please, *please,* let's go there.'

'I haven't seen the sea in Mangalore, let's go there too.'

It was like a trip to an amusement park, with non-stop highs. And even though the Gadbad ice-cream was a gross monstrosity, we weren't put off. If someone had said bat wings were the traditional specialty, we'd have been willing to try those too.

However, not everyone was willing to share our enthusiasm.

'Left or right?' Ganga Singhji barked at Jayant.

'Stret,' said Jayant, our local stringer, in his strong Mysore accent, then changed his mind a little while later: 'Laift, laift.'

Ganga Singhji had already gone past the turn.

'Why didn't you tell me before?' Ganga Singhji scolded him in Hindi.

Jayant muttered under his breath.

Naghma and I knew what this was really about. Ganga Singhji had lost his sense of control. He liked to chat up people in the local paan and cigarette shops when he stopped to buy his gutkha. He wanted to tell them about his cool job at

NDTV where he only drove the bosses and the famous guests around, and he wanted to talk about his days in the army and the four people he was now taking around the country. He could do none of this because no one understood what he said. He couldn't even convey his displeasure to Jayant.

I was very upset about Ganga Singhji's rudeness to Jayant, so I had a word with him. 'But, madam, how can they not know Hindi?' Ganga Singhji couldn't understand why these people in south India, always slurping their curd rice, were allowed to get away without knowing the national language. So he snapped at or mocked everybody who didn't know Hindi – the pedestrian who couldn't give him directions, the toll booth attendant, and even Jayant.

'It's his macho north Indian attitude,' said Naghma, irritated with Ganga Singhji. 'They really think they are superior.'

She'd also noticed that Mohammed and Nishant joined in whenever Ganga Singhji made fun of the people around us. And their Bollywood-instilled Madrasi stereotypes tended to really annoy Naghma and me.

'It's been so many days, yaar, since we had roti,' Mohammed would complain all the time. 'I cannot remember when I last had a proper meal. I just want roti, dal and chaawal.'

Naghma and I would instantly pipe up: 'Are you kidding? We love the food over here.'

Jayant took us to a small dhaba which was so popular it had a waiting list of a hundred people at lunchtime. We sat down to eat off banana leaves, and were served the freshest rice, sambhar, vegetables and some humongous fish fries. As we were squeezing the lemon on to our rice, we noticed that the boys had decided to order roti and subzi. 'Why are you eating that?' I wanted to say but kept quiet because I knew what they'd think: 'Shut up, woman, you're not our mommy.'

'We're going sari-shopping after the show,' I said, knowing that this might break down some of the cultural barriers.

'Madam, I will also go. I have to buy for my wife and daughter-in-law.' Ganga Singhji perked up immediately.

'Yes, yes, let's go back to the shop we went to in the morning,' said Naghma. The local Congress candidate had campaigned at a Mysore silk sari shop and since then all that Naghma could talk about was going back there. 'What time will you stay open till?' she'd asked the owners when we were leaving. 'We have to do our show and can come back only after that.' The sales manager had assured her that he'd wait till 9.30pm.

'Madam, it's an expensive shop. I will take you to another one,' said Jayant. 'They will give good discount.'

I looked expectantly at Naghma. 'No yaar, let's go to that shop only, they will be waiting for us.' Noble sentiments – and I would have appreciated them, if we were about to give custom to a struggling artisan. The shop in question was actually a large-scale and successful retailer.

Naghma, Sumit, Ganga Singhji and I landed up just after 9 at the showroom, led by Jayant who immediately warned the sales people that we were very, very special customers who'd come all the way from Delhi.

'Of course, please choose whatever you want,' the proprietor said.

'I want to buy a very expensive sari for my wife,' said Ganga Singhji. 'And a less expensive one for my daughter-in-law.'

'Why, Ganga Singhji?'

'Because, if my wife's sari is not nicer than my daughter-in- law's, she'll kill me.'

Naghma chose three saris and I picked out a couple too, but it was Sumit who bought the most for his mother and relatives. Ganga Singhji also found appropriate saris for the women in his life.

'Okay, sir, we'll offer you ten per cent discount.'

'Just ten per cent?'

Jayant started to hyperventilate right there. The man who uptil then had only shown his displeasure by muttering under his breath suddenly found expression in his own language. He went ballistic, clutching his head and then his mouth and then his hair. 'Oh god, oh god. You are paying so much, oh god, oh god.'

The saris were quite expensive and worse, if one removed the tag that said they were from Mysore, one could probably buy similar saris at much less cost in Delhi. The *Election Express* team had been royally ripped off! Like gullible tourists, we'd been taken in by the shine of a fancy store. Jayant couldn't reconcile to the fact that it had happened on his watch. He was only able to compose himself after Naghma bought us all some hot and pure-ghee-smelling Mysore Pak. 'I wish we'd gone somewhere else,' said Jayant. 'It would have been half the price.'

Suddenly, over the issue of overpriced saris we all, including Ganga Singhji, seemed to have made our peace with Jayant. Because his English skills were minimal, we'd kept our chats perfunctory throughout the day, but now we all felt connected to him. I was touched that someone who'd just met us for a few hours cared so much about us paying a little extra.

'Jayant, forget it,' I said trying to put him out of his misery. 'If you want to help us, can you fix an interview with Ambareesh?'

The legendary film actor and three-time Member of Parliament MH Ambareesh had always fascinated me. He was more than fifty years old and a far cry from your conventional good-looking hero; his most distinctive features were his bloodshot eyes and his heavy stature. MH Ambareesh had been appointed Information and Broadcasting minister in the last government, only to resign over the government's failure to resolve a water sharing dispute between Karnataka and Tamil Nadu.

'Yes, yes. His PS, Somu, is my friend but he speaks even less English than me.' Somu, it turned out, was the head of the official fan club of MH Ambareesh.

We wanted to get a sense of why film stars were so popular and so intrinsic to politics in the south. The national media had been quite flummoxed when, at the death by cardiac arrest at the age of 76 of the other legendary actor from Karnataka, Rajkumar, his fans had become so violently upset that there had been riots in the state for days.

What was it that the southern stars did that made the public there go insane? Even in 2009, the latest actor-turned-politician Chiranjeevi was attracting such large crowds that stampedes at his public meetings were killing people. Would he become the next NTR? Chiranjeevi had no time to spare for us, so we were trying to understand this phenomenon through Ambareesh.

Somu said that Ambareesh would certainly give us time. Or at least he'd give us half an hour in a Mandya village. By pointing to his mouth, Somu first made us promise that we would come back to eat with him once we'd met Ambareesh. He found someone who spoke better English than himself and sent us 10 kilometres away to meet the star.

'Are you also a fan club member?' we asked our guide. Apparently, Somu was the president of the fan club and the man he'd sent with us was one of the district heads. They switched their focus from films to politics and became political workers as soon as elections approached. 'Whatever sir does,' explained Somu, 'we do.' The official fan club as a political workers' body was a new one for us on the campaign trail.

'Does Ambareesh use film dialogue in his public meetings?' we asked Somu's friend. He nodded, and then we realized that even if he were to break into a line from a film, we would never understand it. 'What if we asked some of his supporters to repeat them for us on camera?' I suggested to Naghma.

'Yeah, we could do that.' The actor-politician from Bihar, Shatrughan Sinha always loved using lines from his films during political rallies and they were always a laugh, so we thought we'd do the same in Kannada. 'We'll ask them to do his famous dance moves as well,' said Naghma.

Music, movies and politics – you can't get better television than that.

🚌

'Sir, why are you called a rebel star?'

Ambareesh stood before me, supporting his large body on a smaller man's shoulders. I'd been told he was doing this because he was exhausted from campaigning in the heat. It seemed to me that there was something wrong with his legs, but his fans would not hear of it. A gold chain, thick and fitted as a dog collar was wrapped around his neck.

'Hehehehe,' Ambareesh chuckled as the crowd behind him started chanting: 'Rebel star, rebel star, rebel star.'

'I'm actually called Mandya de Gandu.'

'Sorry?'

'Mandya de Gandu, Mandya de Gandu.' The chants picked up.

I couldn't stop giggling. The more they'd say 'Gandu' the more I'd cackle into my mike knowing that north Indian men and women would be rolling on the floor at the use of this crude expletive repeatedly on TV.

'It means King of Mandya,' said Ambareesh, not minding my laughter. 'Actually, Shammi Kapoor was called rebel star after *Junglee* and then I was also called that,' he said.

I found out later that the epithet referred to his anti-establishment image in films, playing the role of the upright citizen rebelling against corrupt systems and politicians. 'Were you a rebel politician?'

Ambareesh smiled: 'I resigned over the Cauvery water dispute but I don't think my resignation has solved the water problem.' Mandya, his constituency, was totally dependent on the Cauvery river for its water supply. 'It didn't help but I couldn't just sit there. If I hadn't resigned, I wouldn't have been able to face anybody when I came back to my constituency.'

I found that quite endearing, actually. The man was a minister, as high up as he could get at that time, and he had given up his seat, choosing to listen to his conscience. I know it's naive on my part to take his statements at face value but I thought he was genuine. There are so many politicians who make mistakes, who compromise their constituency's demands, just to hang on to power. It was refreshing to hear someone say something different. Of course, the problem was that the public was no longer content with either a clean heart or good intentions – they wanted results. They would come to watch you as a film star but if they figured you couldn't deliver the goods, they voted you out. That's why Ambareesh had suffered a shock defeat in the 2008 assembly elections.

We couldn't talk freely to the people about the film star politician – and our translator was also Ambareesh's man – but we witnessed one old man who came up and angrily ticked off the star, venting his anger loudly in the middle of the crowd. Clearly, he wasn't chanting: 'Rebel star, rebel star.'

'What's he saying?' I asked our guide.

'He's complaining about his area's problems but Ambareesh is saying that it's not his fault.'

Before the situation could get out of hand, Ambareesh was quickly whisked off to a waiting car. After he left the villagers and the fan club had a bit of a free-for-all.

When we tried to find out what the dispute was about, we were told: 'Nothing madam, it's a local problem.'

It always was.

Perhaps the biggest triumph that day was watching the villagers and fan club members perform Ambareesh's famous dance moves and lines. We turned on our camera and invited whoever felt like, to demonstrate their favourite Ambareesh moments in front of the lens.

The first one to jump forward was a forty-something farmer who folded up his mundu to reveal a pair of bandy legs and danced to his own tune of 'Mandya de Gandu'. He wasn't the least bit conscious; he just looked straight into the camera and danced.

The skinny farmer was then pushed from in front of the camera by a man who wanted to do a monologue beginning with the Hindi words: '*Kutte, Kanwar nahi, Kanwar Lal bol.*' ('You dog, don't you dare call me Kanwar, call me Kanwar Lal.')

The line could have been straight out of a Bachchan film. 'How come there's a Hindi line in the film?' we asked the guide.

'They use Hindi lines now and then.' The entire crowd was silently mouthing the lines in sync with the performer. Ambareesh was obviously a huge star here but we in Delhi had no idea who he was. Even though south Indian films bagged most of the National Awards, we seldom watched them. Even the Malayalam film god, Mohan Lal, had to work in a Hindi film *Company* before many of us discovered him.

'Why is it that these actors are so alien to us?' I asked Naghma. 'I've not watched any of Ambareesh or Raj Kumar's films but I've watched the Hong Kong filmmaker Wong Kar Wai?'

'It's because it is cool to watch Wong Kar Wai,' said Naghma. Trust her to be brutally honest.

'No, no, that's not entirely true,' I protested, knowing that there was much truth in what she said. 'I love Rajnikanth so I wanted to watch his last film *Shivaji*, but I couldn't find a show with English subtitles.'

Actually, now that I thought about it, ever since we'd crossed Goa, I recognized very few of the references to popular culture. For instance, one could recognize Mohanlal in some advertisement hoardings, but one couldn't find the Shah Rukh Khans and the Sachin Tendulkars.

Even the model for Pepsi looked unfamiliar: 'I think he must be a big star,' said Naghma. 'His ads are everywhere.' The young male model's bearded visage was everywhere and he looked very, very hot. When we Googled him, we learnt that the model was the actor Chiranjeevi's son, Ram Charan Teja. Pepsi had bagged him as part of their cola war strategy.

In south India, his father Chiranjeevi used to be the brand ambassador for their rival, Thums Up. So, just before the elections, Pepsi had signed up Chiru's son as their poster boy. We, in Delhi, were completely unaware of this marketing coup.

Maybe it was inevitable considering the vastness of India; communication gaps were bound to happen. No wonder, when we came back to see Somu, he honoured his north Indian media friends with a special preparation of north Indian delicacies: tandoori chicken, dal makhni and roti. All Naghma and I wanted was to eat off banana leaves, but Nishant, Mohammed and Ganga Singhji were thrilled.

They needed to be indulged before the long week ahead. We were just to stop for one show in Kanchipuram and then were to spend the entire week ahead traversing through Andhra Pradesh. From Kanchipuram, we would embark on a three-hour journey to Tirupati, then a few more hours to Kadapa and then, the marathon eight or nine hour drive to Hyderabad. And finally five more hours of driving to Vijayawada – our last stop of the week.

It was a tremendous opportunity to get to know the Telengana and Rayalseema regions of Andhra Pradesh, crucial to the Congress Party's performance in these elections, both in the parliamentary and assembly polls. But, it was mindboggling just trying to figure out how we were going to get to all these places, leave aside, reporting on them too.

🚌

'I'm worried about Ganga Singhji,' I confided to Naghma. 'He's exhausted and we have to drive around like crazy. I think we should hire a taxi to take us around the city in Hyderabad so that he can get some rest.'

I then gave Ganga Singhji a bit of a pep talk to prepare him for the 3,000 odd kilometres he'd have to cover that week. As usual, he embraced the task with enthusiasm. 'Don't worry, madamji, if I can get couple of hours of rest, I'll be fine.'

I had visions of myself being a cruel tyrant driving Ganga Singhji to a heart attack, but I loved him for not carping. After all, Naghma and I were getting our mugs on air every day. That, and the fact that we were being paid, was our motivation. Ganga Singhji could as easily have been relaxing at his cushy job in Delhi and not haring through the southern countryside at all.

I was also concerned about our lack of preparedness. The bad news was that we didn't have any stringers in Andhra Pradesh, so we would have to fend for ourselves. There would be no unpaid translators and no local fixers to help us out. We'd have to find stories and conduct interviews all on our own. If it was up to me, I'd just have done one or at most two places in Andhra Pradesh, because of the lack of logistical help. But we were on the bus and we had to make our way to Orissa by road, and it would take all week to cover that distance.

'Don't worry, Sunetra, we'll find stories,' said Naghma, 'Haven't we done half the country already?'

That's true. I'd realized by now that in comparison to planned journalistic ventures, and pursuing a particular story, impromptu stories worked better. So, for instance, when we were in Tamil Nadu's Sriperumbudur, we tried to do a profile on Shipping Minister and Dravida Munnetra Kazhagam veteran, TR Baalu.

The man had money to throw around in his campaign with Scorpio vehicles whizzing about distributing mineral water and fruit juice to the crowds. What turned out to be a nice TV piece, though, was the clothes that the party-workers were distributing to the villagers – all of which bore political motifs. Old women wore synthetic saris with the DMK symbol of the rising sun; men wore mundus in party colours; and young kids sported bandanas, scarves and t-shirts with the political emblem on them. It gave us an instant flavour of the colourful campaign without requiring too much spadework.

I knew that these were the most appropriate stories for the *Election Express*: stories that captured the local colour, but I was a bit nervous about going in completely blind. We needed to know people. So I called friends in Delhi and searched for contacts of local journalists. Through their amazing network, my friends gave me the number of a local journalist, Trimurti, in Tirupati, who in turn gave us a reference to senior Kadapa journalist, Narayanan and a Telugu publisher in Vijayawada called Ashok. They all seemed very confused about what we wanted to achieve in their respective towns but we felt a lot more assured just talking to them.

Andhra Pradesh's state elections were perhaps a bit more exciting, since Chiranjeevi was contesting those polls – one of his seats being Tirupati.

'So what would you like to do here?' said Trimurti of Tirupati, home to the famous Tirumala temple.

'Umm, something about elections and the temple and Chiranjeevi?'

Trimurti was an agency reporter who was now freelancing for many publications. He knew the city inside out and also knew everyone who mattered. His English was limited and heavily accented but he had a wonderful giggle and a string of insider jokes about his town and its politicians.

'You know, the actress, medem?' he asked Naghma and me. I vaguely remembered the film star he named but couldn't put a face to her.

'She's with the Telegu Desam Party,' he said, annoyed at our ignorance. 'I interviewed her.' We tried to look impressed; it was probably a major feat, considering the other star, Chiranjeevi, couldn't spare us two minutes.

'You know, I called her to meet her,' he started recounting the incident. 'We were meeting in the hotel, so I go there and I start waiting for her but I cannot see her. So I keep waiting and then I call her. I am a big fan so I call her and ask her, "Where are you, medem?" She says, "I am right here". I say, "Where, medem, where?" And then she walks in front of me,' he says, waiting to deliver the punch line, 'You won't believe, medem, so fetty and so blekky. Even blekker than me!'

Trimurti was so let down by the actress' TV deception, he had to share his disappointment with the first two TV people he met! Naghma and I had to hold our stomachs because he made us laugh so much. 'No, medem, I'm serious, I think they put paint, she was so blekky.' After that, we knew that we were going to be friends with Trimurti; especially as he delivered this story again and again, on demand.

He was also the first one to introduce us to the concept of faction politics:

'Please do not say anything, just take a picture of the house,' said Trimurti. We were in a nice neighbourhood to interview a politician and Trimurti's behaviour seemed really strange.

'Let's walk and talk. That house you saw, it was snatched by his father at knifepoint,' he said, referring to a mainstream Andhra politician. He was obviously serious about the threat, which is why he didn't want to be heard. 'He was a faction leader who worked with gangs and they would just snatch away people's properties with threats.'

Apparently, in Andhra Pradesh, this kind of factionalism, which I only remember from Hindi movies of the eighties, was rampant. Faction leaders were deeply involved in politics and even today, group wars were common in the Rayalseema region to gain control of an area. I met my friend, the Additional Director General of police of Andhra Pradesh, Vivek Dubey, who told me that it was a reality that still existed. 'It doesn't matter how educated you are, whether you are a doctor or an engineer. When you come back to your village, to your home, you have to work with the local factions.'

Back home, we only saw that aspect of Andhra Pradesh which boasted the IT city, Google and the Indian School of Business. No wonder, when we were in Kadapa, the Telegu Desam Party was celebrating the fact that after decades, they'd managed to open a party office in the heart of Chief Minister YSR Reddy's constituency, Pulivendula. I thought the TDP candidate was exaggerating when he said that they were fighting against extreme conditions and terror tactics, but not allowing the opposition to have a party office, I think, was pretty extreme. And this, from the liberal Congress Party.

The other extremists we met were the temple authorities. The reason we were running around a temple was because everything in Tirupati was controlled by the temple authorities, and of course, the government was involved. A bigshot bureaucrat was the real god behind the Lord of Tirumala. The candidates were trying to influence the temple; candidates from all over the country were seeking blessings from the temple and one former temple trustee was even contesting the elections himself.

'Is everything run by the temple?' we asked Trimurti. He nodded, telling us that the main scandal hitting Tirupati elections was that temple employees were being *threatened* to vote for the Congress Party. 'They make that much difference?' I asked like a fool.

'70 per cent of Tirupati's employment is dependent on the temple, medem.'

Unfortunately, we weren't meant to please these gods in human form. The *Election Express* team treated them as regular interviewees, hustling them for appointments and refusing to invoke them in style. We met the IAS god at a BSP meeting. He was probably embarrassed to be spotted at a party meeting which is why he refused to speak to us there. 'Come to my office,' he said curtly.

At his office, where we had to take our shoes off to enter, Trimurti was summoned to explain the circumstances of our visit. We sat and waited for a frustrating half an hour. 'Why do we need him anyway?' asked Naghma. 'It's boring to interview him in his office.'

'I thought we could just get our background information from him about the new things that they were doing here.'

'But why is he taking *so* long?'

That's true. We really had no time to placate so many gods. I got up and asked his secretary to let me in.

He looked at me like I'd committed a cardinal sin. 'He will call you when he wants,' he said disapprovingly.

That just upset me further. 'Look, we don't have all day, either he meets us now or we go.'

They ignored us.

'Okay, we are going,' Naghma said and strode out to the car, but I barged into his room.

'Yes?' the big fat man looked at me contemptuously.

'We are actually in a hurry because we have to leave Tirupati today, so if you're busy, we'll leave.'

Trimurti's face fell! He had used all his contacts to warm up the IAS chap and I, a stupid journalist from Delhi, was insulting this god.

'That's up to you, you didn't take any appointment in advance.'

'Okay, Trimurti, let's go.' And I left, knowing full well that this was going to damage Trimurti's relationship with the god but I just couldn't help myself; we were in a race against time and we had to put our show together. As we were about to go, a waiter brought out a tray of fresh juice for us. In my anger, I thought we should reject it but the gang decided otherwise and drank it in the car; it was truly divine.

Trimurti was upset. He kept shaking his head in mortification, shocked at how we'd treated his contact. 'I'm really sorry, Trimurtiji, I know that he was an important source for you, but we really had no time.'

'He's a big man, he's a big man,' Trimurti kept saying.

To the god's credit, he wasn't vindictive. He allowed us entry into the temple on the hills. But even there, there were smaller gods – all refusing to grant audience without proper invocation, for which we had no time. I was convinced that we'd have to rehabilitate Trimurti in some other town by the time we were done treading on toes over here.

'These are very important people, medem,' Trimurti said. 'That officer has to sign lakhs of tickets for the people that come to visit the temples, so he finds it difficult to give time.'

'I understand, Trimurti, but we don't have that time so we are going to just interview pilgrims and not them.'

That was easier said than done. Everything – from the queues, to the crowds, to the cleaning, to the food – was handled by bureaucrats. We had a piece which we wanted to do on the jumbo ladoos but to procure one, we had to get tokens.

'Forget it,' I said. 'We'll just show them being made.'

'I want to eat one as well,' said Naghma. 'They are famous, aren't they?'

Trimurti held his head in his hands. He couldn't believe he'd had the misfortune of meeting people like us – impatient, rude and now, clearly greedy. 'That's a difficult demand to fulfil,' he said and Naghma's face fell.

So we gave the big and small gods a miss, and struggled our way back through the crowds and the hilly roads to complete our assignment. As we made our way back to main-town Tirupati, tired and hungry, we noticed a jeep standing by a picket.

'One minute! Stop!' said Trimurti, jumping out.

'Oh god,' I thought. 'He's gone to meet another officer I don't want to interview.'

We dreaded the wait and kept glancing at our watches as we were dangerously close to airtime. We thought of leaving Trimurti there in the hills, when we saw him return clutching a big white plastic bag. 'For you,' he smiled, handing it to Naghma and me.

Inside, were those divine, ghee-dripping, nut-filled, half-kilo-each ladoos that Tirupati was famous for.

14

Of Other Gods and Naveen Patnaik

'You have to visit the Ameen Peer dargah in Kadapa, that's where AR Rahman goes,' my Andhra journalist friend had advised me on the phone. 'That's of course if you've had enough of tracking the faction-ridden politics of the Rayalseema region.'

Composer AR Rahman was like a no-brainer of a story at the time because of *Slumdog Millionaire*'s success. Whatever he said was being written about, whatever he did and wherever he went and especially where he prayed, was big news.

'Not just AR Rahman, even Abhishek Bachchan and Aishwariya Rai pray at the same dargah.'

That decided it. We were going to go to the dargah whether there was a story there or not.

'It's becoming a religious tour, isn't it?' I said to Naghma. First the temple town of Kanchipuram, then Tirupati and now a 300-year old dargah in Kadapa that was visited by film stars across the country.

'Don't forget we have more coming up,' said Naghma. 'There's the Jagannath temple of Puri and Konark.'

I knew that Naghma loved visiting temples from our earlier trips to Ujjain and Haridwar. In Haridwar – while I hung back worrying about the crowds and the dirt – Naghma had been totally moved by the Ganga arti. In Ujjain, instead of using the free time to sleep, she'd dragged us all to see the temples. Of course, I still have nightmares about the time she made us take a dip in the Ganga during the Kumbh Mela. It was at night and the water was slimy but Naghma thought that it was the appropriate thing for us to do after visiting so many temples.

Her editors had obviously tapped into her interest which is why she'd been sent for the Kumbh Mela all over the country, including the Allahabad one where she'd befriended some weird, pot-smoking sadhus. 'Do you know one of them came to see me in Delhi?' she had told me later.

I was fascinated by the fact that Naghma was more of a Hindu than I was, and that when we went to the temples, she wouldn't just be an observer but actually participate in the rituals. I remember once straying into a Catholic congregation as a teenager and feeling extremely awkward and unsure during communion. I didn't know whether it was like prasad; I wasn't sure whether I could go ahead and eat it or not.

But Naghma looked comfortable at any place of worship.

'Do you ever think they might stop you because you're Muslim?' I asked her.

'No, no one's ever stopped me,' she said. 'And they always know.'

We actually witnessed this at the Kamakshi temple in Kanchipuram. We were using the temple as a truly resplendent backdrop for our live links, when the head priest dropped in. He was very friendly and as religious leaders often are, very political:

'Election show? Of course, of course,' he'd said. 'Advaniji always comes to our temple, and so do Murli Manohar Joshi and all the other leaders.' Sensing that we weren't very impressed, he continued: 'Do you know that I was the person who first brokered the alliance between Jayalalitha and the BJP?'

To prove his point, he'd dragged us home. His living room was adorned with pictures of him with LK Advani, Venkaiah Naidu, and Murli Manohar Joshi. We finally believed him.

'Don't share the news with anyone but we are going to do a Mahayagya here for the BJP to win in the elections,' he said.

I'd heard of placating the gods for electoral gains but if the Kamakshi temple had ceded to the BJP, then who would conduct yagyas for the Congress?

'I tell you, I have done predictions for the elections and they are always right. Last time I said that the UPA would win even though everyone said the NDA would win, and I was right.'

'Who will win this time, sir?' We couldn't resist asking.

'The NDA will get 166 seats and with the help of its allies, it will form a government and LK Advani will be the next prime minister.'

We were blown away! He wasn't just playing it safe and giving us a trend, he was actually willing to stake his reputation on the line. 'We will check with you once results are out. Are you sure?'

'Yes, I am hundred per cent sure.'

Obviously, the head-priest's calculations had gone a little awry or maybe, the large-scale prayers weren't quite to specification, thus earning the displeasure of the gods and turning them away from the NDA. But we looked impressed enough by the head-priest for him to offer to take us for a private tour after the show.

🚌

'We must go, we must go,' said Naghma. How could we not, even though at the gate of the temple it clearly said, 'Only Hindus allowed'? I was a little nervous but we had a special invitation from the head priest. He'd indulged us completely, letting us photograph ourselves with the temple elephants even though cameras weren't allowed inside. He had taken us to the sanctum sanctorum, giving us an exhaustive commentary along the way. 'A lot of women come to the temple to fulfil their wishes for a child,' he said. 'After coming here, within a year they will be given a child, it is guaranteed.'

He instructed another priest to conduct a puja for us. The man came close to me and asked me my name and personalized his prayers for me. When it was Naghma's turn, I froze. He asked her her name, she told it to him, then he asked her to repeat it. I felt like a trapped animal who, along with her friend, was going to be insulted for being in a place they weren't meant to be.

But the priest calmly continued the puja, concluding the ceremony by giving us six green glass bangles each. 'Thank you, sir, thank you very much,' we said to the head priest at the gate. I suddenly felt touched by the experience. They were obviously strict about the only-Hindus rule which is why they had a sign on the gate but they chose to overlook our defiance, respecting Naghma's faith. This was the kind of accomodating religion that I could identify with.

'How did you guys get in?' said Nishant as he was coming out with Sumit. Mohammed hadn't bothered to go in.

'We were given a royal tour.'

'But did you see that sign? And he also asked each person's name.'

'Yes, that was just to conduct a personal puja, I think.'

Nishant shrugged, indicating that he wouldn't have taken that risk if he was in our place.

There was no such risk in Tirupati. No signs proclaimed the temple an all-Hindu zone. Naghma kept saying that she wanted to visit the temple but there was simply no time to brave the thousands-long line in Tirumala. It was too hot, we were too rushed for time, and there was no breathing space for spirituality. 'Can't we at least have the lunch that is served to pilgrims?' pleaded Naghma. We stared at the rows of men and women sitting cross-legged on the floor and licking their fingers en route from the banana leaf to their mouths. If there was one thing you could be certain about in religious places, it was the quality of the food – it was always a meal fit for the gods.

But we had to content ourselves with the divine ladoos.

'No, madam, it is impossible. You cannot go to the dargah,' said Narayanan, a fellow journalist and our local contact in Kadapa.

Uptil the moment we'd requested a visit to the centuries-old Ameen Peer dargah, Narayanan had not said no to anything. He was the perfect host, helping us beat the heat with frequent stops at Cafe Cuddapah to refresh ourselves with sugarcane juice or ice-cream.

'Why, Narayanan, sir? We really want to go.' We'd even got ourselves a peg for the story – using the dargah as a perfect symbol of communal harmony to interview leaders of the community about their hopes from the elections.

'No, madam, it is open only till 10am, after that it will close till 4pm.'

That was when we were scheduled to leave. 'Narayanan, sir, let's talk to them. I'm sure they'll make an exception for us.'

He looked at us as if we were not just crazy but also completely delusional for thinking that a special place like the dargah would remain open for us. 'Not even for the President, madam,' said Narayanan kindly, because he knew that we were really disappointed.

'Narayanan, sir, maybe not Madam President, but I know that if anyone can, *you* can. Please, sir, please.' If there's one lesson I have learnt in my years in television it's to never be afraid to grovel. And here my grovelling seemed to embarrass Narayanan sir so much that he got on the phone immediately. 'Let us go there and see, but I don't know if they will allow us.'

They were gracious enough to let us in. It was so hot, that we almost burnt the soles of our feet as we had to take off our shoes to enter the dargah. The caretakers of the dargah didn't once let on that they were doing us a favour by letting us in. They seated us in the shade, letting us cool down with fizzy drinks. They smiled and answered our questions and patiently sat through our interviews. Even though we asked them questions specific to the Muslim community in Kadapa, they refused to be bracketed. They insisted that their problems were like anyone else's in the city, and what they wanted, they wanted for everyone there.

Naghma had covered her head, but they didn't ask me to cover mine. Later, they asked if we wanted to offer our prayers. We all did, actually. I remembered how I'd been coaxed into tying a thread and making a wish at the Fatehpur Sikri dargah during Pakistan President Parvez Musharraf's infamous trip to India in 2001. My wish had been granted in less than a year, but I had taken seven years to return to untie the thread.

So Naghma, Nishant, Mohammed and I put away our cameras and mikes for a while and took time-out. I thanked god for a fantastic trip so far, and prayed that the rest of it went off as splendidly. I suspect that the guys prayed for the trip to end soon, or maybe, for better food. It quite made up for the not-so-liberal atmosphere we'd faced at the Golden Temple in Amritsar, where you were reprimanded if your head-scarf slipped off your head. It made up for the warnings we got to stay away from the Jagannath Temple in Puri. (When we'd told a senior police officer friend in the state that we'd been to every temple and were planning to visit Jagannath next, he'd said: 'You shouldn't bother, especially not you,' pointing to Naghma. 'It's not worth it. These people really insult you.')

Not a very inviting proposition, so we'd kept well away.

Anyway, there was so much more to see. Before I had planned this trip, I hadn't even heard of Kadapa.

Kadapa, a town which doesn't even have a hotel – only government guest houses that transformed into ghostly buildings by night; Kadapa, where sugarcane juice is sold not just from street-side carts but in fancy air-conditioned cafes in multiple flavours; Kadapa, where you can go into a pokey, red-bulb lit room and get the best prawn biryani and fish fry ever; Kadapa, where my friend Narayanan taught me a lesson I'd forgotten as a journalist.

It was a lesson in dealing with politicians. In this particular case, the TDP's Shrikant Reddy – a Stanford-educated professional. We were doing a piece on him and because we'd left our hotel really early, we didn't decline when the candidate's family offered us breakfast. Narayanan had come along too but we didn't spot him at the breakfast table as we wolfed down the dosas and upmas and watermelon juice that Reddy's family served.

After breakfast, I found Narayanan hanging around the house and asked him why he didn't come in. 'I've eaten, madam, and I do not want to go into their house and eat. I never do that.'

Why?

Because that way he didn't have to think twice before criticizing him.

I felt really embarrassed. I am not saying that eating Reddy's dosas would make me go soft on him or accepting a meal makes us obliged towards a politician. But hobnobbing with them has become so much the norm in Delhi that the local reporter's view was really refreshing.

In a way, though, it's tougher for local journalists. They have to live in the same community as the people they write about. If the neta of a small town decides to, he can really harass a journo. Children's admissions to school have been known to be stopped, and electricity supply disrupted – there are a hundred small ways of harassment. It made me think about the hospitality we so readily accepted on this trip. The problem is that, in the boondocks on an assignment like this, the neta is usually the only one who has access to clean water and food for hungry hacks like us. The way to be fair is perhaps to eat with *both* parties. That way we cannot be accused of being unfair to one!

Local journalists like Narayanan are also not scared of banging on about the real, local issues. They have their ear to the ground and are dogged about being anti-establishment. So, for instance, when a big diplomatic event is held at a place the national press will write about who said what, the implications on world peace and nuclear disarmament, blah, blah, blah. While the local press will talk about how to provide security for the visiting dignitaries, how poor, slum-dwellers were beaten and kept out of view, in detention. Or they'll write about how one road that has never been built, gets built overnight for the VVIP's visit. They'll also write about how the local administration could have done a lot more with the money and built better drainage or fixed a few more roads. The national media looks on derisively thinking that the local media is so limited in its worldview!

But actually, it's we who should be laughed at. We are so caught up with what's happening in Delhi and at political parties' national headquarters, that we forget to talk to the real people, to ask them what matters to them and what decides their vote. And then, when the election results are announced, we desperately try to backtrack and understand what really happened.

The 2004 election results were a case in point. We were all so taken with Pramod Mahajan telling us that India was prospering and shining, that we were blind to the truth. We had the noblest of intentions – we *wanted* to show reality, we *wanted* to show real issues, but we also wanted to show them in a manner that viewers, sitting in their air-conditioned living rooms didn't tire of them and switch to a rival channel. And some of them may be a sensitive souls who live in Malabar Hill and feel for the people of hot and humid Madhubani, but believe me, when each and every person on screen is crying out for bijli, sadak and pani over and over, even the biggest bleeding heart of them all reaches for the remote. The local press doesn't bother with readers' entertainment all that much. And thank god for that!

🚌

Meanwhile, we had the most considerate viewers keeping track of our journey. Here are a just two of the many emails we received warning us of the heat and the cyclone:

Hi Sunetra,

Your Hyderabad edition was good. But you spent most of the time in offices and with netas. You did not interact with common people I guess. I am surprised and felt proud that EVMs are manufactured in Hyderabad and also Customer service is provided from Hyderabad. Use Prakasam barrage in Vijayawada as background for tomorrow's show if possible. Vijayawada is politically sensitive place. It revolves around two castes Kamma (Chandra Babu) and Kapu (Chiranjeevi). Earlier Kapus used to support Congress. Now they moved to Chiranjeevi Party. Cyclone is expected in coastal Andhra Pradesh. So be safe while travelling there. Thanks, Rohin Sudini, New York

The Election Express in Vijayawada is something delightful to watch. Ms. Choudhury will have to bear the temperature of Vijayawada which is so hot and so are the political temperatures. One thing you should not miss to see is Vijayawada Railway Station and Pandit Nehru Bus Station. Please show all the glimpses of Vijaywada.

PS Srinivas, Surat.

While these messages expressed their concern and appreciation from a distance, some viewers had even got hold of our phone numbers by citing an emergency to our offices.

'Hello, is that the *Election Express*?' said one gentleman from Rajamundry. We really thought we had a stalker on our hands. (Like the man from Jamshedpur who wanted us – actually just Naghma – to come and stay with him while we were in town. He would call us morning and evening to check when we were coming to Jamshedpur. He would keep saying that he wanted to serve Naghma; that it was his *duty* to look after her while we were visiting.)

The man from Rajamundry said, 'I just wanted to call and say that when the *Election Express* bus is travelling to Vizag from Vijaywada, our town is on the highway so please do make a stop here.'

'I'm sorry, sir, we cannot do that as we have to get to Orissa over the weekend.'

'I wish you could, you see, my family and I have been watching the show every day, we've been reading your blogs and we'd really like to see the team.'

'Sir, I appreciate that but it's not possible.'

'Okay, then, can I come and see you in Vijayawada because it's just a 3-4 hours drive from there?'

I instantly heard the alarm bells go off in my head. 'I think you shouldn't bother, sir.'

'No, no, it's no bother. You can't believe what big fans we are of the show.'

Why would a grown man who claimed to be a doctor want to travel such a long distance to come and see a bus? I seriously did not get it. 'He's a psycho, I think,' I said to Naghma as soon as I hung up.

'He could be seriously interested in the show,' Naghma said. 'My nephew, for instance, keeps talking about the *Election Express*. He's told all his friends in school to watch it.'

'But, Naghma, your nephew is five years old,' I pointed out.

'Arrey, I know people who are watching this show like a serial, I tell you,' said Mohammed.

I wasn't convinced. And braced myself for a twitchy, nervous psychotic making an appearance on our set in Vijayawada. He did appear, but Dr Deepak Ray was no psycho. He was an oncologist who'd taken the day off to visit the show as his elderly father really liked it.

'Don't you have lives to save? Or other, better things, to do?' I asked.

'Not really,' he smiled. He'd brought us a box of sweets and seemed to know everyone on the team, even Ganga Singhji. When I saw him taking pictures of the bus, I realized just what an impact the show had had on viewers.

'Why do you and your father like the show so much?'

'Because we care about our country, we care about the issues that face our country. We really want to know what's happening.'

I guess that must have also been the reason why Yousufuddin, his wife and two children turned up to see us in Hyderabad. And a viewer called Phillip Joshua too. They all wanted to discover India, they all wanted to know what was happening in their country, they couldn't take time out to do it themselves, so they were doing it vicariously through us.

Naghma had heard from some producers in Delhi that election programming wasn't doing so well. People wanted to watch funny videos on YouTube rather than watch political shows like ours. But people like Dr Deepak Ray were telling me that if we were honest, if we really showed how it was on the ground, if we echoed the voices of real India, then they were willing to listen and they were willing to watch.

Actually, by that point in the journey, when we were almost 10,000 kilometres away from home, we no longer cared that much about ratings or even viewership. All we wanted to do was to travel and meet lots of people and some politicians. Politicians like the chief minister of Orissa, Naveen Patnaik and the former chief minister of Bihar, Lalu Prasad Yadav.

🚍

The very posh Mr Patnaik had not granted an interview to any news channel or newspaper so far in the campaign. He'd made headlines at the beginning of the election campaign when he had ditched his right-wing alliance partner, the Bhartiya Janata Party, after it had been linked with attacks against Christians in Kandhamal. Naveen Patnaik had read out a brief statement in English and Hindi in his clipped English accent and in a matter of minutes had unequivocally ended a decade-long partnership between his BJD and the BJP. Till that point no one had seen it coming. Pappu – as Mr Patnaik had been referred to by his chums from St Stephen's back when he was a socialite – had taken everyone by surprise.

'We want to meet Pappu, we want to meet Pappu,' Naghma and I had begged our senior colleagues Sampad Mohapatra and Purusottam Thakur. Sampadji was in his early fifties but displayed no signs of fatigue from journalism. Whenever I met him, I felt reassured about sticking it out in this profession; he was proof that you could work as a journalist all your life and still not end up being a cynic.

'Sunetraji' – (Initially, I'd get embarrassed when a senior person like Sampadji would refer to me in that way) – 'we've tried earlier. We went and stood outside his house but he didn't talk. But' – (what I loved about Sampadji was that he always held out hope) – 'if you go for his rally, he may decide to talk to you.'

It wasn't an ideal situation. What we really wanted was to spend a day with Naveen Patnaik, to get a sense of the kind of books he read, to hear more of his posh, clipped accent. We wanted to know what it had felt like being part of the jet-set in New York, mingling with the likes of Gore Vidal and Jackie Kennedy. What made him give it all up to come back to Orissa to save his father's party, the BJD, after his father had died? We wanted to understand how he had transformed himself into a crafty Indian politician and whether he sometimes yearned to go back to his old life.

Our curiosity about Pappu could only have been satisfied if we'd had the kind of access to him that we'd got while doing a show called *Follow the Leader*. In that show one almost got into bed with the politician being featured. We were present when they woke up, when they brushed their teeth, when they played with their pets, when they had breakfast – tailing them through the entire day. We'd mastered this format at NDTV and many prominent politicians had obliged us to the point that viewers weren't really surprised to see someone like, say, Uma Bharti stuffing her face at breakfast. But Pappu's aura of mystery seemed as if it would stay that way.

So we headed off to Kendrapara, an area about 40 kilometres from Bhubaneswar, from where the other Page Three regular, Jay Panda, was contesting. Sampadji had suggested we go there because it was going to be the last stop in Patnaik's chopper ride, as at 6.30pm that day, according to Election Commission guidelines, contestants had to give up their choppers and then take to the road to campaign. We stood at the edge of the stage waiting for Patnaik's chopper to arrive in the dusty town of Kendrapara.

It was a decent turnout – the reason why catching a politician at a rally was next to impossible unless he let you take a chopper ride with him. They had to cram in so many far-flung areas in one day that they just had about half an hour in each place. If you were lucky enough to be invited on board the chopper, then you had to be prepared either to stick it out with them the entire day or to be stranded in the middle of nowhere, with no transport to get you back to civilization.

As soon as Naveen Patnaik's chopper appeared on the horizon, the village women started ululating. It's actually an eastern ritual and marks auspicious moments at temples and weddings but only in Orissa had I heard it being used to greet politicians. The crowds went crazy, and while it must be admitted that some of the admiration was directed at the chopper, a considerable amount seemed to be inspired by Naveen Patnaik's charm. Naghma and I could feel the chemistry that he had with the people.

As he moved towards the stage, we noticed how frail Patnaik actually was. He was walking slowly, as if he was on the point of collapse. He was the only politician we'd met who actually looked tanned. For no reason at all, I felt I really liked him. Noticing our faces looking pleadingly at him from the bottom of the stage, he acknowledged us with a 'namaskar'.

'I think he indicated he'll talk to us after this rally,' said Naghma.

'Did he?'

The crowds couldn't wait to hear him speak. They cheered as other speakers introduced him. Naveen Patnaik looked exhausted but he continued to smile at the crowds. When the local leaders finally finished, he took out his written speech.

'He speaks Oriya?'

'No,' said Purusottam. 'That's why he's reading from a script.' There was no hiding the fact that Naveen Patnaik didn't know his mother tongue. In fact, when he ad-libbed in his speech, he lapsed into Hindi.

I know that the elite of Bhubaneswar was very snide about the fact that Naveen Patnaik didn't know the language of his people. But as far as I could tell, it didn't take away from his relationship with them. He wasn't covering up the fact at all, so perhaps – I thought – the junta cared more for honesty than language skills. He couldn't be on the road to becoming chief minister for a third time just by being a famous politician's son.

'Sir, we've come from Delhi to see you,' we said as soon as he came off stage, fawning over him as if he was a rock-star. Naveen beamed and then herded both of us to a corner and gave us our interview. It wasn't really Pulitzer-winning material but he did talk about his reluctance to join any of the two main political coalitions, he also talked about why the people liked him, and about how dumping the BJP was the wisest thing he had done. It was short and it was done standing in the midst of a screaming crowd, but he answered all the questions we had and was very polite. Delhi Newsroom was also thrilled to play up the low-key Pappu's rare interview.

'He's really nice,' we gushed to Purusottam later, like two impressionable schoolgirls. I was very impressed with Patnaik's working of the crowds. It proved how some people were accepted by the masses even though they were completely different from them. Naveen Patnaik shared very little with his constituents – he'd been born into wealth and aristocracy, he had been to the finest schools and universities and he had chosen to be single unlike other politicians who quickly got married and had children. Even now he hardly mingled, not even with the upper crust in town. He was known to be a smoker but hadn't been seen smoking even by his party colleagues. (The rumour was that he sneaked into loos to grab a drag.) And he had no clique in his party, with very few sycophants and hangers-on.

'It's his clean image,' Purusottam explained. 'His party-men are really scared of him. If there is even a single report of a corrupt man in his party, he just kicks him out.' And that seemed to really work. Throughout our travels in his state, from Gopalpur-on-Sea to Puri to Balasore to Baripada, all that people said about their chief minister was that he was a good and honest man who got their work done.

One particular story really impressed me.

We were returning from Kendrapara, when we crossed an Ambassador car with a neon light on the front seat, where Pappu sat. 'He moves around like *that*?' I asked Purusottam.

'Of course, and this is only during election time. But do you know what he does every day?' He paused dramatically before continuing: 'Every morning, whatever the weather, in 40 degrees plus heat, or in the rain, he drives from his home to his secretariat with his window rolled down.'

'Really?'

'Yes, he'll sit in the front seat and he'll keep greeting people, doing namaste to them. He never puts the air-conditioning on.'

That was really brave of him considering how hot it got in Bhubaneswar. I couldn't think of any other politician who would do something like that. I tried to imagine how I'd feel if Shiela Dikshit popped her head out of her open-windowed car and waved at me when I was at a traffic light in Delhi. (I like her anyway so I'd probably have leaned over and given her a peck on the cheek!) 'Wow, Purusottam, that's really cool. People must really like that?'

'They do, they do, the rickshawallah, the local cop, they all see him passing by and he greets everyone.'

My friend Rasheed Kidwai always tells me about the morning ritual that many leaders like Indira Gandhi and others had – of meeting people in the morning. It was a direct contact with the citizenry and they maintained it for that reason, but it is a ritual that's been forgotten in Delhi in these days of paranoid security. Even party-workers can't meet their leaders, forget about common people like us.

But smart Pappu had it all figured out.

'Do you think there's been development, Purusottam? To me, Bhubaneswar looks like a clean, organized capital city.'

'I think he has done good work,' acknowledged Purusottam. The roads were to die for across the state, there was cleanliness all around and even the traffic was more organized.

'I think, the real litmus test was the Saliya Sai slum,' said Naghma. 'Compare that to the dirt of Delhi slums.' It was true. We had gone to the worst part of the city and we hadn't felt disgusted. People were poorer, of course, but they were not living amidst filth and squalor like they did in Delhi. And there definitely wasn't that air of complete decay about the place that so many places in Delhi exuded.

Perhaps the most visible instance of what Naveen Patnaik had done in the city was in the boundary walls of the place. The city's municipal commission had come up with the inspired idea of getting a hundred local artists to paint the walls using local styles like the Patachitra. Some places sported paintings of the traditional border of Sambalpur saris. So flyovers and roads were vibrant with the colours of local art. There was no other place in India, nor any other politician who had the vision to give a platform to local art and beautify their city. It was just evolved thinking. When we spoke to some locals, we realized they were all responding to this change in outlook, whether it was the local rickshawallah, who knew little about art, or the eminent dancer, Aruna Mohanty. 'I can feel the change in the city,' she told us. 'These paintings really gladden my heart.'

Actually, Pappu Patnaik had gladdened *our* hearts.

We had to travel 10,000 kilometres to meet one, but we'd finally met a politician who really made the system work.

15

Bihar and Beyond

Sometimes you don't have to travel very far from a big city to discover pockets of abysmal poverty. Shivgarh village, after all, was just 10 kilometres away from Jhansi. But you have to travel about 300 kilometres from Bhubaneswar to arrive at Sundardih village of Mayurbhanj district.

We hadn't planned to go to Sundardih village. Sampadji had told us about the large tribal population in the state – almost 40 per cent – and suggested we highlight their problems by meeting a firebrand tribal leader called Draupadi Murmu. She'd been a minister in the state government and was now contesting for the Bhartiya Janata Party in Mayurbhanj. When we called her, she said she'd wait for us at a local hotel.

When Naghma and I arrived at the decrepit government hotel in Baripada we were told that Murmu was waiting for us in her room. We went in and found at least five men cramped into a small room watching TV. As there were only two chairs, three of them were sprawled out on the bed.

Initially, I thought that Draupadi Murmu was in a separate room and this room was for her aides. But the men signalled for us to wait there. Most of them went out, and it was only then that I saw a curtained-off area of the room, the dressing area. Draupadi Murmu was in there. Below the knee-length curtain, I could see her adjusting her saree.

As she took her time getting ready, I wondered how women politicians like her maintained their privacy. After all, most aides tend to be male and sometimes they totally call the shots. I work with male colleagues all the time but I still wouldn't be able to get used to having a crowd of them hanging about my room at all times. People like Draupadi Murmu would have to get used to having strange hangers-on, not all of them men of refined sensibilities and etiquette.

But when I met Draupadi Murmu, I felt reassured. Tall and strong, she didn't look suppressed at all. On the contrary, she looked like someone quite capable of thwacking an errant aide with the back of her hand.

'I thought that we could eat lunch here first,' she smiled at us. 'There is nowhere else to eat and the food is good.'

We never needed to be persuaded too much about that.

Over a lunch of mixed vegetables, dal and rice, Draupadi Murmu told us why someone like her — with no family connections — had decided to jump into politics. Because she'd been successful in politics, her two daughters were getting a good education, she explained, but the rest of the children of her community were still neglected. 'You should see the way things are in the villages, there are no drains, no water, nothing,' she said.

Was it possible that Naveen Patnaik was only fixing things in the big cities or on the main connecting roads? Till recently, people like her couldn't even crib about the state government as they were part of the alliance. But now that Naveen Patnaik had gone his own way, the BJP was free to pick fault. But somehow, I felt that Draupadi was not cribbing for the sake of hitting out at Naveen Patnaik.

'Can you show us a village like this?'

'Of course, we don't even have to go far.'

So we followed Draupadi Murmu's Scorpio to the end of Baripada, towards Sundardih, about 10 kilometres away. The roads grew narrower but remained smooth. Orissa's roads couldn't be faulted. We travelled through fields for half an hour before we arrived at a settlement.

Sundardih was a settlement of about forty mud houses. There were a couple of cement houses too, funded by the Indira Awas Yojna – a government scheme that gave below-poverty-line families a sum of 25,500 rupees to build their house – but they were in terrible shape.

'Do you see that hand-pump there?' said Draupadi Murmu pointing to a corner. Two young girls were busy filling buckets from it. 'That's the only water supply to Sundardih,' she said, adding, 'and there's no electricity.'

While Shivgarh had defied every stereotype of poverty, Sundardih reinforced each of them. The mud huts housed skinny, wasted men with bare chests. They all crowded around us, just as in Shivgarh, but the difference was that they weren't smiling. Draupadi left us for a bit to talk to her constituents, the women of the villages. I noticed an electricity tower at the edge of the village. 'How can you not have electricity? There it is.'

'That's not meant for us,' a young man smiled. 'That's for Bhubaneswar.'

How cruel it must be to be able to see a power line from your house and not know when it was going to lead to you? No wonder the old men were crying and not smiling.

I'd spent a half-hour in Shivgarh after we'd switched off the lights from our bus, and I still had welts from the huge mosquito bites on my arms and legs. But no one had brought up water scarcity as a problem in Shivgarh, while here more than a hundred people were fighting over just one hand-pump.

The villagers told me they were really proud of two boys from their village, one who'd completed his technical education and the other who had passed a preliminary exam for a job. There were four or five others among them who were educated till at least higher secondary level, but none of them had a job, so they all worked in the rice fields. I thought, surely these kind of circumstances would be prime fodder for existential angst. 'Doesn't it make you angry?' I asked some young men of Sundardih.

Their smiling faces belied the question. 'No, we're not angry.'

'When you think of people your age in Delhi and in Mumbai, what they have, doesn't that make you think that it's unfair that they have so much more than you?' I persisted.

'No,' said one. 'We know that if we had the same opportunities, we'd also be able to achieve as much if not more.'

I didn't know what to say, really. On one side, there were the starved old villagers who were crying for Draupadi Murmu's help. They didn't see their vote as a form of empowerment. They were simply going through the motions – voting for the party they had always voted for. Too tired even for anger.

The young boys on the other hand were living in the same circumstances, yet they were hopeful. They didn't feel any different, any inferior to men in any part of the country, and they were certainly not cynical about politics and democracy. They were all going to vote even though the politicians had done precious little for them till now.

I couldn't figure it out. 'Don't you feel you're missing out on something? Like TV for instance?'

'No, we watch IPL all the time. We just have to walk two kilometres to get to a place with a TV.'

Like everyone else across the country, from the actor Shah Rukh Khan to the teenagers glued to their iPods in Delhi, these boys too were into the IPL.

Maybe, their aspirations were a little different.

'What do you want to be?'

'We want to be in the army.'

'Why?'

'Because we want to serve our country.'

I hadn't heard anyone say *that* in ages. Not in all my travels as a journalist. Nor even from my colleagues in the Delhi newsroom. So, that day, my conversation with these boys ran as a stand-alone piece on prime-time television.

It was surprises like these that lined our journey; surprises that knocked down all my preconceived notions of the dispirited and disenchanted poor. We didn't always have time to appreciate all of them, of course, but we tried to mark as many as we could.

For instance, when we were driving around Mayurbhanj, Mohammed suddenly called out, 'Guys, look, there's a group of men sitting about watching TV.' It was the middle of the day so it did seem strange to have men do that instead of working in the fields. When we turned around, and went back, we found them watching an Aamir Khan film. There were at least fifty men sitting around the television set. 'Why aren't you working?' we asked.

'How can you work in so much heat?'

That's true. It was more than 45 degrees Celsius. But I, with my clichéd notions of the harsh rural life, would never have imagined that when the temperatures soared and it was too hot to work, the farmers would take a communal break from the fields, to chill at a matinee. Hell, that's what *I've* always wanted to do.

Or even that boys in Jharkhand villages could speak up to six languages. We found that out at Matihana village, near the West Bengal border, where we'd stopped for our show. Several village boys hung around while Naghma and I did our links live. They'd hear me speak in English on air, then speak to Mohammed in Hindi and then answer a call in Bengali.

'How do you speak English so well and yet speak Hindi?' one of them asked.

'I don't know, I was taught when I was young, I guess. What languages do you speak?' I asked him.

'Santhal, Munda, Bangla, Oriya and Hindi,' he said.

'That's amazing, you speak so many languages.'

'Yes, but what I really want to learn is English.'

Being able to speak so many languages would have been appreciated in any school, but his. But the one language that he thought would get him a job, he wasn't being taught.

'Why don't you demand that English be taught in your school from your local MP?' I asked him.

'We've never even *seen* our local MP,' he said and went on to tell me that the TV star Nitish Bhardwaj who had played the role of Lord Krishna in *Mahabharata* had once been elected their MP. They'd been very excited because they thought that he wouldn't be like a typical politician, that he would do more for them. But, he'd remained as elusive as his divine TV persona, never once blessing them with a darshan.

We were so charmed by the boys we agreed to their demand for a tour of our bus. As soon as they entered our server area, one of them said, 'Yes, I know this. This has to be your control room.'

How were they so smart? I wondered if I'd been in their place – going to a state-funded school with no roof, no proper toilet, and teachers perennially absent from class – would I have managed the knowledge they had? Would I have had the vision to dream their fantastic dreams?

In a way, the meeting with the Matihana boys had set our perspective right. We'd had a troubled 24 hours travelling through Maoist country. The first problems had arisen when we were entering Jamshedpur. We weren't expecting to reach before midnight and, by our standards, that wasn't particularly late. It wasn't until we started looking for a dhaba to eat, that we realized that most of them were closed.

'Boss, I think we should just drive on ahead,' Nishant had said. 'It's voting day tomorrow. The stringer told me that there is a red alert tonight.'

'Yeah, but we've got to eat, yaar,' said Naghma. She and I were treating 'red alerts' in the city with the contempt we thought they deserved. Anyone who's a crime reporter will tell you how cops issue such alerts before every significant national day – Independence Day, Republic Day, Diwali, New Year's. It's their way of covering their arse if an untoward incident occurs, so they can say, 'Yes, as you know, we had issued prior warnings of an imminent attack.' It is a standard line and in fact, lots of times, cops even make 'preventive' arrests of old suspects just to get some praise: 'We've caught Jarnail Singh, a desperate criminal who was planning to attack the capital.' (The other thing I've never understood is why the Delhi Police uses the word 'desperate' to describe all criminals. It's almost as if they are forgiving the poor sod for being addicted to a life of crime!)

Seeing our dismissive attitude, Nishant had decided it was better to give in to us than to argue with us. So, we'd stopped at the Mota Line dhaba on the road to Jamshedpur. The lights were on but the charpoys were stood up on their side to block the entrance. The owners, two big Punjabi men – truck drivers who had stayed on to feed the highway hungry – said they could give us dal and roti.

'Why have you blocked the entrance?' we had asked.

'Arrey, these Maoists had sent fliers to shut our shops and boycott the polls,' he said. 'That's why everyone is closed since yesterday but we cannot give in so easily.'

Long live the Punjabis and their bravado, we thought.

But as we got ready to get on our way, the dhaba men had some grim advice for Ganga Singhji. 'Keep the inside lights on while you drive.' And Ganga Singhji had kept his foot firmly on the accelerator all the way to Jamshedpur.

The next day things went fine till early afternoon. It was polling day so we recorded our pieces at various polling stations. We did a recce of the areas in the city that *weren't* handled by the Tatas and then we figured we would wrap up our work by three, in time to set off for Kolkata. The plan was well on track till we met our local Bengali contact.

'What? Travel back today? You must be joking!' he thundered when he heard.

'But, what's wrong?' I asked.

'Haven't you heard? There's been a landmine attack in Ghaatshila. It is very risky.'

Unfortunately, Nishant was quietly listening in.

'But the attack is over, na?' Naghma said.

'Yes, but it is very risky,' he said, his eyes growing big and round. 'The Naxals might try to attack again. It is not safe to travel till tomorrow. They will try to attack the electronic voting machines which will be taken back after polling is over.' According to our contact, there was no other route and by travelling on it we were inviting death.

'But Naxals have never attacked the media, as far as I know, have they?' I tried in vain.

I could see Nishant whispering something to Naghma and her brows furrowing in response. 'Usually, they don't,' said Naghma. 'We'll be travelling in the afternoon not at night. Are you sure it isn't fine?' she asked our contact again.

'No, no, it's not safe. The attack in Ghaatshila took place just now.'

I was desperate to get to Kolkata and it was at least six hours away. The alternative to our plan was to travel at 4am the next morning. I knew that if I woke that early, I would be tired through the day and Kolkata was going to be a busy shoot. Also, by now, we all knew that we weren't always punctual. Some of us had delayed the entire team, sometimes by as much as an hour. It was just too much hassle.

'Look, let me call the superintendent of police and see what he says,' I said because I wasn't willing to accept the threat. I knew the Maoists were too much in love with getting good publicity to actually attack our red bus. Then again, as Naghma had pointed out, they might have planted landmines on the main road and we could be the accidental victims of explosives meant for security forces or polling officials.

'Sir, I'm calling from NDTV,' I said to a very busy SP in the middle of election duty. 'Sir, we have to travel from Jamshedpur to Kolkata by road and we were wondering if it's safe to do so this afternoon, considering the attack on Ghaatshila and everything?'

'Yes, it is safe.'

'So, we can go ahead?'

'Yes.'

I looked at my Bengali contact in triumph.

'What did you expect him to say to a reporter?' the contact said sarcastically. 'He isn't going to admit to the *media* that it is unsafe to travel in his area.'

Naghma looked like she agreed with him.

I didn't like the way this was going. 'Okay, I'll call up the DGP,' I said.

The same routine was repeated.

Again, our contact said, 'Do you think his security is over there? If something happens, if the Naxals kidnap you, local policemen don't even respond to SOS calls.'

Naghma said, 'You know he's right. I remember when we were travelling through the Naxal belt in Bihar and these people came and blocked the road. We kept calling the police for help but they never came. They kept making excuses.'

I knew now that I was alone in wanting to go. If Naghma was convinced that we should stay put, that meant that the team would stay back. I knew that I couldn't do anything about it. I didn't want to go against the wisdom of the entire team. So I just kept cribbing loudly.

'I can't believe that we are giving into this,' I muttered. 'Our contact is a Bengali and Bengalis are always a bit scared,' I kept repeating, forgetting that I was a true-blue Bong myself.

Of course my ill humour finally pissed Naghma off. 'Fine, if you want to go, then let's go. I'm not scared.' I knew that of all the things that Naghma was, she certainly wasn't a coward. And by indirectly implying that she was, I had rubbed her the wrong way. I instantly felt bad and tried to make up. I was actually angry with Nishant for not having the gumption to say what he had himself, instead of whispering to Naghma that I was putting the team's life at risk.

'Okay, guys, we will not go today, we'll go tomorrow morning,' I said finally. 'But everyone has to be in the car by 4am.'

That was the final word.

Till lunchtime, when a new plan was hatched.

🚌

'What if we went by train?' I said.

'The trains leave at night and they'll reach early in the morning,' said the local contact.

'That's perfect,' I said.

Naghma nodded. 'We can sleep on the train and be fresh by the time we reach. The bus can leave early tomorrow morning.'

It seemed a perfect solution and though we were breaking the rules a bit by travelling by train it was to counter a Naxal threat. We felt relaxed, at last, as we dug into our Chinese meal of Hakka noodles and honey chicken. But it wasn't meant to last.

Just half an hour later, Mohammed announced, 'I'll come by road tomorrow morning.'

'What? What are you saying?'

'I don't want to travel by train,' declared Mohammed looking away.

I was so very angry. 'Why didn't you tell us this before, Mohammed, over lunch?' He said nothing, while Naghma and I glared at him. Nishant wasn't around.

'We'd decided this together and we agreed it was fine with everyone,' I said.

'I have too much equipment and I don't want Ganga Singhji to travel alone,' he replied.

For the first time on our trip, we were going to have a slanging match. 'I can't believe you guys are so irresponsible!'

'Nishant will be there with you, I'll just come a little later,' he said.

'No, we cannot shoot without you,' I screamed back. 'You may be very late and then there's no point.'

'Okay, then let's leave now,' Mohammed said.

'Fine,' we replied.

So I immediately gave directions to Ganga Singhji and a shocked Nishant was told to check us out of our hotel. 'I thought we were going by train,' he said.

'No, Mohammed doesn't want to,' I said. 'We will leave by road in 15 minutes.' Naghma and I were on the same page on this, and we didn't want more tantrums from the boys, so we just went and sat in the car. Most of our stuff was already in the car and Ganga Singhji was loading the last pieces on the carrier when Nishant suddenly appeared.

'Please give me my things,' he told Ganga Singhji.

Ganga Singhji looked a little blank.

'What do you mean, Nishant?' asked Naghma.

'Nothing, I'm taking a flight.'

'You are my camera-person, you have to travel with me.'

'I am not going to risk my life.'

'You think my life is not important?' asked Naghma.

'I don't know about you but my parents are waiting for me.'

'You don't think I have parents who are waiting for me?' I couldn't make out whether Naghma was crying. She just seemed really angry.

I threw in my two bits. 'Look, nobody is going to die. The Naxals have never attacked the media. Come on, Nishant, let's go.'

'Who changed their mind? We all agreed to go by train.'

'It's both you boys,' said Naghma. 'First Mohammed kept quiet during lunch and backed out and now you are backing out. Look, if you leave now, I will tell office to send you back to Delhi. There is no point in you joining me anywhere. If you are working with me then you have to come along with me everywhere. You decide,' said Naghma, finally.

Faced with this ultimatum, Nishant came and sat down in the car. Mohammed had kept his peace during this exchange and sat down quietly too. Ganga Singhji revved the car and the bus followed. We started on the single lane road that was going to take us to Kolkata, via Ghaatshila.

The first two hours of the journey were the most stressful as they took us through the vulnerable areas. My bravado started to dissipate once I saw armoured vehicles moving on the road with only security-men peeping through. When I saw the heightened level of security, I knew that Naghma, like me, was feeling guilty and scared. We had browbeaten everyone to take the Naxal route because we wanted to work harder on our Kolkata show.

If anything were to happen to anyone, we'd be fully responsible.

Every time the armoured vehicles passed us by, Mohammed would say, 'Gangaji, please overtake, we do not want to move with them,' while I held my breath. None of us had the guts to say anything. Ganga Singhji drove like a man possessed and we went through the tricky areas in record time. We'd been so stressed, we stopped immediately after we were out of the danger zone, at the Mota Line dhaba.

Naghma and I sat in the car, while the boys got off. 'Look at them,' said Naghma, pointing to them laughing together. 'They've made up with each other again.'

'Yes, but I was very angry with them today,' I said.

We never spoke to the boys again about what had happened that afternoon.

🚌

Kolkata gave us the opportunity to get a much needed break. Naghma took the weekend off and visited her sister's family, the boys enjoyed the pleasures of a big city with good food and booze, and I got to see Sudeep after five weeks.

'Have I lost weight?' I asked him, really hoping that he would say I had.

'You look good,' he replied, sensing it was a trick question.

I knew that weeks of eating fish, prawns and other fresh foods had not made me any thinner. But I indulged myself further with Kolkata's rolls and more seafood at Mocambo. After two nights of joy in the City, we set off for Patna on Sunday morning.

'I'm not working in Patna,' I announced as we set off. 'Naghma is organizing everything in Bihar.' Our road trip was reuniting Naghma with her entire family. After meeting her sister in Kolkata, she was all set to meet her parents in Patna. She wasn't just from the city, she'd also reported extensively on the state. I had only reported on the floods in 2000 and the elections in 2005, so this was just my third visit.

'You know how it is in Bihar,' Naghma warned me. 'It's not going to be like you fixing up to meet Yashodhara Scindia weeks in advance. We'll just have to wait around and take chances.'

Well, we knew some things for sure. One, Lalu Yadav really liked Naghma. So we had a great chance of doing an interview with him. The railway minister always made great copy and his antics always amused everyone so he was a sure bet for us.

Two, there was no dearth of stories in Bihar. Bihar has been this inexplicable, anarchic land for the English media ever since I'd joined journalism. It was the place where you could be sure to see the most heart-rending poverty; a place where poor people were reduced to eating rats because they had nothing else to eat, a place where law and order didn't exist or at least didn't adhere to the norms that existed in other parts of the country. (Which is why, for instance, police punished under-trials by gouging their eyes out.)

For us the story was simple: Had Bihar stopped being India's basket case ever since Nitish Kumar had replaced Lalu Yadav as the chief minister?

Did they now have the same rules and standards that applied to the rest of the country?

I'd also heard that Bihar was finally talking about development and not just caste. It sounded fantastic because for the first time I was hearing people talk of the declining crime rate and an improvement in schools and roads as poll factors in Bihar, instead of just how the Kurmi and the Yadav castes were going to vote.

'Sunetra, you will see,' said a friend from a national daily who'd been the Patna correspondent for many years before moving to Delhi. 'Patna now has roads that can outclass Delhi's.'

Well, they certainly weren't on view entering Patna. Nor did one have to actively look for signboards announcing that one had entered Bihar's borders – after experiencing double-lane delight all through the country, even in unlikely and poor states like Orissa, we suddenly found ourselves slowed down by a road so constricted we wondered if our bus would be able to go through. Only in Bihar was the national highway so narrow that you could reach out and touch the houses and shops that were lined up all along on either side!

One of these houses, along the cramped highway, belonged to the chief minister himself; his mother still lived there. If curious travellers paused to stare at the local landmark, it would have caused an inter-state traffic jam!

No, even when we reached Patna by evening, we couldn't see the change.

'I come here thrice a year so I thought I wouldn't be able to spot it,' said Naghma. 'Do *you* see signs of development?'

I was coming back to Patna for the first time since Nitish Kumar had taken over and no, it had been three years, but I couldn't find any 'Delhi-like' roads. In fact, I could swear that the new flyover at the centre of the city was a little askew. 'People think that we are trying to talk Nitish down, that we are cynical,' said Naghma. 'But I really think a lot of it is hype.'

I thought perhaps I'd notice some change in Bihar when I stepped out in broad daylight and spoke to regular people – not just journalists – but even then I couldn't spot any.

Actually, there *was* something different about my hotel in Patna. The Maurya Hotel (which committed robbery by charging 60 rupees for a bottle of water) had suddenly found female executives to run their lobby! The only people manning the lobby the last time round had been political hangers-on. A couple of the political types still dotted the landscape but they were relatively few, considering it was election season. The young women were clad in red chiffon saris, though I noticed that the same women had been on duty at night and then also the next morning. The hotel now obviously considered it safe to have female employees to greet people, without worrying about them being sexually harassed.

'We could never imagine going out alone, forget about going out with our wives and daughters,' jeweller Sanjay Dayal told me at his shop. He was one of the hundreds who had been a victim of a kidnapping blitz in Bihar. 'Now, I feel totally safe in Patna. We have a social life.'

I found it hard to believe that a man who was taken at gunpoint and then held hostage for a few days before being released after the payment of ransom, could feel safe again. But Sanjay Dayal said that he really did. He told me how earlier, retailers like him were routinely visited by heavies demanding extortion money. This too had completely stopped.

When taxi-drivers, restaurant-owners and sundry others started echoing Sanjay Dayal, I had to believe it; and when I visited Mona cinema, I was completely charmed: the cineplex near Gandhi maidan can compete with any posh cinema complex in Delhi or Mumbai. So it doesn't have multiple screens, so it shows you only a movie at a time, and so it doesn't offer coffee choices like a latté or a mocha, but it looks clean, indeed almost plush. And night shows have made a comeback too. The cineplex manager told us how they were almost going to sell the place because of bad business during Lalu Yadav's regime, but now that people felt safer, they had come back to the movies. For the first time in two decades, families were staying up to watch the late night show!

So, maybe, it didn't matter that most of Patna was still hidden under a layer of dirt. It didn't matter that flyovers were taking too long to build. Sudeep once told me, elections are all about perceptions, and Patna perceived Chief Minister Nitish Kumar to be strong. Patna believed that, like the rest of the country, it was finally on the road to development. The people had given Lalu fifteen years with his mantra for the empowerment of the backward castes; they could certainly give Nitish a few more years for his empowerment of Bihar.

Heady on this high, Nitish spoke with us for just a couple of minutes. He was straightforward and forthcoming but we knew that a trip to Patna wasn't complete without a trip to Lalu's.

🚌

'What are you roaming around in the heat for?' Lalu asked Naghma as soon as he saw her. 'No wonder you have gone dark.' We had gone to see him at the airport. The airport had become the latest media hub for the local and national press; after all Lalu Yadav, Nitish Kumar, Ram Vilas Paswan – all came there in the morning to hop on board their choppers and be flown to far-flung constituencies. It was an opportunity to ask them questions, to counter controversies, to basically get sound bites.

'We've come to cover the elections,' Naghma volunteered.

'Okay, come home in the evening.'

So, we landed up at his home that very evening. We weren't sure whether he'd give us an interview as he'd figured out that things weren't going very well for him that year and it was best to keep the media at arm's length. We had to admit our fascination with Lalu went beyond his losing or winning. He was such a performer on camera, with his howlers and his clever lines, his tufts of ear hair and his comic hair style.

But when we reached him that evening, he was sitting almost alone. I had lots of expectations from his frequently televised home. I'd expected to see cows roaming about freely. I'd expected his wife and former chief minister Rabri Devi to be nipping in and out, fussing over her nine children. But whatever I had expected, I wasn't getting any of it.

Lalu sat quietly with his spittoon and a handful of men in the courtyard of his home. Everyone was subdued as was our expected source of entertainment. Next to him was a large plasma TV, it was switched off now, but we were told it had been on a few minutes ago when we had been beaming live from outside his house.

We sat without speaking for what seemed like ages. Lalu attempted some desultory small talk – how hot it's been, how he feels sunburnt, the dust kicked up by his chopper and the poor people who stand in the heat to meet him. I noticed he was obsessed with his skin and his tan. His cheeks were ruddy but he was obviously careful to not let them darken further in the heat of campaigning.

Then Naghma remarked on how quiet it was and that was all that Lalu needed to explode. The media, according to him, had conspired to paint him and his party, the Rashtriya Janata Dal, in ridicule. He was upset because our exit polls had written him off although he was sure that he was sweeping the polls. I wanted to tell him that the media couldn't be bothered to turn vindictive against someone, least of all Lalu. I wanted to tell him that exit poll results were taken with a bucket of salt even by TV insiders and that, if anything, the media loved him.

But I figured that he didn't really want to hear all that. Lalu Yadav was just in a mood to vent. He said he had stopped putting up the funny-man face for TV cameras – a factor that many read as Lalu's desperation. I don't know about all that. What I do know is that he looked like a man who was down and out and trying to put up a fight. There was nothing funny in what he said.

'You are roaming around in a bus?' he asked Naghma finally. 'Let us see it.' So like many others across the country, Lalu Yadav demanded a tour of the election bus. He walked inside and was impressed. But there was one criticism.

'Don't you have a toilet?'

'No, sir,' I said.

'The bus I have, it has a toilet.' He seemed pleased, but then quickly added: 'After the elections, you should give this bus to me. I'll use it for my own campaigning.'

Maybe a big red bus is what he needed to win back people.

Maybe, just maybe.

16

The Beginning of The End

I'm a great believer in signs. For weeks while we were on the road, we took the bus to the toughest, most distant of places – to villages with bad roads and no power, on roads that that were melting because of the extreme heat, and on roads booby-trapped by the Naxals. We did all this but we still managed to get on air. So when, at the end of the sixth week, we failed to make it on air, I knew it was the beginning of the end.

Before the failure to transmit, it'd been a fantastic day. Instead of shooting our stories, we had recorded them earlier and were moving 500 kilometres from Patna to Lucknow. It was that rare pleasure of travelling without the pressure of deadlines or the stomach-crunching anxiety about hunting stories. We had developed a strange mindset where we were happiest when we were moving. It meant that we were free to just stare out of the window and let our minds wander, lulled by the scratchy remix hits on 25 rupee MP3s. We could nap in the car now, because unlike before, we weren't stressed about having to arrive at a place and immediately delivering a 30-minute show. We knew that if we'd pulled it off for six weeks, we could do it for a couple of weeks more.

The drive from Patna to Lucknow could almost be described as languorous. As soon as we left Patna, we had stopped at a place called Maner. 'Oh my god, this place is really famous for ladoos!' Naghma had said immediately. Even though it was quite early in the morning, there were plenty of sweet shops open, as if hoping to capitalize on their fame.

'Do you think we should get some?' said Naghma hopefully.

Mohammed and I nodded.

'Tell me what you want,' said Ganga Singhji gallantly offering to buy them for us. So, right after breakfast, we helped ourselves to pure-ghee, nut-filled ladoos.

'I've had these before,' I told Naghma chomping into one. 'When I came for the floods in 2000 I wanted to go back with something for Mum and Dad, so Manish Kumar suggested these.' (I was referring to NDTV's main man in Bihar). 'They were truly amazing.'

Immediately I was struck by the fact that I had been to places that other people had barely heard of, let alone visited. I'd been to Maner of Maner Ladoos fame, I'd been to Raghurajpur in Orissa whose paintings were famous across the country, and I'd been to Kondapally to see the beautiful toys they made. If we hadn't travelled by road from Kolkata to Patna, how would I have ever known about the fresh fish they serve you at the government guest house near Tilaiya dam reservoir? I hadn't just bought my mother a Kanjivaram sari, I'd also met the emaciated worker who had made it (earning 4,500 rupees for making three saris over a month). While travelling through Uttar Pradesh, I went to Rampur and discovered what Rampuri chhuris or knives were all about, and why they were becoming extinct.

I was discovering that I could do all this quite comfortably by road. That, although narrow bumpy roads still existed in our country, we found them to be an exception rather than the norm.

🚌

'Please, let's stop for lunch at Varanasi,' said Naghma. Her biggest lament had been that the *Election Express* hadn't covered the beautiful city on the banks of the Ganga. A city that was known for its art, culture and food, a city that was symbolic of secularism in India, a city she'd never been to. We had really tried hard to work it into our schedule but as it went to polls in the first phase, by the time we could reach Varanasi the elections were over. That meant that election stories didn't hold anymore, but there was nothing wrong in stopping for a look around.

'I've heard of this Middle-Eastern restaurant there called Haifa,' said Naghma.

'What, like hummus and fattoush?'

'Apparently.'

That decided it. 'Let's go!'

So while people came from all over the world to seek nirvana and feed their souls in Varanasi, we went to feed our mouths. And sitting there, next to Assi ghat, dipping my tandoori roti styled pita into hummus, I felt pretty near blissed out. But true nirvana came when I took my first sip of thandai...

(Naghma had shown unmistakable signs of aggression when I'd innocently asked, 'What's *thandai*?' 'What do you *mean* by asking me in front of those people, what thandai is?' she had glared at me later. 'I know what it is but I don't know *exactly*, do you know what I mean?' But Naghma felt I'd diminished our credibility by posing the question, disastrously, in front of a few friendly locals. 'I was going to kill you!' she said. No doubt she thought that, sometimes, even the most enlightening journey was not enough to redeem a person. You could take the girl out of the city, but you couldn't take the city, etc.)

That glass of thandai ended up being our last taste of bliss on that trip. When we stopped the bus in Bhadohi, to do the live show, it was as if the show had run out of steam. Both of us, with our faces powdered, rouged and lipsticked, sat waiting to link up to Delhi but, even though the satellite dish on top of the bus was up, all that Delhi received was unending black.

'Sumit, come on, do something! We have to do our show. It has great stories,' we urged him on. Actually we described every show we did like that, but this time Sumit did not reassure us. He kept climbing on top of the bus and adjusting the dish but no matter what he did, it wouldn't work.

'The system has crashed,' he announced finally.

That's it. There was no one to blame, no one to scream at, because the most essential part of live TV, the technology, had inexplicably given up.

'So, how do we go on air?'

'We'll have to get the equipment replaced from Delhi.'

What that basically meant was that not only were we not going to be on air for that day, there was a huge question mark about the next day as well. We broke the news to the Delhi office.

'Hindi has put some other anchor on air for my stories,' said Naghma, looking miserable.

'English has decided to drop the show altogether and carry my stories in a segment in the evening.'

Both of us were a bit shell-shocked by what was happening. We were behaving as if our world was coming to an end because we hadn't gone live from an obscure town called Bhadohi and introduced the world to its carpet industry and its burgeoning crime rate.

The people of Bhadohi didn't really care and no one in Delhi seemed to be bothered, either. We thought our editors would be devastated at being denied their daily dose of their all-time favourite TV show, but it was as if it didn't make any difference.

And we realized that the reason we'd survived so long on the road was because the daily show gave us an outlet for our energies. Even if we had worked like dogs all day, even if it had been a bad day with the heat and no food, when we went on air in the evening it was as if our efforts were showcased. We'd get feedback for almost every show, if not from the editors, then at least from our viewers. And that had made everything well worth it.

Now just one day of being off air, made us start questioning the wisdom and purpose of travelling 500 kilometres a day.

'We have to travel again early morning tomorrow to Rae Bareli to report from there, and we don't even know whether our show will go on air.' For the first time the travel involved seemed just too much of a bother.

After travelling to various minor VIP constituencies, we were in *the* VIP constituency – the pocket borough of Sonia Gandhi. When we arrived at the local government college, it was made emphatically clear to us that we were no longer in some back-of-beyond destination where the media never went. Around ten broadcast vans were lined up to report on the polling trends of this crucial area, NDTV among them.

'What's up, Anant?' Anant Zanane was sweating it out in front of the camera showing the viewer interesting new angles of the Electronic Voting Machine. The cameraman, realizing the urgency of this assignment had done away with the tripod and loaded the heavy camera on his able shoulders, just so that he could swivel more easily from the Rae Bareli voter, to the election agent and then back to a sweating Zanane braving the almost 50 degrees heat and talking about it all – the fierce heat that had kept people away from Rahul Gandhi's constituency of Amethi; the importance of being a Gandhi; and Priyanka Gandhi's emergence as a prime mascot for her mother and brother.

'Let's go have something to eat,' I said to Anant as soon as he'd done his story.

But he said, 'I've had lunch, the Congress guys organized the food.'

The thing about savvy political parties' media management is that they will ensure everything is available to make life simpler for the media. The nice workers of the Congress Party always organized food for everyone. They didn't even bother tracking what the press was saying on air, as who would dare to criticize Sonia Gandhi, anyway?

'I have some fruits in the car, do you want some?' Anant asked. So, even though we were back in familiar territory, we had to resort to the diet of our weeks in exile – fruit and juice. Of course, they went down quite well with Anant's plentifuly supply of stories.

'You know that story we were covering about a PWD engineer's murder?' he asked.

It had been a major story on national TV a few weeks ago. The chief minister had faced criticism because her heavies had got rough with a government engineer for not generating enough funds to celebrate Mayawati's birthday, also marked as a day to give donations to her party, the BSP.

'I got a desperate call from some of her workers,' said Anant. 'They said please, please take off the story – Behenji is giving ma-behen ki gaalis!'

We couldn't stop giggling. Mayawati had taken Dalit and women's empowerment to a new level – the right of a woman to use expletives!

In fact, there is an infamous story about Mayawati and her use of expletives that's been handed down generations of reporters at NDTV. It's now such an old story that the names and details have got a little fuzzy and I'm not going to risk my neck by naming the wrong reporter. But here is how the legend goes – apparently, years ago, when some scandal emerged about Mayawati – there have been so many so again I'm not going to risk naming the wrong one – a reporter was despatched to get Madam's reaction. The reporter happened to be a woman and it was presumably after nine o'clock at night. The reporter landed up at Mayawati's house at Humayun Road in Delhi and asking for Madam, presented her credentials. The assistant went in and soon after the reporter heard a loud voice from the inner room: '*Iss time par aayi hai? Randi hai ya reporter?*' (She's come at this time? Is she a reporter or a whore?'

Another female colleague of mine told me how once Mayawati didn't like the question she asked her at a press conference and admonished her with a '*Chup kar, kameeni!*'

I have to admit though, she always smiles at me sweetly whenever I see her, once even offering me a cold drink (not individually, no). Anant told me stories about her treatment of bureaucrats and there are legendary tales of how she made them do petty and humiliating chores, but a part of me feels a female bonding with her.

It's the same kind of empathy I felt when I walked into Draupadi Murmu's room and realized that her changing room only had a short curtain that ended at her calves, and there were so many men thronging about her. Draupadi Murmu had a quiet strength about her. Perhaps Mayawati deliberately cultivated this crude, cruel image because that's the only way a woman can survive in politics. Perhaps, in adopting a filthy tongue, Mayawati has just tried to subvert a male hegemony that has existed in politics for years.

Then again, perhaps she is just a dirty mouth.

I was very close to a dirty mouth of my own when I realized after returning to Lucknow that the dish problem had not yet been resolved.

'But, they told me that it would be fixed in a couple of hours,' I whined to Sumit.

'It is fixed, we can go live,' he said.

'You call this fixed?' I thundered. 'We cannot move the bus from the hotel and have to do our show from the most boring location. How can you call this fixed?'

Every day, Mohammed, Naghma and I had discussed and debated our backdrop for the show – the statue or the palace? The river or the bridge? Our long deliberations and its results were appreciated far and wide, or at least in the production control room of NDTV office. Now we were reduced to being ordinary reporters, standing in front of a sad road in Lucknow with nothing to show in the backdrop other than the blue streetlights that matched the BSP's colours.

Again, no one missed our superlative backgrounds; no one cared about the fall in standards due to technical snags in our show.

Needless to say, a weekend in Delhi was now a necessity. Engineering was going to spend the two days fixing our equipment. Ganga Singhji, Nishant and Mohammed could hardly contain their excitement at the prospect of going home. They didn't even want to have another meal on the highway because they couldn't wait for home food. Naghma and I pissed them off by insisting that we stop for dinner.

'I don't want to see the people in office,' said Naghma. I knew exactly what she meant. While Nishant couldn't wait to rush to office to regale our co-workers with stories of our misadventures, I felt they were too precious for me to share with all and sundry. For me, the memories of Bhuri, of Hirendra, of the hundred other people I'd met over the last few weeks, couldn't be randomly strewn between commercial breaks or between scripts of APTN and Reuters. They needed a proper introduction, a beginning, a middle and an end. Most of all, these were stories that needed to be given perspective and respect.

I couldn't deal with the vapid 20-second attention spans of TV types, who'd glaze over when I described the amazing aspirations of Sundardih village. Anyway, I didn't know where to begin.

When Sudeep came to pick me up from office that evening I also realized that it would be the first time in two months that I would be saying bye to Naghma. That's when I realized that I didn't really need a reprieve from her. I realized how lucky I'd been to have her as my travelling mate.

'Aren't you happy to be home?' Sudeep asked, feigning hurt. Of course I was, but I just wasn't that excited about city life anymore. I may have craved Mediterranean and Italian food when I was travelling but I was very happy staying in for the weekend, only venturing out to see my parents and a couple of friends. The rest of the time, I regaled Sudeep with my stories. He understood that I had had a life-changing experience and heard me through.

'Where do you hit the road again?' he asked.

'We're going to quickly cover Haryana, Himachal Pradesh, Punjab before we finish again in UP.'

UP, because that was the only accessible place left to cover in the last phase of polling. And UP, because we wanted to finish with Pilibhit – Varun Gandhi's constituency. It was the constituency that most people had known as his mother Maneka Gandhi's constituency till he had changed all that with his Muslim-bashing speech. The *Election Express* had been about voters throughout its journey and perhaps one set of voters that needed their voices heard over the din were the voters of Pilibhit.

🚌

But before that, there was a nasty surprise waiting for us on Monday early morning. Rohtak, our stop in Haryana was less than two hours away so we were leaving from office at eight in the morning. When we got there, we saw our car but no Ganga Singhji. I saw some other drivers hanging around. 'Where's Ganga Singhji?' I asked them.

'Ganga Singh has gone on leave, so I am coming with you.'

The new driver's name was Subhash and we didn't know him. At that point, he could have been the nicest man on earth and we wouldn't have cared.

'Why? Why did Ganga Singhji go?'

'He had some work at home, he's gone to Haldwani.'

Apparently, Ganga Singhji had called up Mohammed and told him that his daughter wasn't well and was suffering from a suspected case of jaundice. He'd rushed to his village in the hills to take care of her and had promised that he'd be back as soon as he could.

'But that's awful!' Naghma and I both felt like crying. It was another sign that things were not going to go well. It had taken so many days to adjust to Ganga Singhji and he really took care of us. How could we ever adjust to a new person?

The new driver was not in an enviable position. Throughout the journey to Rohtak we complained bitterly. I was careful not to hurt Subhash's feelings but Mohammed and Naghma could not contain themselves. They felt that Subhash was a bad driver and his skills weren't a patch on Ganga Singhji's. Then Subhash made the error of switching off the air-conditioning, again getting on everyone's nerves.

'Ganga Singhji would never do that,' said Mohammed. 'He would always keep the car cool for us.'

I was getting a little frantic because even though I understood the problems of having a new person around, I wanted to make the best of what we had. But no one seemed to share my feelings. Then it started raining. Everyone was ready to throw up their hands and start crying. Usually, the boys and Ganga Singhji would dash out and cover the luggage on the carrier with a plastic sheet. Subhash tried to do so too. But when the vehicle was moving against the hard, wind-enhanced rain, the plastic came undone.

'Didn't you do it properly?' I asked Subhash.

'I did,' he said, making it very clear that he wasn't going to risk getting wet by trying to stop and fix it. 'It's raining so hard that it fell off.'

None of us said it but we all thought, 'This wouldn't have happened if Ganga Singhji were around.' That evening, all our clothes had to be put out to dry in the hotel because they'd got royally soaked in the downpour.

The problem wasn't just with Subhash's driving skills – which, Naghma insisted, were worse than Appu Ghar rides – it was also his attitude. Ganga Singhji was a people's person and even though we used to have problems with his high-handed behaviour with the locals, he used to keep all of us in good cheer with his smiling face. Subhash didn't look too happy being out on this trip with us. He dragged his feet on everything and lacked Ganga Singhji's initiative. He also made no secret of the fact that he would much rather have been in Delhi.

When Ganga Singhji called one evening, Subhash said to him, 'Why have you gone and left me with this lot?'

The team was equally frank, saying, 'Please, please, please come back,' to Ganga Singhji. Ganga Singhji promised that he would be back for the last leg of our journey, towards Pilibhit, but he never came. Ganga Singhji had decided that his last journey across the country, from Dausa to Daman and from Kasargod to Kanchipuram to Konark had been the ideal time to call it quits.

We learnt that he had put in his papers and had asked for an early retirement.

There was no early retirement for us, unfortunately. And even though we were only 80 kilometres away from home, the scope for surprise was undiminished.

We'd just finished filming with one of the youngest MPs in parliament. Rohtak was Deepender Hooda's territory and we'd gone to find out how the shy-looking boy in parliament, (and the first politician I'd met who was younger than me) did in the rough parts of Rohtak. It was bound to be easy for him as his father was the chief minister of the state. But it is always fun also to watch a preppy from an American school trying to connect with his constituency.

'What's your favourite line to the people?' I asked Deepender.

'I tell them that my exams are coming, so if they think I've not worked hard, then they should fail me, otherwise they should give me really high marks and make me come first.' Playing the innocent schoolboy obviously worked for Deepender, but then we wanted to see what perhaps wasn't working for a rich state like Haryana.

'We have a strange custom here in Haryana,' said our contact. 'Here girls don't vote till they are married.'

'What?'

'It's true, it's true, you can come with me now to the girls' college and ask.'

It seemed a little strange because just a short while ago, I'd asked Deepender what he was doing about the high rates of female foeticide in his state And he'd brushed me off by saying, 'Yes, it is a major problem and we need help from the media, from people like you, to help change the mindset.'

Just a bunch of glib words which actually didn't mean anything; words that airbrushed the reality that so many unborn girls had been killed. Men from Haryana villages now had to run to states across the country to find brides.

So we went to the post-graduate college and because it was examination time, we found lots of young women and some men around the place. I thought it was an encouraging sign to see so many women over there. If their parents could let them out to study, surely, they would allow them to vote?

I went up to the first group of women and they all seemed nervous and unsure, especially after spotting the two big cameras with me. I asked Mohammed and Nishant to wait while I broke the ice a little.

'Hi, what are you guys studying for?' I asked.

They told me they were about to take an exam for the Masters of Politicial Science degree.

'Do you guys vote?' I expected them to nod shyly. Only one of them spoke up, 'I do,' she said, chirpily, then added, 'for my grandmother.'

She explained that her grandmom was too old so she'd accompany her to cast her vote.

'What about you guys?'

They all shook their heads.

It was so shocking that I didn't want to talk to them any longer without having it on film. Once Nishant and Mohammed were filming again, I asked them why. They were very calm about it. Even though they were all post-graduate students, they didn't seem to think there was anything amiss about them not having the sanction to vote.

'In our society, we do that after we get married.'

'Why?'

They giggled.

'Don't you want to vote?'

They all nodded. One of them explained, 'See, our parents think that there's no point getting our voter's card made because we'll have to get it changed after we get married, so they leave it for once we are married.'

'Why can't you get the cards made yourself?'

They all smiled.

'Did any of you have fights at home over this?'

This idea also seemed highly amusing to them. One of the girls was married and she confirmed that she only started voting after she got married.

'Did you get married *because* you wanted to vote?' I asked, sending her into a fit of giggles.

Naghma and I spoke to lots of women on campus and they all said the same thing. We wished that we could have gone to their homes and asked their parents why it was like this or even asked the sarpanch, but we really didn't have the time to pursue it like a story. All that we established was that most of the women in this college, or at least the thiry-odd we spoke to, had no hopes of voting before they got married. They didn't look particularly harassed or suppressed but they were discouraged from exercising a right that most women in the country were taking for granted.

The strange thing was that I couldn't understand how it must have been living there in the 80's when Rajiv Gandhi reduced the voting age to eighteen. Did they just assume that Gandhi was only talking about men? In a way, the whole fuss about the youth vote was like a myth in this part of the world.

That's why I really wanted to meet Shruti Chowdhary, the Congress candidate from Bhiwani. She was young and a first-timer in politics, but was that only possible in Haryana because she came from an established political family?

I will never know because Shruti Chowdhary's chopper developed a technical snag and she couldn't make it to her appointment with me.

'I saw your show,' Deepender called me later – however busy politicians are and however big they become, they make sure they get to see and read every bit of media they occupy. 'The girls in that college...' he said. 'It was in a way something I never knew.'

The college was just a few kilometres from his home and I found it strange that savvy politicians like him didn't even realize they were missing a vote-bank. If it had been anybody other than Deepender, I would have thought they were lying; that they had chosen not to pursue the young single women's vote-bank, because they didn't want to upset their families.

'You must do something about this,' I told Deepender, rather naively, in my save-the-world way.

'I think I will, you know,' he said, and we left it at that.

My office found the story a little incredible, actually. It wasn't the kind of thing you left hanging in the air, or did in an hour – like we had to on the *Election Express*. The story needed to be pursued in a more in-depth way. I wanted to ask the Election Commission if it knew what was happening under its nose. I wanted to find out if there was anything it could do. After all, here we were as a country, celebrating powerful women like Sonia Gandhi, Mayawati and Jayalalitha.

And here they were in Rohtak, studying for MAs and not voting.

We'd now been through Rohtak, Bhiwani, Shimla and Anantpur Sahib in Punjab, and were looking for a piece to wrap up our show in Chandigarh. 'You know whom we should meet?' said Naghma. 'We should meet Fiza.'

Of course. Fiza could be our case study about the role of women in Haryana politics – a government lawyer who had made the mistake of falling in love with Haryana minister Chander Mohan. Both of them had changed their religion so that Chander could legally marry a second time. Chander became Chand and Anuradha became Fiza. They were featured in the news for many days in various romantic poses before Chand returned to his first wife, leaving Fiza in the lurch. On the face of it, the story was a steamy affair that had nothing to do with the *Election Express*. But Naghma and I were just curious to meet Fiza and we found our excuse in the little fact that Fiza was campaigning against Chander Mohan's political family in the elections.

Could a spurned woman create a dent in politics?

We would find out.

Getting in contact with her did not prove difficult. She'd provided ample entertainment to local TV channels by first presenting public displays of affection, then playing the outraged jilted lover, complete with all the theatre of threatening suicide in front of the cameras.

'She's not picking her phone,' I told a journalist friend of mine who had given her number to us.

'Don't worry, just go there, she's lost her job so she's always at home.'

So we landed up in the housing colony in Panchkula where she lived, at about 3:30 in the afternoon. Once there, it wasn't difficult finding her house as neighbours directed us right to the door with the words, 'What has she done now?' Some of them even lined up on their balconies, fully expecting some fresh drama to take place. Outside the double storeyed house, we rang the door of the ground floor portion. A maid came out.

'Is Fiza in?'

'I don't know.'

'Where is she?'

'She lives upstairs but I don't know if she is there now.' Fiza hadn't answered our calls till then. We knew we were being terribly intrusive but since we'd come so far, we made our way upstairs, and rang her bell. No response. We rang it again but there was still no answer. We proceeded to knock on her doors. 'Her secretary also told me that she must be at home,' I said, collapsing wearily against her balcony wall, as her neighbours ogled.

'Let's go,' said Naghma. 'She's not opening the door. She probably doesn't want to speak to us.'

Disappointed, we were making our way back to the car, when I pressed redial on my phone again. 'Hello?' a sleepy voice answered. Saying a silent word of thanks, I explained who I was and why we'd come to see her. She asked us to come up to her floor and wait.

It took ten minutes for her maid to open the door.

When Fiza finally walked in, I noticed her face was swollen, as though she had been sleeping for a long time. She was dressed in low slung jeans and a fitted top. When she bent her jeans went lower still and I remembered thinking how different she was from other government lawyers I had seen. It wasn't that she was just attractive, she was also incredibly aware of it. As soon as she saw me she pulled me by the hand. 'I want to show you my house,' she said, pointing to an unkempt living room. 'That is my bedroom and here's where I work out.' Her treadmill was positioned bang in the middle of her room. I found it a little strange that she was keen to show me her house. It was like she suddenly had a girlfriend over – which I obviously was not. I felt bad that I was part of the hack-pack, feeding off her heartbreak.

'Where should we have the interview?' I asked Fiza.

'We can do it either here, or, downstairs, in my ground floor house.'

'Haven't I told you not to leave clothes around?' Fiza turned to reprimand the maid, who'd opened the door initially. It was then that I realized her maid actually worked in the portion downstairs, where her mother stayed. I imagined how the neighbours would be giving them grief; and that while Fiza didn't care, her mother probably found it easier to disown her own daughter, at least in front of outsiders. Her mother didn't come out at all during our visit but we could hear the maid speaking to someone inside.

'Just wait here for a bit while I fix my face.'

When Fiza came back, she was ready with full studio make-up on but she hadn't changed out of her low slung jeans and tight t-shirt. 'What will you ask me?' she said, giving last minute touches to her straight shoulder-length hair.

'Just about your campaign in the elections,' I said quickly. I didn't have to tell her that actually. Ever since Fiza had been left by her husband of a few weeks – one of the most powerful men in the state, the former chief minister Bhajan Lal's son – she only spoke of one thing. It was the same thing she repeated at election rallies as well: How Chander Mohan once loved her passionately, which she proved by showing his text messages, and how his family had now taken him back to his first wife. Her only political point was that people should vote against Chander Mohan and his brother Kuldeep Bishnoi for this breach of faith. So their opponents paraded her about, almost like a circus exhibit, for entertainment value.

'He used to say "Fiza, I love you, I can't live without you". See, see, it's right here,' she said, showing me her mobile phone which had these messages in English. The messages were full of intimate terms of endearment. Fiza had shown these to the media freely. Because she asked, I looked at the messages but I didn't want the camera to record them.

It wasn't fun to see a woman disintegrating in front of the whole world; it was just sad.

17

The Bus Stops Here

'Is there a nice hotel in Moradabad?'

'Madam, how nice a hotel do you want?' asked our stringer, Bhishm Singh. 'We have five-star hotels here.'

A five-star hotel in Moradabad? Now that was a novelty.

But, having learnt from previous experience, we weren't willing to take his word for it. After all, the owner of a very nice hotel in Bhubaneswar had promised to fix us up in a comfortable place in Balasore. We thought, being the owner of a nice establishment, he knew what he was talking about. But on entering the room in Balasore we'd realized that we could have done very well without its 'five-star' embellishments. There were pink velvet curtains matched with a mouldy velvet bedspread and they got to me to such an extent that I was gnashing my teeth all night long. The luxury loo boasted a red commode and sink – both of them stained.

Bhishm Singh, though, proved to be a man of his word. Moradabad's luxury hotel could be spotted from miles away from the highway. It was like a beautiful Mughal palace that rose like a gleaming white mirage amidst Moradabad's dirt and dust. As we drew up to its glassy interiors, we realized that the inner decor lived up to its flashy exterior. The lobby was vast and shiny with women receptionists in western suits. 'How can there be a place like this in Moradabad?' I asked Naghma. 'I don't think people come here to holiday.'

'It's for the NRIs and businessmen, I think,' she said. 'Remember, this is the centre of the brass business.' Well, thank god for that, because by then, our tolerance for dodgy hotels was running thin. Yes, the Moradabad hotel was a bit over-the-top. Yes, the chandeliers everywhere made its decor look archaic and yes, it was spooky to get off the elevator and walk into a floor that was completely unlit, perhaps to save electricity. But the fact that the sheets were clean and there was no trace of velvet made us sleep well enough to regain the strength to tackle the rest of our journey.

The remainder of our journey had a few changes. Subhash, like Ganga Singhji, also jumped ship. Of course, this didn't create as much unhappiness, as none of us had warmed to him. When he realized that Ganga Singhji wasn't coming back, he begged office to replace him and in his place, we got the silent but stable Baby John, who, much to the amusement of everybody else, I insisted on calling Babyji.

Babyji was low-profile and with his deft driving, ensured that we all had nothing to complain about. Anyway, we were also a little miffed with Ganga Singhji leaving us midway and not coming back, so we eased up on the incessant comparisons with him.

'Why did he have to lie to us that he was going only for a short while?' Naghma and I would say to each other now and then. But we also realized that he had done the hardest part of the journey, covering thousands of kilometres in the hottest parts of the country. Just for that, we figured, we really ought to cut him some slack.

In Moradabad of course, the question was whether the city was going to cut Azharuddin some slack. The former Indian cricket captain was going to contest from Moradabad for the very first time, having joined the Congress Party only a couple of months before. The seat was with the Samajwadi Party and the Congress Party hoped that Azhar's status as a Muslim would win over the sizeable minority community and his position as a prominent cricketer would win over other communities. That's why, when we were entering our hotel, we saw a Congress fixer showing the Delhi Jama Masjid's Imam Bukhari the way. He stopped when he saw us:

'Ah, the media,' the Imam said. 'How do you think Azhar is doing?'

It was a classic situation. A highly important person was asking *my* analysis of an important political situation. He and his posse looked expectantly at me. They were waiting for pearls of wisdom to drop from my mouth, and I was sweating under the glare and the pressure.

'Umm, it depends really,' (the classic buying-time strategy). 'We've only just arrived and from the sample we've spoken to it can go either way... What do *you* think?'

That was a masterstroke. I hadn't committed myself to anything, not giving away my ignorance or inability to analyse and also flattered the other person by pretending to be interested in what they had to say.

'We are just trying our best,' he said, smiling. 'We have come to meet people in Moradabad.' In other words, to endorse Mohammed Azharuddin. I knew that the Imam Bukhari did endorse various candidates in Delhi, which is why he was so politicised but I didn't know that his influence spread to other parts of the country.

'Do you think he is effective?' I asked Naghma later. 'I mean will people vote for Azhar just because of the Imam?'

'I think it's more of a symbolic gesture,' she said.

The next day when we went to one of Azharuddin's meetings, we realized just why he needed all the symbolic gestures he could get. Azhar and his sons were coming to offer their prayers at the local mosque and although it wasn't a campaign appointment, officially speaking, everything always turned into one so close to elections. Congress workers were distributing party flags and masks among the local children. Everyone had gathered there to catch a glimpse of the former cricket star and local party-workers were out in full strength, all offering to get us a word with the candidate.

'Last time, Sangeeta Bijlani had also come,' they told us, referring to Azhar's wife, a former model and actress. 'You should have seen the kind of crowds that were there *that* time.'

I could imagine. Sangeeta Bijlani stepping out onto the dusty streets of Moradabad in her designer sunglasses and shiny long hair was no less a sight than a chopper landing in far-flung villages.

They both pulled crowds but could they pull votes?

The Samajwadi Party which had won the last three times was so uncomfortable by his star power, they were trying to make Azhar's second marriage to Bijlani an issue, which perhaps even they knew, hardly mattered to anyone. In speech after speech, they carped on about how he'd left his first wife to marry Bijlani, how he was accused of fixing matches which is why he had to stop playing, etc., but when we stood outside that mosque that day, this really didn't seem to matter to anyone. They all seemed completely taken by him, even though when he spoke to the people, perched on top of his SUV, we couldn't understand a word of what he said. Public speaking was definitely one skill that the Congress was not counting on from Azhar.

Then again, the Samajwadi Party's number 1 leader also had a problem with that, and it had never held *him* back!

We finally got our interview.

Azharuddin spoke to us with his two sons in tow, and all he spoke about was how much he loved Moradabad. 'I am building an emotional bond with the place,' he said.

When we asked him about all the nasty things his rivals were saying, he replied, 'They will say all that they have to say but it's the people who matter.'

If he really believed that, why hadn't he brought up the issue of polio in his speeches? After all, the World Health Organization was calling Moradabad the polio capital of the world. While the disease had been more or less eliminated from most parts of the globe, Moradabad had the dubious distinction of still reporting cases. Why? Because of dodgy vaccines and the dirt. Both furthered the spread of the water-borne virus.

Two doctors, Dr Vineet Gupta and Dr Atul Mehrotra told me that if Azhar and other politicians really cared, they would ensure the polio campaign was so successful that the disease was actually eradicated from the city. Then again, if the people really mattered, wouldn't he have promised to do something for the brass workers of the city who were reeling under recession? They were the reason why that shiny hotel had sprung up in the first place and why buying agents from Walmart and other department stores were lining up in Moradabad, generating valuable resources. But the politicians didn't care to improve their condition, and so when the results came out, it seemed that the voter had such limited expectations, they didn't much care about all these things either.

They tossed out the Samajwadi Party and voted for Azharuddin to be captain of their constituency.

I didn't know what lesson to take from that victory. Did the voters of Moradabad actually see an agent of change in Azharuddin? Or were they so sick of the Samajwadi Party's performance that they decided to toss them out after three successive elections and give their votes to the only other opponent, a there-is-no-alternative (TINA) candidate, Azharuddin. Or was Moradabad, just another instance of what was happening across the country – a vote for the Congress and the UPA to come back to power?

If the people of Moradabad were starved for real issues, the problem was heightened a hundred-fold in nearby Rampur. The story of development and whether the government had done any work in the area was buried under a misogynistic fight. Actress Jaya Prada was supposed to be fighting a battle against former royal Begum Noor Bano but she was actually fighting a sexist attack from her own party-men.

The Samajwadi Party heavyweight Azam Khan was really pissed off because he thought he was more precious to the party than some southern star who he had helped to win in 2004. But the party didn't agree, so Azam Khan hit where it hurt the most – he attacked Jaya Prada's modesty.

'Look, she's just famous for her Anarkali dance,' he told us, not even blinking about saying derogatory things about a woman to two women reporters. 'I haven't watched her dance but I heard that she's really good at it. So she should just stick to doing that.'

'Don't you think you are being hurtful by saying things like that? Don't you think you are taking this fight to a really low level?'

'Hurtful? She's an actress, she can look hurt whenever she wants to,' he said. Azam Khan did not just threaten with low barbs like this. He also threatened to wean off Muslim voters from the Samajwadi Party. I couldn't fathom how the Muslims could feel all cuddly towards a man who spoke so derogatorily about women. But, obviously, Azam Khan believed it boosted his macho image.

The rumour doing the rounds was that he was surreptitiously helping the Congress candidate. Just how, we only got to know when we went to meet Jaya Prada.

Why would someone like Jaya Prada want to drag herself through the dirt of politics? I couldn't get that question out of my head. It has to say something about life in Andhra Pradesh that former film stars and cricketers, who were surely flush with funds, would still want to drag themselves through the grime of heartland politics. Even if Jaya Prada didn't spend all her time in Rampur listening to the barbs of people like

Azam Khan, surely even a couple of months of such insults were too much for any normal person?

🚌

'You know what they are doing, right?' said Jaya Prada to us, as she sat surrounded by a crowd of her aides and supporters, all male. 'They are distributing nude morphed pictures of me. And those morphed pictures have come straight from Noor Mahal.'

As she said this, Jaya Prada broke down. Her aides gawked, perhaps understanding only key bits from her conversation with me in English. But they all had no problems understanding the pictures that I was shown later. They showed her in a shower cap, looking stunned at being caught in that position.

Her supporters claimed the pictures were morphed. But how would they explain the concept of morphed pictures to Rampur constituents? Her constituents were so conservative, that every time she went outdoors to meet them she had to ensure her head was covered. Azam Khan called her tears theatrics but standing there, while she quietly sobbed in the middle of her uncaring, unsympathetic male entourage, I couldn't stop myself from reaching out and holding her hand. As soon as I did that, she embraced me, holding me as she wept. I've always been careful to maintain the distance between interviewer and interviewee, reporter and politician, but that afternoon, I understood the cost that women have to pay to take up public life.

They say that in India no one cares about the personal life of a politician, but that statement should be amended – no one cares about the personal life of *male* politicians, how many mistresses they have, who they are going out with, how they treat their family.

When it comes to women, however, it's all fair game. Azam Khan did not attack Jaya Prada about her failure to increase school enrolment rates, or about her failure to start development projects. He just used sly innuendo, talking about her close association with Amar Singh, about her dancing skills, and her so-called 'theatrics'.

In a way, it kind of illustrated to me, just how much out-of-step these politicians were with the voters of this country. Voters like the never-seen-electricity villagers in their own state's Shivgarh who only wanted power so that their children could study in the evening. Voters like the tribal children of Jharkhand who spoke six languages but wanted to study English. Voters like the young men of tribal Orissa who believed in the idea of India, who believed that their leaders were working to improve their lives.

Voters like Mohammed Asif who hung around with us the entire day because he was unemployed and he truly believed that if he endeared himself to us, we would help him get a job. Though that's not what he said when he first met us. 'I can take you to Jaya Prada,' had been his opening bait at the railway crossing at the entrance of Rampur. When we'd asked who he was, he said that he worked with her and he'd been despatched especially to meet the media and guide them to her. We'd believed him, and let him ride with us, but it was only when we finished interviewing her and he still hung around, that we figured he wanted something else.

'I'm doing my BSc from Jamia University,' said Asif. 'My home is in Tanda but my father lives there with my stepmother. They've got a room for me over there but they'd be relieved if I found a job for myself. Didi, can't I work with you all?'

His plea was to Naghma who, of the two of us, appeared more sympathetic to his tale. I knew that I had no career opportunities to offer him, and virtually no contacts either. But Naghma really wanted to help him. And Asif, seeing that willingness in her eyes, was not letting go of us. He came with us when we went to report a political clash between the Samajwadi Party and local goons, he came with us to look for artisans who made Rampur chhuris, and he took us to sample some Nawabi cuisine. Over the delectable 15-rupees-a-plate kebabs, Asif tried to draw us to his constituency:

'Why don't you come to Tanda? I can show you around there as well.' It wasn't a bad idea and if we couldn't help Asif get a job, then the least we could do was to tell people about where he came from. There'd be so many other young people in Tanda like Asif, I was sure, who were dying to get out, who were willing to do anything to get a job. But we were pressed for time. We only had time to make quick visits to Badaun and Uttaranchal before our last stop on May 13.

Pilibhit. The constituency in Uttar Pradesh had dominated headlines ever since we'd left Delhi, two months ago, in March. The place from where BJP's un-charismatic youth icon Varun Gandhi was caught on camera threatening to cut off the arms of the Muslim community if they dared touch Hindus. Of course, he hadn't used the word 'Muslims', preferring the street lingo instead. Since then, he'd been charged under the National Security Act; had claimed that the video evidence was false; had gone to jail; had succeeded in dividing his party, the BJP, along the lines of those who supported him and those who did not; and now had come out of jail to campaign again.

Through all these headline-making events, we were busy covering other parts of the country where Varun Gandhi's voice did not reach. We wanted to believe that his voice didn't matter in diversity-drenched majority parts of the country, but we couldn't make the assumption until we went to Pilibhit ourselves.

It was the last morning of our *Election Express* journey, the last phase of polls. I hadn't slept at all, trying to imagine what my life would be like after 7.30pm that day. I could feel an existential emptiness in my heart because I knew that the last two months had been the biggest, most assiduous assignment I'd ever faced.

Everyday I'd stood up to the journalistic test of being only as good as my last story. But after today, would I be content to go back to my old beat, running between the Congress office and Parliament? Would I feel fulfilled sitting in studio instead of jumping off the bus daily, stepping into a new town and a fresh set of stories? I knew I'd be happy to see my family but would I get bored sleeping on the same bed every day, especially now that I'd got used to the unexpected? I knew that the travelling had generated unlimited supplies of adrenaline in my system; it had worked to remove all traces of fatigue from my body, and I was now addicted to it. Would the lack of travel leave me craving my next hit? What could *possibly* be a good follow-up act to this?

🚌

If we had thought that meeting people in Pilibhit would be our finish with a flourish, we were totally mistaken. When we stopped to speak to villagers just outside the town, they said things that would have made liberal India cringe: 'Varun Gandhi is our hero.'

'Why?'

'Because people now know Pilibhit. He has made Pilibhit famous.'

'We will all vote for Varun Gandhi.'

'Varun Gandhi has done something for us.'

This wasn't just a handful of people speaking. We got this reaction from young and old, and from women as well. And when we went to Muslim dominated parts of town, they first abused us for making Varun Gandhi a hero, and then they shouted, 'Why don't people listen to *us*? Why don't they listen to what *we* have to say?'

They were so upset at being drowned out by Varun Gandhi's diatribe, they got aggressive and started banging on our windows. 'Today, you'll have to listen to us,' they screamed, scaring us a bit. 'We will not let you get away,' said one man, trying to snatch away our car keys. Naghma and I stumbled out of the car, trying to explain our point of view but it is a bit difficult being heard when you have twenty people trying to shout you down, assuming you are from the enemy camp. The community here obviously felt so alienated from the rest of the country, they just assumed that they had to be heard by force.

'Listen to me,' screamed Naghma, amazing me by how strong and loud she could sound. 'Listen to me! I know what you're saying because I am a Muslim too.' Everyone was a bit stunned. They didn't look apologetic but they toned down their aggression a bit. As Naghma talked it out with them, I felt really sad because it'd been the first time in our two months of touring India that she'd been forced to state her religious identity. She'd been forced to use it because nothing else would have calmed the crowds.

Those angry young men didn't care that we'd spoken to every group across the country, not just headline-makers like Varun Gandhi. They didn't care that we'd come to their colony to speak to them. They were just paranoid that being from the national media, we'd only give voice to the majority. Naghma's loud proclamation stunned them into their senses a bit, and they let us go after we recorded their statements.

We wondered whether Varun Gandhi would talk to us. He hadn't spoken to the media for a very long time. With a legal battle on his hands, that's what his lawyers had advised him. But you never knew with him, so broadcast vans stood lined up along his guest-house all day. They were all waiting for him to break his silence, or witness some last-minute theatrics on Pilibhit's polling day.

Our bus pulled up there too, drawing envious glances from all the other networks.

'I cannot believe that you've spent two months in this,' said Randeep, my colleague at NDTV who was on the Varun Gandhi beat. He had climbed into the bus and was sprawled out on a seat along with a couple of other reporters from Delhi.

'I know, and our last day of the journey is with Varun Gandhi,' I said. 'Why won't he speak to us, Randeep?'

'You can try,' he said. 'Maybe, you'll be as lucky as that other guy.' Randeep winked at me. The other guy was a TV reporter who'd finally managed to steal some time with Varun Gandhi. The story goes that the reporter was just warming up to ask political questions when Varun said, out of nowhere, 'You know the other day, I was sitting on the beach.' The reporter was a little surprised and wondered where this was going.

'I was sitting there and reading this book and I was truly happy.'

The reporter looked at Varun, expecting him to finish his story. But after a few minutes, he realized that *was* the story. Varun was lost in some kind of reverie of his own and the reporter came back, flummoxed.

We'd all giggled over chai and biscuits as the reporter had tried to describe Varun's expression.

We didn't mind even such a meeting with Varun Gandhi, so we really put in several requests with his aides. Alas, there was no response. So when the last show of *Election Express* went on air, it projected Pilibhit without the infamous Varun Gandhi. It had stories of his uncle and Congress candidate, it had stories of the flute makers of the city, and it had a story about the Muslim community, but it didn't have any interview with the man who'd made Pilibhit *the* constituency that election. I also did a closing piece on the crew of the *Election Express*. It featured Mohammed, Nishant, Sumit, drivers Jiggy and Thomas and Babyji.

When the credits rolled for the last time on the *Election Express* we were all there in front of the camera, thumping each other on the back – the journey was over, we were going home to life as usual.

'Listen, Varun Gandhi's meeting some aides inside,' Randeep called to inform us. 'Why don't you guys go in?'

Our show was over, and really, we had no business to meet him anymore but we were still curious to meet Varun Gandhi. So Naghma and I sneaked in. Unlike the other reporters, we hadn't been camping there for days and his guards didn't recognize us so we weren't stopped. He was sitting in the front lawns of the guest-house, addressing his workers. At regular intervals, the assembled throng would go, 'Jai Shri Ram!'

Naghma and I went up to him. He was in his trademark bright yellow Fabindia kurta.

'Hi,' he said, as soon as he saw us. 'I'm not speaking to the media.'

'We know, but we just thought we'd talk to you before we left.'

'Okay, go in and wait for five minutes.'

We did as we were told, waiting in a living room with no furniture except a bed that served as a sofa and a couple of plastic chairs. There were a few other people waiting there for him as well.

Varun Gandhi walked into the room a short while later. 'Please give me a few minutes,' he said indicating to the others to leave.

'I don't know whether you've watched the *Election Express...*' I began by way of introduction when he cut me short –

'I haven't watched any TV, I've been busy with my campaign.'

'Well, from what I hear, you've been on TV a lot.'

'I don't know, I haven't had the time to watch,' he said. 'You know Margaret Thatcher, once gave me some great advice.'

We looked impressed so he explained, 'I once met her and when she spoke to me, she told me she doesn't read the papers so she doesn't know what they write about her.'

We didn't really know what to say to that.

'So there's been a good turnout today. 61 per cent, I think,' I said, trying to change the subject, 'Do you think it's because of you?'

'Yes, of course.' He went on to tell us how he had managed to mobilize the entire BJP cadre in Uttar Pradesh. He felt that he could be credited with the BJP's change in fortune in the state.

'But don't you regret saying what you did?'

'I was misquoted.'

'But we all heard it.'

'The tape was edited.'

'So you're not a Muslim-basher? You did not call them Katwas?'

'No, I did not. I said that votes would be "cut" and they edited it to sound like "Katwa".'

There was actually no point to that. We had all heard the tapes and it didn't sound edited at all.

The Election Commission had also not found it to be edited but the 29-year-old man wasn't about to confess to us. Even if he did, there was no camera. 'You know, when I think about those times, it's like I wasn't even there, it was somebody else.'

'Was it like an out-of-body experience for you?' I asked.

'No, no,' he said. 'An out-of-body experience was when I was 19 and the girl I was seeing, was cheating on me.'

'So what do you want to do now?' asked Naghma.

'I really want to enjoy all kinds of experiences – love, life, sex, everything; I really want to live my life.'

'You're 29, surely you have your whole life to do that?'

'Oh, don't get me wrong,' he quickly said, 'I've led a Byronic existence till now. I just want to meet people and have a full life.'

And then came something familiar. 'The other day, I was in my car and I thought of my last holiday,' he said, and our antennae went up. 'I thought of the time that I was last on a beach and I was reading. I was reading a kinky book by Murakami and I was really, really happy.'

I was adamant that I wouldn't be thrown off this time.. 'Were you thinking about it because you were happy like that again?'

'No, I was just thinking that I'll never be happy like that again.'

After about half an hour of this strange exchange, we came out and headed for our last night halt in a hotel in Bareilly. Naghma and I were both quiet. I thought like me, she too was overwhelmed by the end of our journey, by the type of people we'd met by all that we had seen. Then suddenly she said, 'Listen, the book that Varun was talking about, the one by Murakami,' I looked towards her, 'I have that book and there's nothing kinky about it. Why did he say that?'

Who knew? Like many other things on our journey, it would remain one other mystery that we had stumbled on.

Epilogue

January 2010

The turn of the year was always terrible for news flow and I was bored. 'Guess what?' Naghma sidled up and whispered in my ear as I sat in my corner of the newsroom in front my computer. I perked up hoping it was some kind of salacious gossip – confirmation, maybe, that two of our *married* colleagues really were having it off; perhaps the bosses were bumping someone off the prime-time slot, maybe she had access to one of those slanging-match emails that I hadn't seen – I didn't care what it was as long as it was entertaining.

Naghma, encouraged by the hungry look in my eyes, continued: 'One of the admin girls caught hold of me today. She was saying the usual stuff about how she really enjoyed the *Election Express* and how it was a great show...'

I was obviously going to be let down hugely.

'She then told me that they are trying to sell the bus!'

I was shocked. 'What? No way!'

'Yeah, she said that they are selling it for like six lakh rupees.'

I don't know why but I felt indignant. How dare they sell our bus? Shouldn't it be preserved in some kind of NDTV museum that housed the memorabilia of fine reporting? Did the people who took this call not *know* that we had become world-famous in small-town India for achieving and notching up more mileage than even Rahul Gandhi? Or were we labouring under a misapprehension?

Not that we hadn't had enough time to get over such delusions. When we got back to office after the last counting day on May 14th, we may have been greeted by a round of applause in some parts of the newsroom, but Naghma and I were soon brought down from our Red Bus pedestal. For the election results day, she was dragged down to the studio and locked inside till they declared a government and I, more cruelly, was thrown outside the residence of Samajwadi Party general secretary, Amar Singh.

It was as if our editors realized that we've had way too much fun, way too much freestyle journalism. It was time to get back to the grind, to our routine of being an MC-BC.

'So Sunetra, how many kilometres did you cover?' Dr Roy asked me when I went live that morning.

'Almost 15,000 km.'

'You travelled *all* that distance to arrive at Amar Singh's door?' I could hear the mirth that this generated in the studio between Prannoy Roy, Barkha Dutt and the other guests. It was kind of ironic but then isn't everything that has happened in Indian politics since then?

Amar Singh, the socialite socialist, whose house I was stalking then, is out of the Samajwadi Party – eight months after the election result. The game of 'Who do you love more' that Mulayam's son Akhilesh and his trusted general played was just the follow-up. The *Election Express* witnessed one of the first rounds when we visited Rampur. At that time, Amar Singh had used Jaya Prada as a pawn. And Azam Khan was his opponent not Akhilesh. We watched as Amar Singh won that round, getting Mulayam to back Jaya Prada's candidature and even getting her to win the election, but which one of us political reporters would have ever predicted that he would be out of the party before the year ran out?

No one knew at that time that Amar Singh's real grouse was with Netaji's family members (or if they knew, they didn't announce it publicly), that he would start blaming Akhilesh openly for losing the Firozabad elections for his wife and they definitely didn't know, that Mulayam would finally have to give up all his high-profile contacts like the Bachchans to choose his son over Amar Singh.

But maybe, the *Election Express* got an inkling that the time for small parties to expand their base across India had not yet come. The Samajwadi Party wasn't the only one with a lacklustre performance in the 2009 elections.

Mayawati may have flexed her muscles by getting her candidate Madhavi to stand for elections in the backwaters of Kerala apart from every other constituency across the country, but they all knew that it wasn't more than a token gesture, much like having female candidates in that region for the first time. Of course, political commentary can sway between two extremes and the other extreme also turned out to be untrue. Soon after pundits declared the resurgence of the big national parties and the death of regional ones, the BSP trumped the Congress in the Uttar Pradesh by-polls. The

Elephant's progress may be slow but it was steadily holding on to its area of domination – Uttar Pradesh.

One can hardly say the same for one of the Big Two parties. Almost a year later, I cannot recall any region in the country that had been floored by the BJP's performance or the promise of LK Advani's leadership before the elections. And since then, we've all witnessed the public decimation of the party. Varun Gandhi may have rightly claimed a record victory when we met him in Pilibhit but he was wrong about reviving his party's fortune in the entire state. His championing the Hindu cause turned out later to be a liability, cited as a mistake by his own party-men and seniors like Arun Shourie and Jaswant Singh. As it turned out, the fans of BJP we met during our travels were still taken up with Atal Bihari Vajpayee and unfortunately Mr Advani just couldn't fill his shoes.

The head priest at Kamakshi temple in Kanchipuram who had predicted Advani as the next prime minister had obviously got his astrological calculations wrong – but he wasn't alone. The party's celebrated election managers made the same mistake and the last I heard – they are all getting away with it as well!

And what of the Congress? I admit, despite doing such extensive travel, we had no clue that the Grand Old Party was going to come so close to getting a simple majority. An overwhelming mandate that would make the Left parties' role obsolete, that would shatter ally Sharad Pawar's dream of becoming the prime minister (with our naive endorsement provided he turn the entire country into a Baramati model) and re-instal Manmohan Singh in the top job. We had no doubt, however, that some of UPA-I's rural policies had a lot to do with this stupendous victory. After all, hadn't we seen the Bhils line up to work for the NREGA scheme in the area outside Udaipur? In the arid desert of the region, they were happy to get work building roads but maybe, by next elections, their expectations will be higher. (They might not be so tolerant of the fact that they are getting Rs 60 instead of the promised Rs 100 per day under the scheme.)

We had seen how the tribal boys of Sundardih village in Mayurbhanj district were optimistic, they wanted to serve their country, but they also believed that their government saw their potential to be IPL players; they believed that just because they had no electricity did not make them any less than their peers in big cities. Will the Congress government be able to live up to their dreams and the dreams of the Matihana boys who wanted to study English?

The politics, the language, the traditions, the food, may have been different in every part of the country we travelled to. If there's one thing that binds us all in India, it's our aspiration for a better life, for a better job, for better governance. It's the weight of that aspiration that challenges the Naveen Patnaiks and the Nitish Kumars, the Bhupinder Hoodas and in fact, every politician in New India.

What sets apart Mayawati is that she understands this new aspiration which is why while the Samajwadi Party still continues to look at the English language as the enemy to be tamed, Chief Minister Mayawati has made its instruction compulsory. Nitish Kumar has got the popular vote because while he took his state's GDP to the number 2 position after Gujarat, the Bihar Congress was still busy describing its speaker Meira Kumar as a 'chamar'!

The big lesson for journalists like me – it's always easier to sit in a comfortable armchair in the confines of an air-conditioned office, and analyse the results. But if we want to survive as chroniclers of historic events, as witnesses of change, as trend-spotters who don't just report the obvious and tell stories that the outside world hasn't heard before, we have to get out there. In the words of my wise editor, we have to get the dirt in our fingernails, the dust in our hair and only then can we call ourselves reporters.

For now though, I'm thinking about raising some cash. Could I squeeze the red bus into the parking lot next to my home?

I'd like to hold on to it, for NDTV, at least till the next elections.

Acknowledgements

Been there, done that, and written the book. I think after 15000 kms on the road over 50 days and covering 40 cities, we can safely put that TV critique behind us: studio-bred TV reporters are scared of getting their hands and hair dirty in the field! But I wasn't writing this book to prove anything. I had to write it down to tell myself and anyone else, how much fun travelling and reporting in India can be. After a decade of journalism, I thought I knew a thing or two about this country but this journey taught me that a lifetime wasn't enough and there were millions of stories to always keep me hungry for more.

Of course, if it wasn't for NDTV's vision of defying global recession to bring out the ambitious *Election Express* campaign, none of this would have happened. Radhika and Prannoy Roy came up with the concept, were generous with budgets to allow us to do such extensive coverage, at a time when other news organizations allowed no travel at all. I will always, always be grateful that Barkha Dutt and Sonia Singh chose me for this assignment, taking me out of the newsroom and sound bite stories to explore election journalism any way I wanted. Barkha's threat of allowing me to go only if I could pull off the entire two months, worked wonders whenever my spirit wavered.

For me, the true heroine of the book is my colleague and co-traveller Naghma Sahar. Apart from her natural instinct for rural reporting, Naghma also knew how to seek out the best of every place we went to – stories and local delicacies. All our efforts (especially the skilful camerawork of Mohammed Mursalin) and bumblings on the field were then glossed over and packaged beautifully by the very young, talented team of Priyanka Khaneja, Ankush Arora and Nida Malik.

I do want to acknowledge the extensive help from journalists across the country – Avtar Singh in Dausa, Naseem in Agra, Dev Shrimali in Gwalior, Atul in Shivpuri, Vinod in Jhansi, Sanjay in Udaipur, Nilesh in Vadodara, Manish in Surat, Anand in Daman, Kishore in Nashik, Milind in Baramati, Frankey and Sujoy in Goa, Manju in Mangalore, Jayant in Mysore, Vaidyanathan in Kanchipuram, Trimurti in Tirupati, Narayanan in Kadapa, Ashok in Vijaywada, Purusottam in Bhubaneswar, Raju in Baripada, Kaushik in Jamshedpur, Bhishm Singh in Moradabad, Surender in Rohtak, Ashwani in Shimla, Braj in Chandigarh, Asif in Rampur and Dinesh in Nainital. My colleagues Harsha Kumari Singh, Vasanthi Hariprakash, Sanjay Pinto, Sam Daniel, TS Sudhir and Uma Sudhir, Sampad Mahapatra, Alok Pandey, Monideepa Banerji and Anant Zanane gave invaluable advice and suggestions which I couldn't have done without.

My friend, the accomplished author Rasheed Kidwai, was the first to push me towards putting my experiences down in a book, pushing me with references of publishers. The other big motivator was my brilliant photographer friend Mustafa Quraishi who told me to not let two months of my life go to waste. For a first time author, there could be no better publishing mentor than my editor Nandita Aggarwal – she always knew the right thing to say and do.

Friends and colleagues like Prachi Bhuchar and Manika Raikwar helped me along the way with suggestions of titles in the middle of a news bulletin! Senior Editor Ayesha Kagal encouraged me by giving me the first rave review of my book (even though she may have been biased). BFFs are great for encouraging every idea even if it is the worst in the world. Nina, Kaushik, Suneel made sympathetic noises about all my writing blues and helped out by taking me out for a drink or a meal where they assured me that the world was waiting for a book like this.

But, if we're talking about soothing frayed egos, nothing can beat family. I only had to announce to my two sets of parents that I was attempting to write a book, and it seemed I'd already conquered Mount Everest. Ma and Papa were convinced it was a sureshot bestseller while my in-laws, both accomplished authors, were unrestrained in their encouragement. I love them all for being the best pep squad ever. Bhai and Vasudha, Neelanjana and Suranjan cheered on from the ringside and the title is a collective product of their labour. That's what family is for, I say!

Finally, Sudeep has influenced this book even before it was conceived. He taught me how not to be scared of adventure, how to appreciate it, how to savour it with all its challenges. Sudeep made travelling nine hours non-stop on bumpy roads without proper amenities, feel glamorous; hearing my stories as if I was doing something heroic. He took time out from his demanding career to hear me crib whenever it got tedious and then later, read each word I wrote. Journalist partnerships are often dodgy but Sudeep makes it work for us every single day. Here's to the time we go back on the road again, this time, together.